The Soviet City

Ideal and Reality

James H. Bater

Explorations in Urban Analysis

General Editor R. E. Pahl

Already published:

Volumes in preparation:

The Soviet City

Ideal and Reality

James H. Bater

SAGE Publications ● **Beverly Hills**

12/11/85

General editor's foreword

This is one of the first cluster of books in the series *Explorations in Urban Analysis*. The original idea for the series came from Jim Dyos, who saw the need for books which would be readily available for students, who would not be at a stage to use the magisterial monographs in his *Studies in Urban History*. It was natural that he should approach the same publisher with his proposal for the new series and I was excited by the prospect of working with him when I was invited to be joint editor. It is tragic that Jim Dyos's untimely death in the summer of 1978 meant that he did not see the publication of any of the volumes he so enthusiastically encouraged our authors to produce. However, he played an active role in planning these first books in the series.

Professor Dyos's scholarly work in urban history speaks for itself. What is not so well known is the enormously painstaking care with which he undertook his editorial responsibilities. He never lost patience with authors and his good-humoured encouragement brought the best out of those who worked with him. He would give generously of his time to smooth down the jagged edges of an author's prose style, and he cared for all the details of the production of books for which he was responsible with singular devotion and energy. He was a model editor and a wise and companionable friend.

In the preamble to our series we said we wanted 'to encourage authors to make connections, to draw on other traditions from those with which they are most familiar', and then Jim added, 'to think afresh'. Insofar as the series does that it will be a fitting memorial to him.

RAY PAHL
December 1979

Table of contents

TO
LINDA, LISA, STEVEN, KEVIN AND IAN

List of Tables

List of Figures

List of Maps

Preface

This book has been written with a view to introducing the undergraduate student to some facets of the Soviet urbanization experience in general, and to selected dimensions of the Soviet city in particular. The emphasis is on continuities and changes, on matching reality with the ideal. To those *au fait* with Soviet sources, it will be immediately apparent that this study is largely a synthesis of other peoples' research and writing. While an attempt has been made to move beyond description to analysis, for many topics this is far easier proposed than achieved. What is contained herein, therefore, is very much an introductory statement. No doubt more questions will be raised than answered. To the extent that further inquiry is stimulated as a result, one of the purposes of this book will have been served.

While a paucity of data at the intra-urban level precludes most kinds of quantitative analysis, it is important for the undergraduate to recognize that there is a wide variety of sources available in English translation, and found in most university libraries, which makes possible an examination of some facets of Soviet urban life. *The Current Digest of the Soviet Press* and *Soviet Geography: Review and Translation* are but two examples of an increasingly large stock of translated materials which has been emphasized quite consciously in this study. Insofar as Soviet town planning is concerned, the most recent guide to the English language literature is the working paper (No. 58) published by the Centre for Urban and Regional Studies at the University of Birmingham, England: *Soviet Town Planning: A Bibliographic Guide to English Language References* by Paul M. White (February 1978). The Bibliography in this book only contains works cited and therefore is in no sense exhaustive, but its perusal will provide several other leads. Thus, for a number of urban-oriented topics undergraduates may themselves experience some of the fun, and certainly a few of the frustrations, of research on the Soviet Union.

In bringing this particular project to fruition, I have been greatly assisted by the knowledge and experience of several people who have kindly commented on parts, or all, of the text. To Ray Pahl, the series editor, to Hans Blumenfeld, Tony French, B. M. Frolic, Peter Nash and Jiri Zuzanek, I am grateful for ideas and criticisms. Not all suggestions have been incorporated. But beyond doubt whatever merit the book may have, it owes much to the efforts of other people. As usual, the deficiencies remain my responsibility.

On the technical side I would like to acknowledge the assistance of Barry Lively, who drew all the Maps and Figures, Jean Fraser and Anne Marie LeFort who typed and re-typed the manuscript. Their assistance has helped to make the preparation of the manuscript less onerous than would otherwise have been the case.

I would also like to express my thanks for permission to quote from a variety of articles in translation, copyright the *Current Digest of the Soviet Press*, published weekly at the Ohio State University by the American Association for the Advancement of Slavic Studies, reprinted by permission of the Digest.

1

Introduction

Throughout history the gathering of people into cities has tended to coincide with the material and cultural progress of society. In short, the city long has been both an agent and example of modernization. But it is obvious as well that the consequences of urbanization have been far from uniformly positive. By the early nineteenth century rapid urban-industrialization wrought enormous changes in the Western, capitalistic city. Very often the change was of a dysfunctional kind. Overcrowding, disease, deprivation and social disorder while not new, were of unprecedented dimensions. For observers like Engels the industrial city had created new opportunities for the exploitation of the masses by the few who controlled the means of production. Political ideology aside, many other observers of the nineteenth-century city were equally pessimistic about the urban future. The growing numbers of the middle and upper classes who sought respite in bucolic suburban retreats apparently shared this perception. Perhaps the pessimism of some observers of the nineteenth-century city is vindicated by the reality of third-world environments in the late twentieth century. Certainly most of the traditional problems associated with uncontrolled urban growth are still evident, along with a variety of ostensibly new ecological and social ills. However, the course of history has been neither predictable nor everywhere the same.

Few countries in the early 1900s were beset by urban problems as serious as those in Tsarist Russia. But with the revolution of 1917 the ideological blueprint for society was changed and new possibilities for charting the course of urbanization were opened up. The transformation of the values of society through the conscious manipulation of the urban-industrialization process is an integral part of Marxist–Leninist thinking. One objective is the removal of differences between town and country-side. Some progress toward this particular objective in fact has been made. However, as we shall see, this is but one facet of the Soviet programme for the planned development of urban society.

There is no question that over the past six decades the urbanization process has altered profoundly the lives of the Soviet population. In 1917 barely one-sixth of all inhabitants lived in cities. Soon two-thirds will. (The major cities, and all others referred to in this study, are included in Map 1.) Moreover, the numbers involved are neither small in absolute terms nor in terms of the share of the world's urban population. In 1979 more than 162 out of a total population of 262 million Soviet citizens lived in cities. Soviet classification procedures distinguish cities (*goroda*) from urban-type settlements (*poselki gorodskogo tipa*), but both are combined to make up the urban population. In general cities are defined as those places with more than 10,000–12,000 inhabitants (depending on the Republic). Urban-type districts are defined as those places with a minimum of between 2,000 and 3,000 population in which between 60 and 85 per cent of the labour force are engaged in non-agricultural pursuits, the particular threshold used again depending on the Republic. At the present time more than one in ten of the world's urban population live in a Soviet city (Khorev and Moiseyenko, 1976, 8). Against the background of uncontrolled and problem-ridden world-wide urbanization, the Soviet experience stands in apparent contrast. Before outlining the scope of our inquiry on the Soviet city, it would be useful to summarize briefly how the application of Marxist–Leninist principles makes Soviet socialist urban society different.

The nationalization of all resources, and the substitution of centralized planning for the market to develop and allocate them, has obvious consequences for the city. With the nationalization of land one of the principal historic forces shaping urban land use was removed. Economics would no longer dictate land-use allocation, planners would.

Privatism in any form is socially undesirable, though when circumstances make prohibition impractical, it is tolerated. Thus, the state-owned apartment built according to prescribed standards, and rented for the most nominal sum, is the desired form of accommodation. However, because of the long-standing housing shortage, private, detached homes have been allowed, and in certain times and places their construction has been encouraged. Cooperatively-owned apartments are more acceptable than private dwellings, but still constitute a compromise with principle. But the land, of course, is state owned and state allocated. While poor housing may exist, in theory any form of segregation according to income or occupation does not. Clearly, the role of the state in allocating housing and land means that ideal and reality may be reasonably, if not entirely, congruent.

The abolition of the private sector has dictated that the state fill the void. With the principal exception of the distribution of produce at market-determined prices through the ubiquitous collective farmers' markets, the state does determine what shall be produced, in what quantity, where it shall be sold and at what price. Uniform products and prices, and norms for number, variety and location of retail outlets, clearly distinguish the process of provisioning the Soviet population from its Western counterpart. The absence of competition in marketing results in a rather different urban landscape. So too does the traditional emphasis on public rather than private means of transport.

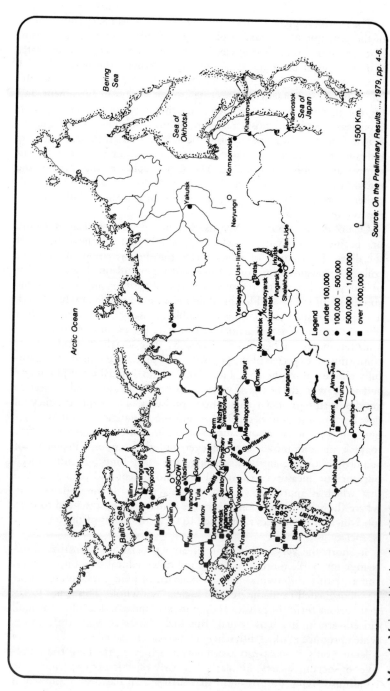

Map 1 Major cities in the USSR

The pervasive presence of state bureaucracy is a necessary concomitant of the principle of centralized planning and the abolition of privatism. The assumption is that the Soviet leaders know what is best for the state, that the central planning apparatus can determine the best course of action, and that such directives are implemented all the way down the line. Theory and practice in this case are not always in agreement, and for the planned development of cities the consequences of any such divergence can be of considerable importance. Solving urban problems demands that town planners either be able to deal effectively with the bureaucratic maze that envelopes the decision-making process, or to find some way around officialdom. The same applies at the level of the individual inhabitant. Having home repairs done, for instance, entails rather more ingenuity than is required to turn to the yellow pages of the Western city directory.

One of the virtues of the Marxist–Leninist ideology is that no region, or specific group within society, should be denied the benefits of socialism. The setting of basic norms for the provision of items of collective consumption, for housing and for the planned development of cities has helped to remove regional disparities and to bring the conditions of labour and life in all Soviet cities to a tolerably high level. To be sure, disparities continue but unlike so many other societies, their ultimate removal is an essential part of state policy and practice.

In return for the benefits conferred by state socialism, a measure of conformity is expected of the population. People are assumed to be gainfully employed by the state. Hence there is no 'official unemployment' and those who do not seek work are labelled parasites and subject to various forms of social and official pressures. The express policy of developing all regions necessitates a measure of state intervention, if not outright control, over population migration. Soviet citizens are not free to pick up and move to whichever city they choose. Problems of acquiring housing notwithstanding, the state long ago introduced bureaucratic measures to forestall such movement and to superintend that which is approved. Conformity in terms of living and working where the state requires one's services is matched by the need to do a job which in most cases is intended to serve the needs of the state, that is, society as a whole.

In short, the very real benefits of Soviet socialism mean that in exchange for cradle to grave security, unlimited educational opportunity, and a steadily improving material standard of living, self-interest must be subordinated to the interests of society as a whole. This is not to say that various forms of privatism do not exist, indeed, flourish, or that all citizens are in any sense equal. But such things as wage differentials which produce marked differences in income and standards of living are tolerated only as short-run expedients in achieving the long run objectives of socialist society. Similarly, the early rejection of experiments in communal living do not mean that such a goal has been dismissed as an integral part of the future Soviet socialist city, but only that at the present stage in the development of socialist society it is not appropriate. In terms of the long run goals of realizing a heightened social consciousness, the dissolution of the various strata in Soviet society, the fusion of the many nationalities and the creation of the necessary conditions for the emergence a communist ethos, the importance of the planned development of the Soviet city is undeniable.

To summarize briefly, the application of Marxist–Leninist principles may be said to differentiate the Soviet socialist city from its Western counterpart in the following ways:

1 nationalization of all resources (including land)
2 planned rather than market determined land use
3 substitution of collectivism for privatism, most apparent in terms of the absence of residential segregation, the dominant role of public transport, and the conscious limitation and dispersal of retail functions
4 planned industrialization as the major factor in city growth
5 the perceived role of the city as the agent for directed social and economic change in backward and frontier regions alike
6 cradle to grave security in return for some restrictions in personal choice of place of residence and freedom to migrate
7 directed urbanization and the planned development of cities according to principles of equality and hygiene rather than ability to pay.

The focus of our inquiry

It is now more than half a century since serious consideration was first given to what the Soviet socialist city should be. During this time extensive research on migration, urban growth, demographic, social and economic change has furthered our understanding of the aggregate dimensions of the urbanization process. In spite of all this research the Soviet city remains very much in a shadow. The reason for this is that the voluminous literature on what the city ought to be is not matched by analysis of what it is. Why? A dearth of published data of any description at the intra-urban level confronts the non-Soviet researcher, while the classified nature of much existing, unpublished information severely handicaps his Soviet counterpart. Assumption and generalization have tended to supplant evidence and analysis insofar as the internal structure and living environment of the Soviet city are concerned (Gutnov, *et al.*, 1968; Jensen, 1976; Davidow, 1976; Fomin, 1974). Therefore, the achievements of the Soviet town-planning experiment have yet to be adequately assessed. It is the purpose of this book to initiate such an assessment.

Limitations of data and space will necessitate a selective approach to our analysis of the Soviet city. What will be presented is very much a portrait, a portrait in which many details will remain obscure and in which the prominent features will reflect as much what is deemed important as they will what available data have permitted delineation. Because a normative style of town planning has been practised for most of the Soviet era, we are able to set available information about particular places against prescribed norms or standards, and thereby acquire some appreciation of the extent to which town-planning theory has been translated into practice. There are some obvious limitations to such an approach, not the least of which is the possibility of ending up stressing problems rather than achievements. But it is only by setting reality against ideal that the Soviet town-planning experience can be evaluated properly. There is also the risk of overemphasizing generic features of the Soviet city at the expense of regional variation. By consciously widening the search for information to include as broad a range of city sizes and regional examples as is feasible, this risk should be minimized. Our analysis of the Soviet city will be organized around five themes:

1 the importance of continuity and historical momentum in urban development
2 the framework for, and process of, decision-making as it affects town planning
3 the tempo and pattern of city growth at the national scale
4 the spatial organization of the Soviet city
5 the Soviet city as a place to live.

The following chapter will establish the need for an historical approach to the study of the Soviet city. Obviously, the transformation of society which occurred in 1917 did not wipe off the map the cities produced under conditions of an absolute autocracy. To understand the urban experience under Soviet socialism, it is imperative that the revolution not be viewed as a hard and fast watershed. Many ideas made the transition from one epoch to another intact. Without knowing something about the evolution of cities during the Tsarist era, what they were like as places to live in, how they were managed and what their problems were, it is not possible to comprehend fully the nature and intensity of the debate during the 1920s over what principles should guide the development of the new Soviet socialist city. The principles for Soviet town planning which were adopted in the early 1930s must be seen in the context of the urban crisis which had taken hold in the Tsarist era.

Chapter 3 examines the evolution of the municipal government structure in which the town-planning function is executed, and describes the general political arenas of which municipal government and the town planner are a part. There are some obvious advantages for town planning in the Soviet system of public ownership of resources and the emphasis on collective rather than personal consumption. The main purpose of the chapter is to establish just how well the decision-making system accommodates the town-planning function.

The fourth chapter deals with the aggregate dimensions of city growth. For the most part the changing spatial and temporal patterns will be examined for the major economic regions (Map 2). Soviet town-planning strategy has been predicated on the assumption that population movement must be subject to state policy. The nature of these policies, and how effective they have been, are the foci of much of the discussion. This chapter sets the groundwork for the subsequent examination of the city growth process as both example and agent of change in society.

In the fifth chapter an attempt will be made to comprehend the reality of the Soviet city. The central questions are, where do town-planning principles and practices diverge, why, and how efficient and equitable is the spatial organization of the Soviet city? The analysis will deal with five facets of the spatial organization of the Soviet city: industrial location and land-use zoning; the allocation and organization of housing; transportation and the journey to work; the provision of items of collective consumption; and the role of the central city.

The purpose of the sixth chapter is to attempt to assess what life is like in the Soviet city at present. The inquiry will focus on three features of Soviet city life: the patterns of daily activity; some social and environmental costs related to town-planning practice; and the role of social planning as an ameliorative force in urban development.

In the final chapter we will assess the Soviet town-planning experience and evaluate the role of the Soviet city as an agent of social change.

A note on sources and interpretations

We have already stressed that the paucity of information at the intra-urban level makes analysis of the Soviet city a difficult and, not infrequently, a rather indirect process. What has been of immeasurable assistance, however, is the spate of sociological and town-planning oriented literature which has appeared during the past decade. Much of this research comes hard on the heels of an albeit rather late official recognition of worker dissatisfaction, and hence flagging productivity. As this issue is of fundamental national importance, the causes of dissatisfaction have been explored with growing frankness. Since the problem is partly related to the conditions of life outside the workplace, the town-planning process has come under careful scrutiny both with respect to the way decisions are made and their consequences in bricks and mortar.

Newspapers, academic and technical journals in particular, are widely used as forums for raising issues concerning the city and the town-planning process. The principal source for newspaper reports is the *Current Digest of the Soviet Press* (cited as CDSP), which offers coverage

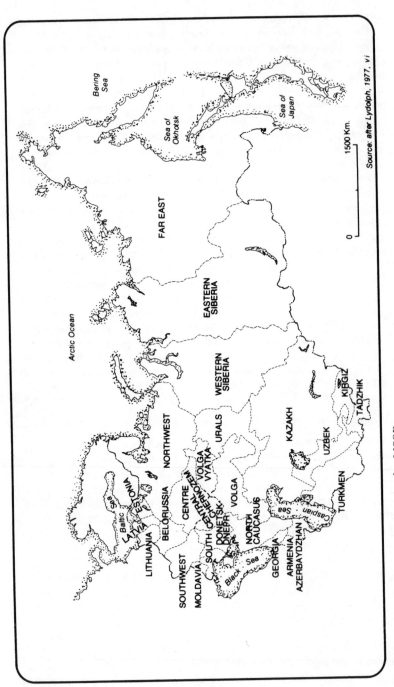

Map 2 Major Economic regions in the USSR

Source: after Lydolph, 1977, vi

not just of the two principal newspapers, *Pravda* and *Izvestiya*, respectively the voice of Party and government, but of a host of other popular national and regional newspapers as well. A number of specialized technical newspapers like *Stroitel'naya Gazeta* (Construction Gazette) and the weekly *Ekonomicheskaya Gazeta* (Economic Gazette) have also been consulted. Along with the academic and technical journals, some reasonable insights into Soviet town planning can be obtained. However, a couple of points should be borne in mind. Firstly, while Soviet commentators have been harsh judges of late in detailing a prodigious list of shortcomings and outright failures, the intent of such critical comment is to set in motion changes in attitude, policy or programme to remedy perceived deficiencies. What we have done here is to set this kind of information against prescribed norms as to what the city should be, thereby providing a basis for assessing Soviet town planning as it is practised. This kind of data base hardly can be claimed an ideal one. Some topics are politically sensitive and therefore not reported very often, or in much detail. For individual cities, and especially the smaller ones, data are at best patchy. While it is possible to reach some general conclusions about the Soviet town-planning experience and the resultant Soviet city, the reader must remember the reliability of the data on which conclusions are based is not what the author would like and is certainly inferior to that available to scholars doing similar studies in a Western context.

2
Ideology and the city

The revolution of 1917 confirmed the demise of the autocracy and ensured the same fate for capitalism. It heralded the rise of an entirely new system, but one in which many values and relationships had yet to be worked out according to socialist principles. The prospects for urbanization under socialism were both exciting and uncertain. This chapter sets out to establish the effect this ideological transformation had on the evolution of town-planning principles; but first we need to know something of the history of town planning and of the city itself during the Tsarist era. We will then be in a position to turn to town-planning developments during the early Soviet period.

The legacy of autocracy

The urbanization of Russia differed in many ways from what generally occurred in Western Europe and North America. There cities developed in response to a host of economic, social and political pressures, with few institutional checks on city growth. In Russia, on the other hand, the development of cities and life within them was very much under the thumb of officialdom from the middle of the seventeenth century until well into the nineteenth. The institution of serfdom, formally abolished in 1861, presented numerous barriers to free migration from the countryside. But the potential threat to political order of a sizeable *lumpenproletariat* was in any case sufficient for the authorities to attempt to regulate the duration of residence in the city. An elaborate bureaucracy arose to superintend the comings and goings of huge numbers of temporary city dwellers (Zelnik, 1971, 20–21). The movement of peasants especially was affected, and as they comprised the largest share of the urban population by the end of the nineteenth century, Russian cities came to be characterized by transience (Bater, 1980). Restrictions on movement and residence also served to check the growth of cities. Thus, despite the rapid urban-industrialization during the late imperial era, on the eve of the Great War less than one-sixth of the Empire's 160 million subjects lived in towns, a proportion very much smaller than in advanced European countries and the United States (Parker, 1968, 308). Not only was the urban population subject to bureaucratic manipulation, but the Russian city itself sometimes bore the indelible impress of the autocracy's concern with town planning.

The emergence of town planning

Town planning in Russia had a relatively auspicious beginning in terms of bricks and mortar, an inauspicious start if the human costs entailed in city building are reckoned. Peter I introduced European rationalistic town-planning concepts to Russia through the construction of a new city, St Petersburg. While town-planning principles were nowhere else put into practice on such a large scale during this epoch, the history of planning in St Petersburg merits examining in some detail since what was done there both reflected the prevailing values of the autocracy and served as a model for new town development and reconstruction elsewhere in the Empire.

Founded in 1703 at the mouth of the Neva river, St Petersburg symbolized Peter's attempt to modernize a state that stood markedly outside the mainstream of European economic, political, social and intellectual development. It is rather ironic that construction should require the power of an absolute autocrat to command the presence of representatives of the social and commercial elite and to dragoon tens of thousands of peasant workmen to a remote and inhospitable corner of the Empire. How many workmen did not survive the harsh conditions of labour and life in the new city cannot be determined with any certainty, but that the toll was in the thousands is beyond doubt. In planning St Petersburg, indeed in town planning generally during the eighteenth and early nineteenth centuries, creating an urban form that properly reflected the glory of the autocracy and Empire was the major concern. The needs or wishes of the individual, aesthetic or otherwise, were summarily subordinated.

In 1716 Peter I managed to persuade Jean Leblond, a student of Le Notre, to become chief architect of the new capital. Within six months a general plan had been prepared. As is clear from Map 3 the proposed new centre was off-centre from the existing built-up area. The obvious rectilinearity of the scheme was further emphasized by regulations pertaining to street widths and building heights. Canals and fountains were liberally incorporated, both as safeguards against flooding and fires and as aesthetic features. Not shown in the plan, but included in its specifications, was a high degree of land-use segregation. Separate areas were set aside for manufacturing and handicraft activities for instance. It was an imposing scheme, but already impractical owing to the massive transformation of the existing city which its implementation would occasion. Still, it embodied many of the design features desired by Peter and demonstrated beyond doubt the importance of developing the city as an integrated whole (Luppov, 1957). The influence of Leblond's plan on subsequent town-planning schemes was probably far greater than its

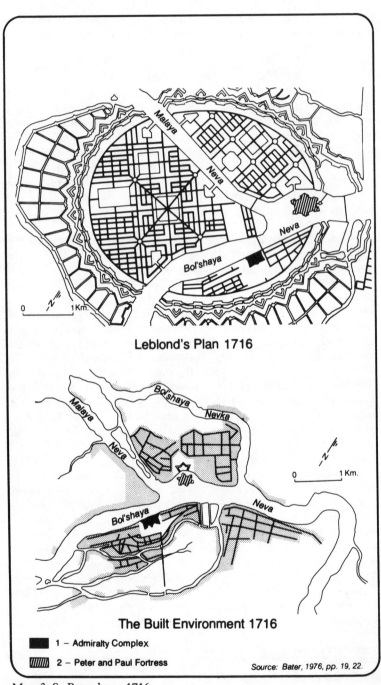

Leblond's Plan 1716

The Built Environment 1716

1 – Admiralty Complex

2 – Peter and Paul Fortress

Source: Bater, 1976, pp. 19, 22.

Map 3 St Petersburg 1716

impact on the layout of St Petersburg, although the grid of canals and oblong blocks (after the seventeenth-century Dutch pattern) intended for Vasil'yevskiy Island can be seen to this day. However, during Peter's time a plethora of decrees had not in fact prevented haphazard construction of inferior wooden buildings, especially on the periphery. But the idea of a general plan being the mechanism by which town-planning principles were to be implemented had taken root.

At the time of Peter's death in 1725 St Petersburg had approximately 40,000 inhabitants, a number much augmented each summer when large numbers of construction workers arrived. The city had been made administrative capital of the Empire in 1712 and this encouraged the rapid growth of the population. Though the figures are not very accurate for this period, it would seem that Moscow, the former capital, had between three and four times the permanent population of the Tsar's new city (Zaozerskaya, 1953, 63). As the total number of town dwellers in the Empire in 1725 probably did not exceed 1.25 million, these two cities clearly accommodated a substantial share of the total (Rozman, 1976, 72).

Following Peter's death St Petersburg itself was deserted by many of its involuntary residents, and most plans for the development of other new towns were quickly forgotten. It was not until the time of Catherine II (1762–96) that the idea of the city reflecting the majesty of the state was once again actively promoted. Under her tutelage the Commission for the Masonry Construction of St Petersburg and Moscow came to play a vital part in town planning and urban reconstruction. Within two decades the Commission's responsibilities had passed far beyond dealing just with Moscow and St Petersburg. It was now responsible for all town planning throughout the Empire. Comprising the best architectural talents, the Commission prepared more than 400 town plans during Catherine's reign. The work initiated by the Commission, and strongly endorsed by Catherine, continued through the early decades of the nineteenth century (Shkvarikov, 1954). So far as the exercise of preparing town plans is concerned, the scale of this endeavour in Russia was probably unmatched anywhere in Europe or America.

The largely geometrical town plans put particular emphasis on the city centre (Map 4, a and b). During Peter's time the cityscape was usually dominated by a single central building. A century later the usual design featured an architecturally harmonious façade surrounding a central square with one or more thoroughfares providing accessibility and the now all important perspective view. Site characteristics and the perceived aesthetic benefits of open space, particularly in the form of parks, also came to play a greater role in design, with the obvious consequence of both softening and 'greening-up' the cityscape. The preoccupation with regularity manifested itself in more utilitarian ways as the pace of urbanization quickened (Map 4, c). In the nineteenth century

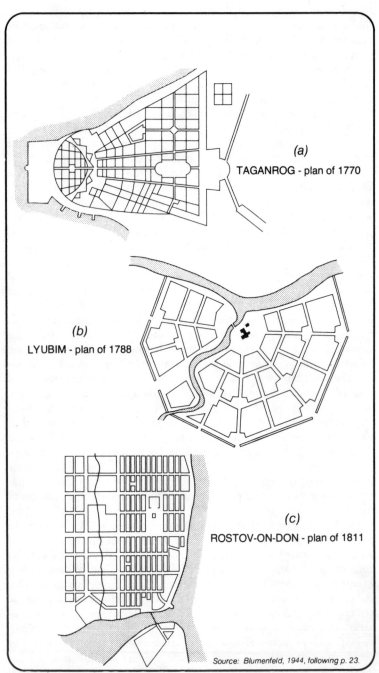

(a)

TAGANROG - plan of 1770

(b)

LYUBIM - plan of 1788

(c)

ROSTOV-ON-DON - plan of 1811

Source: Blumenfeld, 1944, following p. 23.

Map 4 Examples of early Russian town planning

the creation of a multi-nuclear and varied cityscape was often sacrificed to the expediency of a quickly prepared, standardized street plan (Blumenfeld, 1944a, 27).

The fascination at this time with the geometry, and especially the symmetry, of the plan was scarcely peculiar to Russia. Indeed, how could this be so when many of the leading architects were foreign-born and trained, and when the creation of cities like Washington or the layout of Versailles provided such important examples of planning practice? This does not mean that town-planning developments in Russia were unknown in Europe. But it is fair to say that their influence was very much less than Europe's on Russia.

Although the apparent emphasis of the eighteenth- and early nine-teenth-century plan was on external form, it was much more than simply a technical working document. We have already noted that land-use segregation was an integral part of the plan. This went far beyond simply banishing noxious industries to peripheral locations. The plan included provisions for the enforcement of social-class segregation. While attempts to separate classes met with only limited success owing to the costs involved and less than perfect police enforcement, the important point is that town plans reinforced the existing social-class system. The town plan affirmed prevailing social values in more subtle ways as well. While many major thoroughfares provided a perspective, they also facilitated movement. It was no accident that in the design of St Petersburg the three primary radials focus on the Admiralty, adjacent to which was the Winter Palace, the seat of the autocracy and constant ikon of the established social order (Egorov, 1969, 31–6). At the base of two of the radials were the barracks of crack palace horse-guard units, while the Aleksandro-Nevskiy Monastery at the foot of the third radial, the Nevskiy Prospect, symbolized the link between God and the Tsar (Map 5). Ease of movement between barracks and palace clearly reflected the felt need for surveillance and control, a need which was manifested in many ways other than by the conscious manipulation of the street plan. The aforementioned bureaucracy which monitored the comings and goings of the population is one of the more important of them.

By the middle of the nineteenth century the urban population numbered about 3.4 million, barely 5 per cent of the total population of 67 million (Lyashchenko, 1949, 273). Despite the hundreds of documents created to guide the development of new towns and the reconstruction of existing ones, the Russian city rarely gave much evidence of close adherence of ideal with reality. Wood not stone remained the dominant building material, even in St Petersburg. Hence fire continued to take its annual toll of lives and property. Nor was there great uniformity in the form and fabric of Russian cities. After all, as the Empire expanded, regional differences became more pronounced. Cities of the Baltic region such as Tallinn, Riga and Vilnius had their

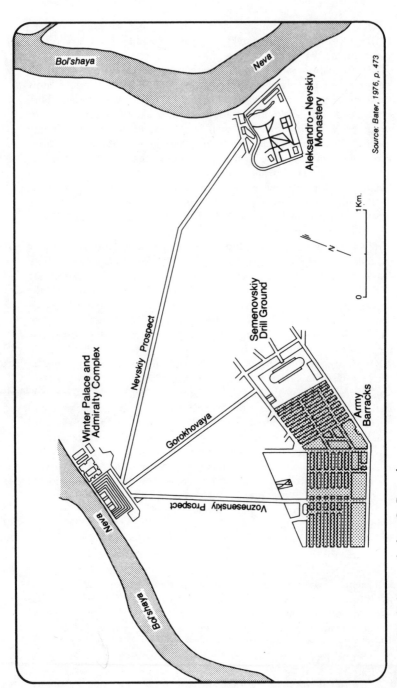

Map 5 Symbolism and plan: St Petersburg

Source: Bater, 1976, p. 473

own distinctive architecture. So too did the more recently acquired Caucasian cities like Tbilisi and Yerevan. Still to be brought into the Empire were the major centres of Middle Asia, but the frontier was fast approaching them. Notwithstanding the fact that few cities were actually developed according to town-planning principles, their importance should not be underestimated. The principles, like St Petersburg itself, often symbolized the aims and aspirations of the autocracy. St Petersburg served as the archetype of classic Russian town planning on the one hand, as the physical manifestation of the attempt to modernize, to Westernize the Russian Empire itself, on the other hand. Similarly, what happens in Moscow during the Soviet era may not always find much expression elsewhere, but Moscow still serves as a model, and in some respects a mirror on society.

From the mid-nineteenth century, the increasing tempo of urbanization dictated a change in town planning. Numbers alone eventually demanded that more attention be given to the material conditions under which people lived, and hence less attention was paid to the external form of the city. But despite the conscious shift in emphasis, it came both too late and with too little force to alter substantially the course of events. Even at mid-nineteenth century speculation in property, rising demand for housing and thus rents, and incipient industrialization were rapidly changing the character of Russian cities.

A crisis of numbers

Between 1850 and 1914 the urban population of Russia tripled. But no longer was there any effective means of controlling urban development. The various architectural and town-planning commissions established in the late eighteenth century had long since atrophied. Their place was to be taken by the Technical Building Committee, established by the Ministry of Internal Affairs in 1885. However, rapid urbanization prevented any attempt by this committee to monitor urban and architectural developments throughout the Empire. In the end the committee busied itself instead with setting technical standards for engineering projects (Starr, 1976, 224). The possibility of an overall regulatory body bringing order out of chaos evaporated. By the close of the century, zoning restrictions and architectural controls had collapsed in the face of unparalleled in-migration.

The new reality ushered in by rapid urban-industrialization soon challenged the very basis of the traditional deferentially-based, and essentially pre-urban, social system. By the late 1800s the notion that town plans might be an instrument for social-class segregation was certainly an anachronism. Moreover, the voluntary isolation of elites in socially homogeneous residential suburbs was severely handicapped owing to the limited development of public transport. Lavish decoration of personal living space might insulate elites from the poor, who even in the ostensibly better parts of the Russian city often lived in the garrets and cellars of the same building. But on the street amidst the seeming confusion of classes and activities the social elites were increasingly dependent upon time-honoured personalized symbols of rank and class to proclaim their status. However, these no longer guaranteed a deferential response from the burgeoning masses (Bater, 1976, 405–8).

Industrialization had triggered rapid urbanization. While a degree of modernization had been brought to Russia, for huge numbers of urban dwellers the consequences were not improved material conditions but unprecedented overcrowding and misery. We need only examine a few statistics on the extent of overcrowding and deaths from infectious disease to gain an appreciation of the dimensions of the urban crisis which took hold throughout the Empire.

Ratios of persons per apartment are the only available measure of overcrowding. While admittedly very crude, they nonetheless provide some idea of the scale of the housing problem. In 1912 in St Petersburg and Moscow roughly nine people lived in each apartment. Of course, floor space is the critical consideration, but if we assume that amongst cities having similar built environments differences would not be excessive, then a comparison of these figures with Berlin, Vienna and Paris is revealing. In those cities around 1910 the ratios of persons per apartment were 3.6, 4.2 and 2.7 respectively (Pazhitnov, 1910, 1164).

Though expansion of municipal services like water and sewage took place very rapidly after 1890 in most major Russian cities, it did not bring supply and demand into balance. For instance, on the eve of World War I at least a quarter of the apartments in Moscow and St Petersburg did without the benefits of running water or water closets (Zhilishchnaya Perepis', 1906, 161; Petrov, 1955, 709). And, of course, disparities existed within the cities. Suburban regions experiencing rapid population growth frequently had neither municipal water nor sewage services. European and American cities tended to be better off in respect to these particular services, not only in terms of the level of service but also in terms of quality. Piped water, for instance, was only of real benefit when free from contagion. In many Russian cities it was often unsafe to consume municipal water untreated.

Acute overcrowding and inadequate sanitary measures ensured that maintaining satisfactory standards in public health remained one of the most urgent tasks facing municipal authorities throughout the late imperial era. While deaths declined in per capita terms over the long run, regular outbreaks of epidemic disease continued to be a part of city life, the dimensions of their impact being clearly revealed by periodic sharp increases in the death rate. Again to use the situation in Moscow and St Petersburg as examples, although the death rates sometimes dropped to the low 20 per 1,000 range, especially severe epidemics, such as that of 1907–9, pushed them up to the 28 or 29 per 1,000 level (Frenkel', 1910, 1407). Moscovites endured 32 outbreaks of smallpox, typhus and cholera in the period from 1883 to 1917 (Sysin, 1955, 718). The record in St Petersburg was certainly no better; indeed, even more people succumbed annually to infectious disease of one sort or another than in Moscow. During the epidemic-ridden years of 1907–1909, more than one-third of all deaths in the capital were caused by infectious disease, and in 1908 a staggering 47 per cent (Kak khvoraet, 1909, 545).

The responsibility for the health and welfare of the urban population clearly fell on municipal government. But three points ought to be considered before judging municipal authorities too severely. In the first place a measure of local autonomy came late to Russia. Though mooted for a long time, the major municipal reform occurred only in 1870. A lack of understanding of, indeed, a lack of interest in, civic government on the part of the limited electorate made the manipulation of municipal politics by cliques with particular vested interests much easier, interests which may well have been better served by policies which did not serve best the public at large. With municipal autonomy came increased fiscal responsibilities. As in cities everywhere, municipal government had limited sources of revenue generation. While municipally owned, profit-making enterprises like the tram system eventually came to dominate the revenue side of the ledger, takeovers and new developments alike took time to effect. On a per capita basis, Russian cities fared very badly in comparison with revenues available to the major European and American cities (Bater, 1978, 55–63). Finally there is the issue of transience. We have noted the temporary nature of city residence on the part of a sizeable proportion of the peasantry. But more important from the standpoint of civic government was that in some cities the social elites similarly regarded their time in the city as a seasonal affair. It was simply a place to rendezvous for the winter's round of social events. The threat of epidemic disease and the growing risk of public disorder reinforced such attitudes. To alter the material and moral environment of the city clearly required commitment to it. To the extent that such commitment was not forthcoming from the social elites, managing urban affairs was rendered less effective (Bater, 1980).

Municipal governments, town planners and architects alike might envy the seeming regularity and regulation of the pre-industrial city and life within it, but the links with those features of the urban past had been shattered by rapid urban-industrialization. The new reality intensified the search for ways of coping. Two basic approaches evolved.

Town planning in the early 1900s

The revival of interest in Russia in the principles of eighteenth-century town planning and architecture partially stemmed from the visible deterioration of St Petersburg, the archetype of eighteenth-century planning. However, at the turn of the century the revivalist school was gaining momentum throughout Europe and this development in Russia was not unique. The idea of designing entire cities, or districts, as integrated systems was especially appealing. Exciting renewed interest as well was the magnificence of many baroque or neo-classical architectural ensembles. Most of the revivalist plans for urban development revealed the eighteenth-century preoccupation with the geometry of the street plan and the need to subordinate the interests of individual property-owners. By their scale and uniform architectural style, state, rather than private, financing was implied. For municipal governments unable to keep abreast of the demands for basic municipal services, the cost of such schemes was simply prohibitive. For central government the cost may have been bearable, but at this time there was a conscious attempt to avoid state involvement in urban development and instead to foster private initiative. Hence, while doing much to enhance the professional status of town planning, the revivalist school made little impact on actual urban development practice (Starr, 1976, 223–30).

Ebenezer Howard's concept of the garden city, especially owing to its emphasis on the provision of decent working-class housing, soon caught the attention of architects and planners in Russia. Within six years of the publication of his book, *Tomorrow: A Peaceful Path to Real Reform* a Russian translation was available. For many Russian urbanists dismayed by the deepening urban crisis, the garden-city concept constituted a viable alternative to the contemporary course of urbanization. Once again, European town-planning experience became the model for Russia.

Of the many proposals for new towns put forward in the early 1900s, few were implemented because of the outbreak of war. The schemes which did materialize often owed a great deal to the garden-city concepts of:

1 centralized control, if not public ownership, of land;
2 decentralized industrial development;
3 low density public and privately owned housing;
4 extensive open space and green belt;
5 a population size intended to facilitate the creation of a strong sense of community.

Given the nature of some of these concepts, it is hardly surprising that some socialists should so actively promote the garden-city idea. This did not preclude the involvement of capitalist interests in the actual development of settlements based on the garden-city model, but most proponents of the concept saw greater scope in some form of government involvement. Despite the fact that the original garden-city idea was predicated on the creation of satellite communities linked to the metropolis by inter-urban railways, the application of the concept to suburban areas was of obvious potential value to existing cities and much effort was expended in attempting to persuade municipal governments of the advantages to be gained from controlling land. Success of satellite and suburban community development was limited. The primitive nature of intra-urban public transport and the limited and recent development of inter-urban systems combined with their being too costly for the bulk of the population to use regularly prevented such developments (Starr, 1976, 230–55; Bater, 1973, 85–102).

Clearly, the 'garden city' movement did not tackle the problems of the city directly, but sought instead to relieve pressures through the creation of small satellite communities and ordered suburbanization. The revivalist movement on the other hand drew inspiration from the grandeur of the eighteenth-century city and offered solutions to current problems based on the overt manipulation of the built environment by the state. The tension between the views that the large city could be redeemed and once again reflect the majesty of the state, and that which saw solution only in small settlements of an essentially rural character, intensified after the revolution.

In search of the socialist city

Upon assumption of political power by Lenin and the Bolsheviks in 1917 there occurred a barrage of decrees which breathed new life into the profession of town planning. No longer would the forces of capitalism so influence the development of cities – socialist principles of town planning would. Land was nationalized, and along with it most urban real estate. The collapse of the old social order dictated new approaches to the spatial organization of the city.

Fundamental changes occurred quickly in many facets of political, economic and social life, but the realities of World War I, then three years of Civil War and intervention, meant that little practical achievement in town planning was recorded. Meanwhile, the national economy disintegrated. The curtailment of an agricultural surplus brought shortages and even famine to the cities. The resultant chaos prompted an unprecedented migration from town to countryside, a phenomenon facilitated because large numbers of peasants living in the city had not severed their ties with the village.

Insofar as the available statistics are accurate, they indicate that in 1914 about 25 million people lived in cities. By 1926 the urban population within the same boundaries was just over 26 million. During the years from 1914 to 1926 there must have been a sizeable diminution in the urban population; just how large is impossible to determine with any certainty (Lorimer, 1946, 32–3). Some indication of the scale of urban depopulation for specific cities is revealed by the following figures for Petrograd (as St Petersburg was called between 1914 and Lenin's death in 1924, when the city was renamed Leningrad) and Moscow. In 1917 Petrograd housed 2.5 million people; in 1920, 0.722 million. For Moscow the figures were 1.7 and 0.925 million respectively (Cattell, 1976, 272). The transfer of the bureaucracy of state capital from Petrograd to Moscow beginning in February 1918 helped to offset the decline.

It was not until 1921 and the introduction by Lenin of the New Economic Policy (NEP) that conditions slowly began to return to normal. By allowing some elements of free enterprise to operate under NEP, the full impact of state socialism was deferred. The Five Year Plans initiated by Stalin in 1928 finally put an end to the NEP accommodation with the old order. Meanwhile, some of the objectives of Soviet town planning were being clarified.

From the Marxist perspective the contradiction between city and countryside under capitalism had resulted in pernicious, exploitive class relationships. Under socialism the gap between proletariat and peasantry must be bridged, a task in which the town planner played an especially important, though yet unclear, role. It was frequently argued that communal living eventually would replace the nuclear family, a line of reasoning which had obvious implications for urban design. And, of course, with the demise of private enterprise, the void had to be filled. The provision of all items of collective consumption would become the responsibility of planners. So too would be the task of ensuring equality in their distribution, both within cities and amongst regions. The tasks were daunting, but at least there was a sizeable number of professionals willing to assume the responsibilities.

The revolution had not provoked a massive emigration of town planners as was so frequently the case amongst other professional groups (Starr, 1976, 236). The reason is not so difficult to perceive for the revolution stimulated, not stifled, interest in the role of town planning and the city. Though actual development was limited, debate over what form the Soviet socialist city should take was intense (Blumenfeld, 1942, 33). The tension between the essentially divergent philosophies behind the revivalist and 'garden city' movements mounted. In no sense did these particular movements, having transcended the ideological watershed owing to their perceived innovative qualities, monopolize the debate over the future course of urban development. But their underlying premises did transfix an ideological split of a more general nature.

Out of the debate of the late 1920s there emerged two principal and opposing schools of thought about the future Soviet socialist city. Some of the underlying assumptions of the revivalist and garden-city movements can be subsumed in the urbanist and de-urbanist schools respectively. The vast majority of schemes propounded under these labels was simply utopian. Many presumed complete reconstruction of the existing urban system. Most assumed almost unlimited financial resources. While still-born owing to the many competing demands for the state's limited finances, a number of principles common to both schools ultimately became the working guidelines for Soviet town planning.

The industrial and agricultural centres proposed by the prominent

Soviet architect, L. Sabsovich, are typical of the urbanist-school approach to the socialist city. A system of essentially self-contained urban centres in which multi-storeyed collective living facilities would de-emphasize distinctions between the agriculturist and the proletarian was proposed. The nuclear family as the primary unit of social organization would eventually dissolve, giving rise to an entirely communal way of life. The notion of a fixed population of approximately 50,000 is one of several features which suggest some links between Sabsovich's conception of the socialist city and the garden-city movement, while the emphasis on high-rise housing owes something to the ideas of Le Corbusier. Yet it would be a mistake to overemphasize the connections. Sabovich's socialist city was not simply a small town benefitting its inhabitants through easy access to the countryside. Much more of 'nature' was to be included in the design of this new community than was characteristic of the garden city, something which the demise of the capitalistic land market clearly facilitated. Insofar as the influence of Le Corbusier is concerned, most of his ideas were of far greater theoretical significance than practical. Extensive development of high-rise housing for instance, was precluded because of inadequate supplies of building materials, inadequate technology and limited finances. His essentially urbanist views, however, did involve him directly in the debate in the Soviet Union concerning the form the Soviet socialist city should assume. In short, the typical scheme propounded by the adherents of the urbanist school emphasized communal lifestyle in a settlement of fixed population size. Some of the other major design considerations included: strict land-use zoning, parallel development of industry and housing, ample green space and recreational facilities, pedestrian journeys to work, minimal development of streets and a non-commercialized city centre (Ilyin, 1931, 179–83; Kopp, 1970, 164–78; Bliznakov, 1976, 246–8).

In the opinion of the de-urbanist school proponents, schemes like Sabsovich's did not chart a new course for urban development at all, they simply replaced large cities with smaller ones. The de-urbanists proposed a totally different future, one felt to be more in keeping with basic Marxist ideology. They wanted an essentially townless, socialist society in which the age-old contradiction between town and country would be abolished once and for all. Representative of the de-urbanist school were the ideas of M. Okhitovich and M. Ginsberg. They proposed dispersing the population over the whole of the habitable parts of the state. Settlement would take the form of ribbon developments. Individual dwellings located in natural surroundings would be allocated as housing, but within easy access would be communal centres for dining, recreation and so forth. In other words, some privacy would be provided in terms of living quarters, but the lifestyle would be essentially communal. All employment nodes and centres of collective consumption would be incorporated into these continuous ribbon developments in such a manner that they would be within specified time–distance bands of their potential users. Mobility was predicated upon near universal use of the automobile. Compared to the urbanists' proposals, those of the de-urbanists were heavily dependent upon technology. The rejection of the city was clearly a controversial declaration. Le Corbusier dismissed the movement as a fad, but whether he was cognizant of all the dimensions of the de-urbanist proposals seems doubtful (Kopp, 1970, 172–3). Still it is hardly surprising that such radical proposals for the transformation of the built environment should remain on the drawing board (Bliznakov, 1976, 249–51). But out of all the rhetoric, debate and drawing did emerge some practical proposals which incorporated several features from both the urbanist and de-urbanist schools. N. Miliutin's scheme for a linear city is a case in point.

Miliutin's concept of the linear city was not original. The idea had originated, as usual, in Europe, and by the late 1920s had a sizeable and international roster of adherents. His development of the idea may be considered of greater practical importance than the others discussed simply because it was employed in the planning of Volgograd (Stalingrad) and used in part in the design of Magnitogorsk. Some parallels between Miliutin's linear city and the urbanist and de-urbanist schools are readily apparent. The linear city incorporated about half a dozen strictly segregated zones (Map 6). Moreover, between the industrial and transport arteries and the residential zone was a green buffer. Though discontinuous, in a broad sense it bore some resemblance to the schemes of Okhitovich and Ginsberg. But the parallel development of industry and housing so as to facilitate a short, pedestrian journey to work is also similar to one of the principles Sabsovich's scheme embodied. The perceived need to create an alternative to the large city and urban agglomeration, both judged to be inevitable by-products of capitalism, led all planners to try to create urban environments which would generate a sense of community. Miliutin, like Sabsovich, reckoned that the best balance between economic provision of urban services and potential for creation of a sense of community, if not a communal ethos, was in a town of 50–60,000 inhabitants. Thus, population totals were to be strictly limited. Okhitovich and Ginsberg attempted to create the same kind of environment but through a quite different physical form. What all had in common though was the objective of breaking down the differences between town and country. By accommodating both agriculturists and proletariat in the same, or similar, housing, some steps toward fulfilling this objective might be made.

Whatever the merits of the schemes the vigorous debate and experimentation of the 1920s produced, few were translated into bricks and mortar. The programme of forced industrialization initiated in the First Five Year Plan of 1928 clearly laid down long term development priorities, and a fundamental restructuring of the Soviet city was not included.

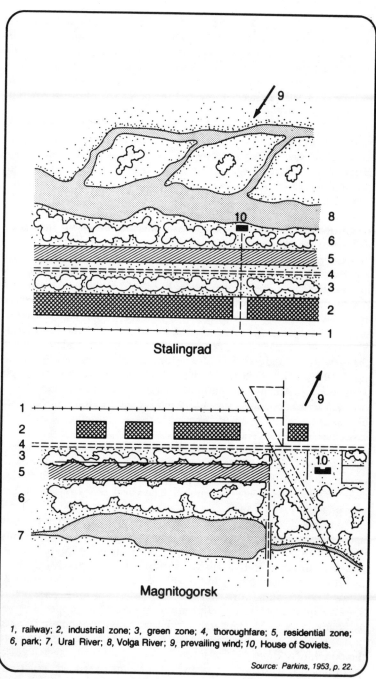

Stalingrad

Magnitogorsk

1, railway; *2,* industrial zone; *3,* green zone; *4,* thoroughfare; *5,* residential zone; *6,* park; *7,* Ural River; *8,* Volga River; *9,* prevailing wind; *10,* House of Soviets.

Source: Parkins, 1953, p. 22.

Map 6 Miliutin's linear city

What the Five Year Plan did was determine the spatial and structural features of urban-industrialization. The task of the planner was clear. He had to prepare the physical environment for the fulfilment of specific objectives within a set time frame. The general features of the new social order were obvious enough, but what about the principles and administrative organizations needed to create the new socialist urban environment for it?

In 1931 it was decreed that further debate about the future form of the Soviet socialist city was redundant. All Soviet cities must be socialist by virtue of their being part of the Union of Soviet Socialist Republics. While this somewhat pragmatic policy statement, coming as it did with the full authority of the Communist Party, served to stifle further debate, and especially the criticism that the existing urban system being capitalist in origin and in form should be eradicated, it did not imply dismissal of all the ideas so vigorously enunciated during the theoretical debates of the 1920s.

Socialization of the housing stock and urban–rural migration had eased the problem of overcrowding in the immediate post-revolutionary period, but the benefits were short-lived. With the programme of rapid industrialization, which the Five Year Plan introduced, the pace of city growth quickened. Once again the demand for housing outstripped supply. Whether de-urbanist or urbanist in origin, theoretical considerations thus had little impact on the actual course of city building during the early part of the First Five Year Plan, 1928–32. What was done was essentially *ad hoc* in character. Until 1930 there was no state-wide administrative structure for putting town-planning principles into practice. The first major agency was GIPROGOR (the state committee for city planning). Over the next half dozen years the centralization of authority continued, with the creation of the State Planning Agency, STANDARD-GORPROYEKT, and of GORSTROIPROYEKT and PROMSTROIPROYEKT (respectively agencies concerned with urban and industrial planning projects under the Ministry of Heavy Industry), being significant first steps (Blumenfeld, 1944b, 53–4). Republic, and eventually city-level urban planning agencies followed.

Shortages of trained personnel soon showed up as the demands placed upon the planning profession soared (Meyer, 1942, 29). It was not until the early 1930s that the products of Soviet architectural and town-planning education were available in sizeable number. To some extent the void was filled by an influx of foreign professionals, many of whom held key administrative positions. It was to be some years before Soviet-educated architects and planners dominated the upper echelons of the administrative hierarchy. The process of Sovietization was speeded up as a result of the general expulsion of foreigners which characterized the purges of the late 1930s.

During the past half century the education of Soviet architects/planners has neither ignored the classical era nor contemporary foreign trends. But insofar as the planning of the Soviet city is concerned, there has been a number of principles which have figured prominently in planning pedagogy throughout this period. Indeed, it is the near universal application of these principles which has helped to standardize parts of all Soviet cities. A few principles have something in common with Western notions of optimal spatial organization, but this seems to be more a by-product of a real concern for humanizing the urban environment than the consequence of a preoccupation with technical efficiencies. As we shall see in the next chapter, town planning in the Soviet Union as elsewhere is very much a political process, and decisions taken as much reflect this reality as they do specific norms or general principles for physical planning (*planirovka*) or economic planning (*planirovaniya*). This is not to say that efficiency and cost minimization considerations have played no role in town-planning decisions. But when basic inputs like land have no price, or have only been nominally accounted for, calculations of least-cost alternatives for example are exceedingly difficult. Just how such factors might be adequately measured in the Soviet economy is a question still demanding an answer. At this point, however, we need only concern ourselves with the nature of the general principles which have guided town planning for much of the Soviet era. We will then be in a position to proceed to an evaluation of Soviet town-planning practice.

General principles for planning the socialist city

Following three years of preliminary work on a scheme for the development of Moscow, some basic principles were finally confirmed with the adoption of a general plan in 1935. Though the 1931 Communist Party decree effectively limited the terms of reference to development based on a moderate reworking of the existing urban form, rather than presuming a new capital to be built from scratch as proponents of both the urbanist and de-urbanist movements might have wished, the principles embodied in the 1935 Moscow plan, which are listed below, did constitute a sharp break with the past.

1 Limited city size

The overriding principle was that of a strictly limited city size. Insofar the 1935 plan for Moscow itself was concerned, an upper limit of five million inhabitants was established. At the time the capital's population was approximately 3.5 million. The optimum city size was, however, generally conceded to be in the 50–60,000 range. At this scale all urban services, items of collective consumption, amenities and so on could be provided economically and yet still permit the forging of a socialist, communal ethos. This principle clearly implies that urban growth somehow be monitored and controlled. Thus, in 1932 an internal passport system was established and the right to a residence permit (*propiska*), and hence a housing allocation, was made dependent upon having employment, and remaining regularly employed. A bureaucracy necessary to administer permits, similar to that of the pre-revolutionary era, emerged, though it must be emphasized the reasons and objectives differed.

2 State control of housing

Social equity and considerations of hygiene dictated that some regulations be introduced to control the allocation of housing space. Indeed, as early as 1922 a sanitary minimum of nine square metres of living space per urban inhabitant was adopted, and it remains the basic norm. Because housing on a per capita basis is still below the norm in most cities, over the years nine square metres of living space has served as the maximum allocation possible in most circumstances. Exceptions do exist, and these will be discussed later. However, the principles of importance are those a normative housing allocation process, and the most nominal of rents. Private housing, while regarded as an essentially short-run adjunct to the available supply, in the long run would be abolished.

3 Planned development of residential areas

A variety of approaches to the organization of housing was mooted, but in the end the notion of a basic planning unit or 'super block' accommodating about 1,000–1,500 people was adopted. In it all the necessary day-to-day facilities like schools, shops and so forth would be within walking distance. The provision of facilities to meet day-to-day needs combined with a measure of local autonomy was expected to go some way toward creating a sense of neighbourhood. Groups of living complexes comprised the next highest organizational unit in the provision of housing—the *mikrorayon*. It would normally have between 8,000 and 12,000 inhabitants and provide higher-order services not required at the level of the 'super block'. The next level in the spatial hierarchy for the allocation of services and employment would be the residential complex. There is therefore a logical progression in the development, servicing and spatial organization of residential areas.

4 Spatial equality in the distribution of items of collective consumption

The spatial allocation of consumer and cultural services was to be carried out in accordance with the general principle of equal accessibility. A normative approach to the overall provision of items of collective consumption is intended to ensure a high degree of equity within, and amongst, cities.

5 Limited journey to work

Journeys to work were to be short, and public, not private, transport was to be dominant. Norms were established to govern the time spent journeying to work. In large cities a forty-minute trip to work was deemed the maximum acceptable. Prescribing journey to work times was intended to insure the rational location and staging of both housing and employment nodes.

6 Stringent land-use zoning

In order to reduce the length of the journey to work housing and employment centres should not be far from each other. But as industry was to be the major employer in cities, proximity raised the possibility of environmental pollution of one kind or another. Thus, strict land-use zoning was required. Where necessary adequate green buffers would separate noxious industry from housing.

7 Rationalized traffic flow

Within the city traffic patterns were to be rationalized. Heavy traffic flows were to be accommodated by designated streets so as to minimize both congestion and noise. Industrial areas were to be served by integrated transport systems whose routes were to be strictly segregated from residential areas.

8 Extensive green space

Open space in the form of parks, recreational areas and green belts was to be an integral part of urban design. Public ownership of land facilitated its conversion to park and green space in built-up areas: moreover, green space was to be far more extensive than was characteristic in the Western, capitalist city. Additionally, there was to be a clear-cut delimitation of the built-up area and therefore no scruffy, rural–urban fringe. One of the first tasks in accommodating the implementation of the generous norms for per capita allocations of green space was the determination of municipal boundaries. Few cities had clear administrative boundaries in the early Soviet period.

9 Symbolism and the central city

The 1935 Moscow Plan also established the guiding principle for the development of the city centre. During the 1920s, it had been suggested that the future Soviet socialist city would not have a distinguishable centre. Instead, it was now to be the nucleus of the social and political life of the city. By means of unified and uniform architectural ensembles, thoroughfares and squares, the city centre was to cater for massive public demonstrations. The design problem was one of striking a reasonable balance between occasional public functions and the ordinary day-to-day purposes these same thoroughfares, squares and buildings had to serve. The objective was to have the resultant ensembles reflect the glory of the state—a sentiment and purpose rather reminiscent of eighteenth-century Russian town planning. As the cultural and political uses of the central city were emphasized, the customary central city functions were downgraded. The result was the conscious decentralization of administrative and distributive services into fully developed secondary centres.

10   Town planning as an integral part of national planning

Because the planning process began at the national level, it was thought possible to direct urban growth at the regional level. The general principle governing location decisions was that industrial development should be directed away from the large cities and existing agglomerations to less industrialized, rural or minority group regions. To help fulfil this objective, the location of new, non-city-serving industry in Leningrad and Moscow had already been prohibited earlier in the 1930s. Such measures, and this general principle guiding future decisions, were assumed sufficient to prevent development of urban-industrial agglomerations, a phenomenon assumed peculiar to the capitalist stage of economic development.

Summary

The Soviet government inherited cities beset by problems of the most serious kind. The onset of civil war eased the burden of over-crowding somewhat, but the cities were scarcely any less insalubrious in consequence. Against the reality of the Soviet urban scene, the debates and proposals which characterized the 1920s appear rather idealistic. Yet many of the fundamental objectives of these utopian schemes eventually became part of the general principles adopted for the guidance of town planning. Most of the principles were products of the new socialist ideology. Yet there are some interesting parallels with the era of autocracy. The sense of order which was pursued but not always realized in the Russian city was very much dependent upon controlling the movement of people to the city and keeping them under close surveillance once there. The very essence of the planned Soviet socialist city is the ability to predetermine growth and adequately accommodate it. This demanded tight control over population migration, and to this end bureaucratic measures were put in place. Thus, control of population movement and various forms of surveillance were common to urbanization under ideologies as outwardly different as autocracy and socialism.

The successful realization of objectives in both situations depended upon full use of totalitarian powers. As these have waned, so the goal of controlled urbanization slipped from grasp.

The creation of a Soviet socialist city should bring into existence a new and higher form of society, one in which the traditional values of the earlier societies and religions would be obliterated, in which the primacy of the family unit would give way to collectivism, and in which the internationalization of the many minorities would be expedited. Much depended upon the successful planning of the Soviet city. However, town planning is a political process, one in which longer-term objectives sometimes must be forsaken in the interests of short-run expediency. Clearly, success depends in no small way on the perceived importance of town planners within the larger political arena. In the next chapter we will focus on the decision-making process in town planning.

3

Decision making and town planning

The task of Soviet urban government is broader than that normally associated with cities in, say, Western Europe or North America. While provision of the usual public services and their maintenance are common denominators, Soviet municipal authorities also must see that all the presumed requirements of the citizenry are met. It is in this latter endeavour that the private sector plays such an important part in differentiating the role of the Soviet town planner from his Western counterpart. But irrespective of the scope of the town-planning exercise, in the final analysis the efficacy of town planning hinges on the manner in which decisions are taken and implemented. In this chapter we will attempt to answer the question, how does the decision-making process affect town planning? Before exploring this relationship, however, we need to know something about the development of municipal government and about the larger political arenas of which it and the town planner are a part.

The emergence of the Soviet

In Russian the word 'soviet' means council or assembly and is essentially apolitical. In the context of the Union of Soviet Socialist Republics the word obviously has some political significance. The Soviet in fact is the basic building block of the governmental structure, and is commonly understood to mean a council of delegates elected by groups of workers, soldiers or peasants. How this system evolved and its consequences for the management of urban affairs are worth considering, if only briefly.

Years of economic depression and growing social unrest culminated in 1905 in widespread strikes and mass demonstrations to publicize perceived injustices. Amongst the many important developments of that year, the spontaneous appearance of grass-roots organizations of workers' delegates to coordinate strike activity figures prominently. These 'Soviets', in a few instances even assisted in maintaining a semblance of public order where local government had fallen into disarray. By the autumn of 1905 the formation of Soviets became a more formal, democratic process. For example, following the lead of the St Petersburg Soviet, it was agreed that all factories and trades should elect delegates to the Soviets on the basis of one for every hundred workers. Such a rapid spread of an overtly socialist, grass-roots organization as occurred in late 1905 clearly could not be tolerated under an autocracy. Thus, the stifling of dissent by the authorities included the suppression of the network of Soviets. But it proved simpler to remove the formal trappings of the organization than it did the concept of the Soviet. The economic chaos during the Great War and the eventual demise of the autocracy were sufficient condition to bring about their spontaneous resuscitation.

With the abdication of Tsar Nicholas II in March 1917 the legal underpinnings of the Duma, or consultative assembly, collapsed. Created to appease public opinion after the unrest of 1905, the Duma had served only as an advisory body to the Tsar and thus had no legislative powers. Failure to find a successor to Nicholas brought about an unprecedented crisis. As a stop-gap measure a Provisional Government was created out of the remains of the Duma. It immediately set out to democratize government, both central and local. Moving quickly to some form of democratically elected central government, however, required a measure of consensus. The Provisional Government was handicapped in this endeavour by the very circumstances giving rise to it—world war, a national economy in near ruin and political conflict. Though committed to the task of bringing into existence a Constituent Assembly, the exigencies of the times and the lack of any tradition of consensual politics made a daunting task all the more difficult. Election of the new Constituent Assembly was nonetheless set for the autumn of 1917. However by this time the drift toward a revolutionary solution to the domestic chaos in Russia was underway.

During the eight months of Provisional Government, *de facto* political power was increasingly assumed by the rapidly expanding network of Soviets, the apex of which was in Petrograd, as St Petersburg had been renamed in 1914 in deference to anti-German sentiment. The crisis of 1917 had proved fertile ground for the re-emergence of the Soviets. The importance of the Soviets was reflected by the fact that the Provisional Government early on found it necessary to secure agreement with the Petrograd Soviet on several key policies before implementation. The Soviets were fast acquiring a measure of popular support, something the Provisional Government was having much difficulty sustaining.

Once the potential political significance of the Soviets was recognized by Lenin, the slogan 'All Power to the Soviets' was adopted by his Bolshevik faction of the Russian Social Democratic Workers' Party. To the peasant masses, however, the campaigns to end the war and to redistribute the land were doubtless more comprehensible. In any event, public endorsement of the Soviets brought with it some risk so far as the Bolsheviks were concerned, simply because they were far from the dominant political party in the movement. Indeed, in the First All-Russian Congress of Workers' and Soldiers' Deputies convened in Petrograd in June of 1917, the Bolsheviks could lay claim to barely 10 per cent of the nearly 900 delegates sent by Soviets across the country. If the Soviet was to become an avenue to power, the Bolsheviks had their work cut out.

Throughout the summer and early autumn the authority of the Provisional Government steadily waned, while that of the Soviets grew. Symptomatic of the perceived weakness of the Provisional Government were the attempts to overthrow it in July and September. In the first instance, the Bolsheviks became embroiled in what proved to be an ill-judged venture to effect a coup. Its failure resulted in Lenin having to depart smartly for Finland in order to avoid arrest—barely two months after his return to Russia after years of directing the affairs of the Bolsheviks from abroad. Notwithstanding the attempted coup, the Provisional Government did not outlaw the Bolshevik party itself. Thus the Bolsheviks, under Lenin's supervision, continued to extend their influence in the Soviets. By October they controlled the vitally important Petrograd Soviet. Meanwhile, a second assault on the Provisional Government occurred in September. Fears of perceived socialist tendencies of the Provisional Government and disillusion with the handling of the war effort lay behind an abortive attempt to establish a military dictatorship (Scott, 1961, 580). With each passing week the Provisional Government's ability to control events inspired less confidence.

With a firm hold on the Petrograd Soviet and the support of disaffected sections of the Petrograd army and naval garrison forces, Lenin, having returned surreptitiously to Petrograd, planned the takeover of the Provisional Government. Along with the election of a Constituent Assembly, a Second All-Russian Congress of Workers' and Soldiers' Deputies had been set for the autumn of 1917. On the eve of the opening of the Congress, the Bolsheviks with little difficulty forcibly took over and dispersed the Provisional Government. Presented with the fact of a *coup d'etat*, the Congress adopted a motion that it should administer the country until the election of the Constituent Assembly. The 'revolution' of 7 November 1917 thus did not give the Bolsheviks power. But as the Congress's central executive committee boasted several Bolsheviks, including Lenin, the objective was clearly within reach.

The subsequent election of the Constituent Assembly demonstrated yet again that across Russia support for the Bolsheviks was limited. Amongst the urban Soviets, however, they were faring a little better. And negotiations for settlement of the war and the widely popular appeal to redistribute land were beginning to win some support amongst the rural Soviets. But political power was not so much determined by number of delegates as it was by control over the vital centres of decision making. In this regard the central executive of the Congress was unmatched. And it was in this latter arena that Lenin soon emerged in firm charge. By early 1918 it was possible for Lenin to engineer a decree dissolving the newly elected Constituent Assembly. When the Third All-Russian Congress of Workers' and Soldiers' Deputies convened shortly thereafter, a motion that the Congress assume permanent authority as the government of Russia was readily endorsed. Thus, the spontaneous re-emergence of Soviets as a vehicle for the expressing of grass-roots opinion almost accidentally became the avenue to power for the Bolshevik wing of the Russian Social Democrats.

The Soviet and the city

It had long been obvious that the structure of urban government was in dire need of reform. Thus, it was only a matter of weeks before the Provisional Government issued new rules for municipal elections, the main purpose being to broaden the electoral base. Under the existing Tsarist municipal statute of 1892 the franchise had been severely restricted. In most cities less than one per cent of the population could participate in municipal elections. Under the revised electoral rules all those over 20 years of age who fulfilled the simple and unrestrictive residence requirements would be entitled to vote. Though more democratically constituted, municipal government remained under the thumb of central, or higher, authorities. For instance, in matters related to municipal finances approval from central government was necessary for major property, loan or concession transactions. Even where referral to the Minister of the Interior was not specifically requested, the *guberniya* commissar could proclaim a municipal government decision illegal, thus demanding time-consuming adjudication in the courts. In all, the electoral procedures were democratized under the rules promulgated by the short-lived Provisional Government, but its mandate remained far greater than its limited operating procedures could properly accommodate (Browder and Kerensky, 1961, 259–72).

With the advent of the Bolshevik regime the grass-roots significance of the Soviet was soon firmly entrenched. In the constitution adopted in July 1918 for the Russian Soviet Federative Socialist Republic, it clearly played a pre-eminent part in the new political reality. As this constitution served as a model for that drafted for the Union of Soviet Socialist Republics in 1923, the continuing significance of the Soviet was assured. The enshrinement of the Soviet had important consequences for municipal government (Webb, 1937, Vol. 1, 16).

What the Soviet system ushered in for urban government was, like the Provisional Government rules before, a radical departure from the restrictive policies of the autocracy. The electoral base was broadened, but not to the extent of universal adult suffrage. Though the age of majority was set at 18, many members of the former bourgeoisie holding the franchise because of property qualifications were now disenfranchised for precisely that same reason. Elections to city Soviets were to be conducted so as to have one member for every 1,000 inhabitants, excluding, of course, those who were specifically disenfranchised. The maximum size of the city Soviet was 1,000 delegates, the minimum 50. An executive committee (*ispolkom*) comprising between three and fifteen members was to be the effective decision-making body insofar as day-to-day administrative matters were concerned. But in order to ensure control from above, the principle of dual subordination was invoked. This meant that committees and departments were responsible in the first instance to the Soviet at their own level in the hierarchy, and in the second, to the corresponding committee or department at the next highest level in the system. The Soviet, nonetheless, was to be 'master in its own house'. But as Maxwell (1935, 69) has indicated in his enumeration of the tasks of the city Soviet, the actual extent of jurisdiction was rather ill-defined. He has summarized the basic duties as follows:

1 To take all possible measures to carry out the decrees of the constituted authorities.
2 To encourage the development of cultural and economic life in the community.
3 To give decisions in affairs of a purely local character.
4 To unify all Soviet activities in a single territory.

The adoption of new measures for municipal government must be viewed within the particular circumstances of the times. The Civil War which followed the assumption of power by the Bolsheviks, and the further deterioration of the national economy, ensured that there would be a substantial gap between the principles and practice of municipal government.

From the outset managing urban affairs was complicated as much by the dearth of administrative talent as by the vagueness of statutory responsibilities. Amongst the old administrative hierarchy, few personnel were acceptable to the new order. Amongst the capable Bolshevik administrators, the task of municipal government paled in comparison with the importance of ending intervention, extending control over dissident territories and securing a stable food supply.

In few cities did the Soviet assume its full responsibilities, in many it simply failed to materialize. In the first place, regional Soviet executives frequently pre-empted the role of the city Soviet and its executive. Where elections were held the electoral process did not always proceed smoothly, and the resultant city Soviet was sometimes ineffectual. In short, a general malaise seems to have descended upon municipal government and its election. Amongst those holding the franchise a disinclination to vote reminiscent of the Tsarist era obtained. In 1923 less than a third of those qualified actually cast a vote in municipal elections in the USSR. Apparently the participation rates were somewhat higher in the larger centres than in the small, but in any case the results were far from satisfactory. By 1925 a modified statute for municipal government was promulgated (Carr, 1959, 357–60).

The Municipal Statute of 1925 reaffirmed the pre-eminence of the city Soviet in municipal affairs, something unchanged right to the present time. Any settlement with more than 10,000 inhabitants, or 2,000 electors, could now form a city Soviet. The new statute seems to have enhanced interest in elections, for participation rates increased somewhat (Carr, 1959, 361). Initially elections were conducted on vocational rather than territorial bases. Thus, voting was organized around place of employment instead of residence, at least so far as it was possible. As before the size of the city Soviet varied according to the length of the electoral roll. Although the executive committee continued to assume the major burden of administration, the idea that delegates should be involved as much as possible in the work of government was actively promoted. Large numbers of volunteers helped offset the frequently limited contingents of salaried municipal bureaucrats. And within the larger cities, usually those in excess of 100,000 inhabitants, the city Soviet, its bureaucratic apparatus and host of volunteers was complemented, or in some cases complicated, by the existence of district (*rayon*) Soviets which have similar, though smaller, bureaucratic structures. All told, public participation in municipal government was widespread.

Although there have been reforms of municipal government since 1925, as we will demonstrate later, these have simply reaffirmed its original mandate and the role of the city Soviet in the decision-making process. Voting, however, is now organized on a territorial basis. The apparent autonomy of the city Soviet has some clear implications for town planning, but how does the system work in practice? At this point we need to know something about the larger decision-making environment, and the place of the present-day city Soviet within it, before we can begin to provide an answer.

The decision-making framework in national perspective

So far as the formal apparatus of central government is concerned, elections occur at several levels. As a federal system the USSR embraces 15 Soviet Socialist Republics which in turn contain 20 Autonomous Soviet Socialist Republics, 8 Autonomous Oblasts and 10 National Okrugs. Since the late 1930s governmental authority has resided in the Supreme Soviet (Fig. 1). This bicameral legislature comprises the Soviet of the Union, to which members are directly elected on the basis of one delegate for every 300,000 people, and the Soviet of Nationalities, to which members are elected according to the status of political–administrative unit. For instance, the Soviet Socialist Republic is the highest order of political–administrative unit and from each 32 delegates are sent to the Soviet of Nationalities. The lowest level in

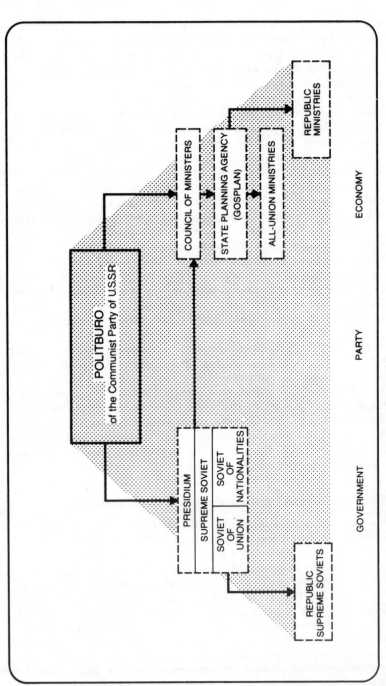

Fig. 1 Simplified structure of decision making in the USSR

the system is that of the National Okrug and from each one delegate is sent to the Soviet of Nationalities. Customarily the delegates are Communist Party (as the Bolsheviks eventually became known) nominees, and elections, while displaying near perfect turnouts, are from the standpoint of the Western observer, politically uncontested. Administrative functions are largely carried out by the Council of Ministers, a body elected from the Supreme Soviet and responsible to it, or the Presidium, another body elected from the Supreme Soviet which can exercise legislative authority between sessions. In theory, the Supreme Soviet, which meets only occasionally, could revoke measures adopted by the Council of Ministers, but in practice it does not. Thus, the day-to-day business of government at the national level falls very much on the shoulders of executive committees of one kind or another, much as it does at the city level. This basic administrative system of Supreme Soviet, Council of Ministers and so on is replicated in each Soviet Socialist Republic. While constitutionally the Republic has great autonomy, it is the nature of this particular Soviet system inevitably to centralize real political and economic decision-making power.

Permeating all sectors of Soviet life is the Communist Party and its manifold congress and committee structures. Most positions of authority are held by Party members whose dual function is to administer and superintend. While Fig. 1 shows the general organizational framework of government and economic decision making, what it cannot adequately convey is the pervasiveness of the comparatively small (some 13 million) Party membership whose principal function is to see that the directives of the POLITBURO, a kind of inner cabinet of the Communist Party, are fulfilled. Still, it probably does not require much imagination to visualize how information flows upward, and channels of communication down through the system, might be manipulated to serve the interests of the Party.

For most of the Soviet era, economic planning has been administered through a hierarchically-structured network of committees, ministries and departments. Basic policy decisions are taken by the POLITBURO of the Communist Party. Decisions of the POLITBURO are accountable not to the government, that is, the Supreme Soviet, but to the Party Congress. In general the role of the Council of Ministers as government is to effect policies laid down by the POLITBURO.

In the realm of economic planning *per se* the state planning agency GOSPLAN plays the principal role. Subordinate to it and other central coordinative committees like GOSSTROY, the state committee on construction, is a complex of ministries, departments and enterprises (Fig. 1). Information required for economic planning supposedly passes up through this system while directives go down. Once basic development priorities have been set by the POLITBURO, GOSPLAN translates them into plan-instructions for the ministries. Ministries exist at three levels—All-Union, Union-Republic and Republic—are numerous in number, and in a constant state of flux. At present nearly 50 are concerned with economic matters. Plan-instructions usually cover a five-year period and theoretically determine what is to be produced, how and by what means, where, when and to whom it is to be delivered. In practice central planning authorities do not make most of the detailed decisions. If they did the system simply would not work as well as it does. On the other hand, to the extent that detailed decisions entirely escape the control of central authorities, planned economic development is frustrated. What has emerged, therefore, is a kind of balance of real decision-making authority between ministries and central planners. Central authorities specify goals, set plans, and it is up to the ministerial decision-makers to do what is necessary to make the system work. The reality of the economic decision-making process is closer to what Alec Nove has called 'centralized pluralism' (1977, 60–64). Ministries almost inevitably become interest groups. But some ministries, and ministers, are economically and politically more important than others. Nevertheless, within any particular ministry all decision-makers have a vested interest in at least appearing successful. Hence, in order to meet the continuously increasing output targets ministerial decision-makers have tended to bring under their control as many inputs as possible. Where they are not able to control all the essential components for increasing production themselves, systems of mutually beneficial personal contacts have been developed to take up the slack, (Andrle, 1976, 31). Where semi-legal bartering or exchanges between production units fail to garner the necessary supplies, production targets are not fulfilled, bottlenecks occur, and positions of authority become increasingly tenuous. Even those in charge of important ministries have been dismissed for perceived failures. Thus, throughout the whole system all participants in the decision-making process have a real stake in making things work, even if in an objectively inefficient manner from the standpoint of the national economy as a whole. While there is no question that the economy functions, and in some key sectors exceedingly well, there is also no question that the nature of the decision-making system produces a number of conflict situations.

In all economic systems there are tensions between regional and sectoral interests. In the Soviet Union the tension is exacerbated somewhat owing to the absence of any spokesman for regional interests equivalent to that of the minister of a branch of the economy. To be sure GOSPLAN contains a regional planning division, and there are Republic level government and planning officials, but in the Soviet system they simply do not have the same profile or political clout as ministers. Thus, in a situation in which an investment allocation must be made to expand production, and the choice is simply one of a better return if new plant is located in an already well developed region as opposed to a less well developed region, ministerial self-interest could well take precedence over regional development needs. The outcome is largely a function of the priorities which will be set by the POLITBURO. In recent years there has been a growing preoccupation with boosting the rate of return on investment. Small cities and backward regions offer fewer external economies and hence become less likely choices for investment allocation—other things being equal.

We have already noted that some ministries are obviously more important than others. Given the reality of differential political and economic powers, the wishes and rights of some decision-making bodies will be overruled. For example, if a particular commodity is in short supply but is required by two ministries, one an integral component of the national defence system, the other being part of the consumer-goods sector, it is pretty clear which ministry would dominate. Similarly, in a conflict of interest between town-planning officials and an enterprise which is part of a nationally important ministry, odds are the enterprise interests would prevail. In the national context of decision making, city Soviets and their various departments simply have not figured very prominently.

Attempts to loosen controls from above, to allow, or indeed encourage, more decision making at the grass-roots level, have been made during the past decade or so, most notably in the 1965 economic reform and in 1973. In 1965 a variety of economic incentives were offered industrial management in an attempt to boost both the quantity and quality of production. In 1973 the association (*obyedineniye*) was created. Intended to replace the enterprise (*predpriyatiye*) as the basic organizational unit in the industrial and resource-development sectors, the association conceivably could include design, production and distributional functions previously under the jurisdiction of several ministries. The purpose of the new organizational structure simply was to promote greater efficiency through scale economies and minimization of bureaucratic interference in production. Despite the intent of the 1965 reform and the 1973 administrative reorganization, the traditional hierarchical structure in decision making has been little altered (Nove, 1977, 81). It is against these hierarchically structured systems of government, Party and economic management at the national level that the government and planning of cities must be viewed.

The contemporary city Soviet and town-planning bureaucracy

As Fig. 2 indicates there are presently three levels of municipal government; Republic, provincial and district. The electoral system continues to produce rather large assemblies, at least by Western standards. For instance, the Moscow city Soviet now has more than 1,100 delegates (*Moskva*, 1976, 15). Real decision-making authority still resides in the executive committee rather than in the Soviet. On this committee sit directors of major municipal departments and Party representatives, usually, though not necessarily, elected from the city Soviet. While in

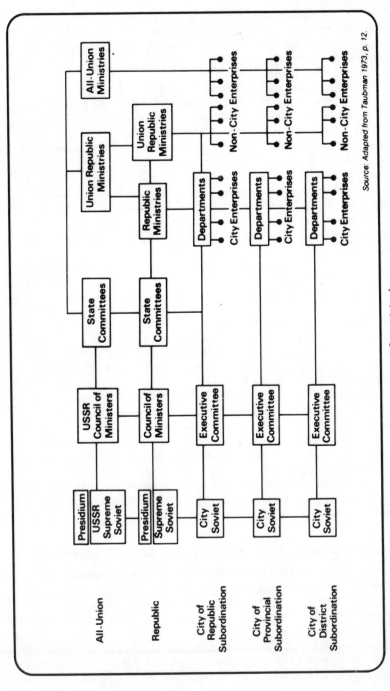

Fig. 2 Schematic outline of decision-making environment of municipal government

Source: Adapted from Taubman 1973, p. 12.

theory the executive is responsible to the city Soviet, in fact it tends to set policies which are then ratified by the Soviet, a not unreasonable state of affairs given the size and sometimes irregular sitting of the latter. In keeping with the principle of dual subordination mentioned earlier, the executive is also theoretically subordinate to its counterpart at the next highest level of the administrative hierarchy. The same applies, of course, to the city Soviet itself and the various city departments (Cattell, 1968, 40–57; Taubman, 1973, 35–8). However, close examination of Fig. 2 reveals an important feature of the urban administrative structure. The various enterprises operating within cities are not all under dual subordination. In other words, some enterprises, and in some cities a very great many, are only responsible to central authorities. The implications of this state of affairs for urban government in general, and town planning in particular, we will develop at a later point.

The size of the architecture-planning bureaucracy in most cities is relatively small. At least two reasons are responsible for this situation. Firstly, it was not until the Khrushchev era that urban problems were acknowledged as national problems. Thus, the development of town-planning staffs had long been of low priority. Secondly, a considerable share of the planning and design work for cities' physical development (*planirovka*) has been assumed by the state committee for civil construction and architecture (GOZGRAZHDANSTROY). This is usually done on a contract basis for client city Soviets. While major cities have staffs of at least 100–200 people, and Moscow more than 500, these are large by Soviet standards. Given the responsibilities of town-planning staffs in the Soviet city, their size is certainly not large compared to the major cities of Europe or North America. The town-planning function is formally linked with municipal government by virtue of the department head normally serving as a member of the executive committee of the city Soviet.

Within municipal government the planning commission (GORPLAN) plays a key role. Its functions include:

1 planning the municipal economy
2 calculating the five-year plans
3 ensuring supplies of raw materials, fuels, materials and equipment for all branches of the municipal economy
4 providing suggestions for improved growth.

Membership of the committee can range from a handful to 100 members (Frolic, 1970a, 104–5). As an extension of the Republic state-planning committee, it therefore tends to act as an intermediary between municipal and Republic interest groups. Annual municipal plans are produced by GORPLAN on the basis of terms of references set by Republic authorities and forwarded to municipal departments, and the responses to these instructions by the various city departments as they have been revised by the executive committee of the city Soviet. Clearly, there is potential for inter-departmental conflicts of interest. If actual conflicts are not resolved by the executive committee, they are resolved by the Party, which often has specialists directly involved in the process of plan formulation. Similarly, conflicts between the city Soviet executive committee and GORPLAN are resolved by the Party. The draft plan is forwarded from the city to the Republic State planning committee in early summer, revisions are made, civic officials respond and by December the upcoming annual plan is ratified. In view of the multitude of ways that available funds might be expended—even allowing for priorities being set by the Republic or State—there is clearly much scope for lobbying by various interest groups. How successful a particular interest group might be seemingly depends to a considerable extent on the degree of Party support for its position. While the structure of the Communist Party is clearly hierarchical, there is some evidence of a measure of independence from central authorities by local Party officials (Frolic, 1972, 44). Thus, the inevitable inter-departmental, if not inter-personal, rivalries tend to be mediated by the local Party organization.

In summary, the bureaucratic structure for town planning is not particularly large in terms of the size of the staff, though its responsibilities are enormous. Available evidence indicates that planners are very much governed by instructions from higher level authorities (Frolic, 1971, 385). While the actual resolution of conflicts of interest are exceedingly difficult to document empirically, it does appear that the Party serves as final arbiter. Whatever the structure of the decision-making system, for an essentially normative approach to town planning to be successful, it is imperative that there be tolerably accurate knowledge as to what the economic and demographic parameters of a city and its immediate hinterland are likely to be within a specific time period, that there be the power to influence events so as to have developments conform reasonably well with plans and that there be the requisite financial resources to realize planned objectives. At present, the nature of such knowledge, influence and finance in the Soviet Union has more in common with cities in markedly different economic and political systems than initially might be supposed. It is the purpose of the remainder of this chapter to examine some features of the actual environment within which the Soviet town planner functions and to briefly illustrate some features of the decision-making process in the 1970s.

Decision making and town planning in retrospect

There are undoubted advantages for town planning in the Soviet system of public ownership of resources and the emphasis on their collective rather than personal consumption (Simon, 1937, 211–20). The existence of a centrally planned economy offers still other advantages, among which is the possibility of a rational allocation and use of resources, physical and human. Since town planning is supposedly an organic component of the planning process at the regional, republic and state levels it should also be so advantaged (Kudryavtsev, 1974, 14). It is thus one of the ironies of Soviet economic planning in general, and the planning of cities in particular, that the allocation and use of resources are frequently described as irrational (Vashanov, 1972, 98–9).

As we have seen, ministries have been the channels through which central planning decisions have been implemented for most of the Soviet period. However, by the mid-1950s the ministerial system had come under fire for spawning autarchic empires in which the welfare of the economy as a whole was sacrificed to individual ministerial objectives. Given that fulfilment of centrally planned production quotas was the basic criterion for judging success, and hence providing rewards, such behaviour on the part of ministerial decision-makers is not surprising. It is equally understandable that the rigid and hierarchically structured decision-making system enveloping the ministerial approach to central planning should be seen as stifling local initiative and impairing economic performance. Still, the Soviet model for economic planning which existed until 1957 did produce remarkable rates of growth in priority sectors of the economy, sufficient to compensate for weaker sectors thereby causing the national economy to expand at a very rapid pace. The casualty of the approach was effective coordination—indeed, even cooperation—amongst the many ministries and their manifold departments or *glavki*. All too often narrow departmental interests took precedence over integration, sectoral and spatial.

The reform of 1957

For town planners operating in the lower echelons of the decision-making system the potential difficulties are clear enough. By the mid-1950s there was growing support for making regional planning at all scales more effective, for devolving greater decision-making responsibilities and, in some quarters, for disbanding the economically and politically powerful ministerial system. These objectives figured prominently in the Khrushchev-initiated economic reform of 1957 in which over 100 regional economic councils or SOVNARKHOZY replaced all but a handful of ministries as the apparatus for central planning. The chequered history of this short-lived attempt to replace ministries with regional economic councils need not concern us, but it is of interest that the problems of town planning were not ignored during this period of reform. Legislation intended to enhance the autonomy of the city Soviet, thereby facilitating town planning, was also introduced in 1957.

That many enterprises and departments in each city did not fall under the town planner's jurisdiction was only a problem if local authorities were either unaware of proposed developments or unable to influence them. All too often, however, reliable information concerning ministerial plans was hard to come by. Last-minute changes in plans were not unheard of and usually boosted the demand for municipal services beyond the ability of the city to satisfy them. If necessary, ministries stepped in and built their own facilities. As a result, it was common for major components of urban water and sewage systems to belong to several different ministries. Similarly, vast tracts of housing remained outside civic administration and control (Cattell, 1976, 259). In theory, such facilities would only be built in consultation with municipal authorities and in accordance with planning norms. The by-passing of both was not unknown, nor was that the most serious issue. The provision of housing, for instance, could conform to all the construction norms. But what of the host of ancillary communal and cultural services required by the inhabitants? These were generally assumed to be the responsibility of the municipal authorities and there the matter stood. The city for its part could only meet anticipated demands from the existing budget. Such unplanned developments usually brought in their wake an unplanned expansion in labour force and in turn an unplanned increment in total population with all the attendant demands for new services and added strain on existing facilities. To the extent that municipal government was unable to control events, short-term town planning became more *ad hoc* and long-term planning, where it existed, redundant.

Legislation introduced in 1957 was intended to clarify and strengthen the role of the city Soviet and its subordinate departments in controlling urban affairs. More specifically, it was the executive committee of the city Soviet which was to have greater power. Through a variety of measures, including the affirmation of political power and transfer of facilities and financial resources, the 1957 reform intended that municipal government in fact be 'master in its own house'. The city was to become the sole agent responsible for contracts for the planning, financing and construction of all housing, municipal, consumer and cultural services. Greater emphasis was to be placed upon town planning, the reiteration of the necessity of a general plan for each city being but one instance. At the time less than half of the cities had such a document to guide development and many of these were outmoded (Svetlichnyy, 1960, 29–36; Taubman, 1973, 22). The system of regional economic councils was also assumed to benefit cities because of the possibility of more direct access to the centres of decision making. The fact that 14 years later the same issues had to be tackled again points to the failure of the 1957 reform. We need only examine some of the principal reasons for its fate.

The SOVNARKHOZ system was not itself enthusiastically endorsed by the bureaucrats and soon proved unworkable. Indeed, within a short period of time there began a steady process of re-establishing ministries in the priority sectors of the economy. The failure of the 1957 legislation to specify how cities were to liaise with regional economic councils ensured that the interests of municipal government were ignored in the shuffle for political power amongst regions, and between regions and the growing number of ministries. Thus, the prospect of greater political power on the part of municipal government did not materialize. Nor did the transfer of facilities, for ministries proved to be reluctant partners when basic services, like water and sewage systems, or housing were involved. The transfer of small industries with local urban markets for technologically unsophisticated products was similarly difficult to expedite, although this met with greater success. However, it was often the case that when agreements were reached, the newly created regional economic councils commandeered the facilities thereby leaving municipal government in the same position as before (Taubman, 1973, 31). But there were gains in the transfer of finances; a massive investment in housing alone dictated that this be so. Direct subsidies from central government cannot be specified with any certainty but available evidence suggests that municipal budgets did improve (Taubman, 1973, 39).

In 1965 the SOVNARKHOZ system was finally abolished and the ministerial system fully reinstated. While the 1957 reform did bring about improvements in housing, communal and cultural facilities, the continued existence of compartmentalized, centralized and generally tangled lines of decision-making responsibility rendered town planning in particular, and management of municipal affairs in general, inefficient and irrational. It was not until 1971 that the Communist Party and government responded to this increasingly serious problem. The response, as usual, involved issuing a barrage of resolutions and decrees intended to set matters right by asserting once more the long-standing legal authority of the city Soviet.

The reform of 1971

Something of the critical flavour of the management of urban affairs which runs through the Communist Party resolution, 'On Measures for the Further Improvement of the Work of the District and City Soviet', is contained in the following extract:

> ... city Soviets are still not making full use of their rights and possibilities for the improvement of services to the population and the integrated development of districts and cities and are not displaying the proper persistence in the resolution of questions of economic construction connected with the implementation of the economic reform. The Soviets are still inadequately coordinating the work of enterprises and organizations of different departmental subordination in the fields of social, cultural and everyday facilities and the production of consumer goods.

> ... many ... enterprises and organizations are directly subordinate to territory and province agencies or to republic ministries and departments. This reduces the responsibility of the district and city Soviets for the state of affairs of their territory and restricts their initiative in the resolution of questions of the development of the local economy and in improving services to the population.

The plans for the construction of housing, and especially of social, cultural and everyday facilities, that are carried out by the ministries and departments are frequently under-fulfilled, but the city and district Soviets and their executive committees tolerate this situation and do not stop manifestations of departmental narrow-mindedness in this matter (On measures, 1971, 1–2).

At the root of the criticism was the failure of municipal government to govern, a state of affairs hardly surprising in view of the numerous centres of decision making over which it had no effective control. The Supreme Soviet and Council of Ministers of central government produced resolution and decree hard on the heels of the Communist Party statement, echoing the sentiment but being somewhat more specific about remedial measures. But these were only models to be used in formulating further legislation at the Republic level (On measures, 1971, 5; On rights and duties, 1971, 27–30). The general directions of change, nonetheless, had been established.

As in the 1957 reform the city Soviet and its executive committee in particular were to exercise more effectively existing legal rights or, more bluntly, political power. Management and planning were to be made easier, more efficient and rational by means of a transfer of non-city facilities to the city Soviet, city-serving industries were to be brought under municipal authority and its financial base was to be bolstered by new sources of revenue. Access to information, power to influence developments, financial resources to realize objectives—all the necessary conditions for an effective normative style of town planning were to be fulfilled. It is still too soon to assess fully whether or not the 1971 reform has been successful, but enough years have passed to reveal any signs of change in the style and substance of Soviet town planning.

Decision making and town planning in the 1970s

Though information is limited, that available suggests more continuity than change in the decision-making process. References to what might be loosely described as the decision-making environment within which municipal authorities, including town planners, must work, continually stress the need for greater coordination. Amongst the flurry of criticisms which followed the promulgation of the reform measures a few relating to transport and housing are sufficient to demonstrate in more detail the nature of the problem and the fact that more than decrees are required to abolish bureaucratic departmentalism.

In the spring of 1971 there appeared in the Communist Party organ, *Pravda*, a short discussion of the transport situation in Gorkiy, a major industrial centre on the Volga river east of Moscow. It was remarked that the management of the tramway and trolleybus system is '. . . shared by the Russian Republic Ministry of Communal Economy, its local territorial agency—the provincial communal economy administration—

and the city Soviet executive committee; motor vehicle transport is under the management of both the Russian Republic Ministry of Motor Vehicle Transport and the province Soviet executive committee' (Sokolov, 1971, 20). It is certainly arguable that the ability to co-ordinate urban transport is essential to town planning in the Soviet Union and it is therefore not surprising that the main point of the article was to voice the demand for a single decision-making authority. A restructuring of the management system similar to that which existed in Moscow was recommended. Elsewhere the public transport situation is equally complicated. In Nizhniy Tagil, a centre of heavy industry in the Urals, tram lines are still owned by a large industrial ministry. Not only is transport planning made difficult for municipal officials, '... ministry and department officials are compelled to concern themselves with matters out of their basic purview—determining the development of municipal services' (Lyubovnyy, 1976, 8).

Time and again the departmental approach to housing has been shown to add to costs and inhibit rational town planning (Kochetkov, 1975, 27; Semin, 1975, 24; Gokhberg, 1974, 129–32). But the problem seems if not intractable then nearly so. It was observed in the 1971 Communist Party resolution itself that '... in many cities the Soviets have no direct relationship to the maintenance, repair and improvement of the bulk of the state housing supply, almost two-thirds of which belong to enterprises, institutions and organizations' (On measures, 1971, 2). As housing remains an important element in the competition for labour, enterprises have been understandably reluctant to give up control or to discontinue the construction of new accommodation. Though there have been occasional reports since of new housing construction being brought under the jurisdiction of the city Soviet, there is little to indicate that existing facilities have been transferred from ministries to the cities (Lyubovnyy, 1976, 8; Semin, 1975, 24; Belchenko, 1974, 15–16). Indeed, the weight of available evidence suggests the contrary. In 1971 it was reported that in Yeniseisk, a fast-growing town in western Siberia '... every Ministry builds its own small settlement with its own services and heating plant' (Sinelnikov, 1971, 22). A year later in Saratov, a city of nearly a million inhabitants on the Volga, it was reckoned that in addition to municipal authorities '... there are 80 other enterprises and organizations of various ministries and departments that function as "clients" for the construction of housing' (Ovcharov, 1972, 31). From Krasnodar in the north Caucasian foreland, from Kuybyshev, another million-people city on the Volga, came similar complaints in 1974 (Gerashchenko and Tsingalenok, 1974, 28; Rosovsky, 1974, 31). In 1975 Kiev's problems were aired. In this Ukrainian capital of almost two million, it was noted that besides the city executive more than 70 organizations of various ministries and departments put up housing. Moreover, these organizations '... generally do not bother about comprehensive restructuring of residential blocks, traffic arteries and

microdistricts, frequently they develop selected sites' (Gusev, 1975, 28).
A different organization is responsible for construction in every residential district of Neftekamsk', a flourishing centre of 60,000 inhabitants
in the oil-rich west Siberian lowland (Mussalitin, 1976, 24). In the
important industrial region of the southeastern Ukraine, the Donetsk
Basin, over 90 organizations are involved in building apartments
(Gokhberg, 1976, 60). In large cities and small, the departmental
approach to housing construction in particular, and municipal services in
general, seems not to have been much affected by the 1971 reform.

It is true that the kind of evidence available tends to stress problems
rather than successes, but it ought to be borne in mind as well that this
attempt to strengthen municipal government did more to clarify its
functions than alter the basic decision-making framework outlined in
Fig. 2.

The town planner's dilemma

That decision making in town planning generally has not been
particularly effective is something which has been commented upon
more than once (Lyubovnyy, 1976, 8; Kravchuk, 1973, 10). Increased
responsibilities have made it difficult for town planners to change this
image. The traditional tasks of gathering data, establishing short-term
plans and attempting to meet the various norms pertaining to urban
growth and the welfare of the population, have been broadened very
considerably (Grigor'yeva and Lagushkin, 1976, 85; Melikyants, 1971,
10). Beginning in the early 1960s growing pressure for a longer-term
perspective demanded that cities take seriously the question of preparing,
and adhering to, a general plan. Most cities now have such a document
—a tribute to the efforts of planning staffs in meeting the challenge
(Belousov, 1975, 4). More recently, the 1971 reform has highlighted
other issues of vital importance to cities, the resolution of which depends
upon widening the traditional town-planning perspective.

It has been argued that a shift in focus from city to city-region is
essential to the successful implementation of long-term plans (Bochkov,
1974, 61; Svetlichnyy, 1974, 140). The need to incorporate more of an
ecological dimension in town planning receives greater publicity each
year (Kochetkov, 1975, 26). Over the last few years social planning has
come to play a more important part in urban affairs. (Deruzhinskiy,
1974, 92–6). And so the task becomes ever more complex. But success
in any one or all of these areas depends finally on the authority of the
planner within the municipal government, and between the planning
commission and the other agents of decision making. While the planning
process in many of the major cities, for instance, Moscow, Leningrad
and Kiev, is indeed admirable in terms of organization, authority and
achievement, it is not necessarily representative. So far as can be
determined the growing responsibility assigned to town-planning

personnel is proving a real burden (Tsitsin, 1976b, 81). The planning process may prove to be less effective in consequence.

In an article in the journal *Planovoye Khozyaystvo* the imbalance between the recently increased demands made upon town-planning personnel and their numbers, above all in the medium and small cities, was described with more than a touch of irony. It was remarked that a staff of three or four was typical of the larger centres, whereas in many medium and small centres the planning commission comprised but one person! (Bochkov, 1974, 62). Similar complaints have been voiced in the past, but there seems not to have been widespread improvement (Grigor'yeva and Lagushkin, 1976, 86; Osborn and Reiner, 1962, 244; Melikyants, 1971, 10–11). The immediate solution is to tap the staff resources of other municipal departments and enterprises, but aside from not always being possible, this measure can scarcely satisfy the 1971 reform's call for more effective control and coordination on the part of town planners. Nor is the existing personnel always the best qualified. Though by no means typical, an account of town-planning difficulties in Bratsk, the new town on the Angara River in eastern Siberia, does illustrate the general point. The chief architect, who is ultimately the final arbiter of town-planning affairs and to whom responsibility for the difficulties was attributed, was relieved of his position when it was pointed out that he was neither an architect nor possessed of any other relevant training. As testimony presumably to his perseverance, and certainly to the problems of staffing in such areas, the person in question subsequently secured the position of chief architect for the town of Ust-Ilimsk, another new town to the northeast (Shinkarev, 1973, 6).

The shortage of trained personnel is real enough and although much effort has been expended in overcoming it, there would appear to be some basis for supposing that this is a contributory factor in the failure of planning staffs to enforce norms and to fulfil the demands of the newly created general plans. Recent studies of the general plans in a number of cities, for example, have drawn attention to the fact that many are now redundant or severely breached (Gokhberg, 1974, 129–31; Khodzhayev, 1976, 43–5). Inadequate numbers of planning staff is certainly one reason for this state of affairs, but so too is the fact that as decision-makers and enforcers of established norms, they are often in a weak position (Kravchuk, 1973, 34; Solovyev, 1971, 13). Planning staffs all too often have failed to integrate some enterprise and departmental actions with town plans and norms (Tsitsin, 1976c, 9). At least partly responsible for the situation is the difference in economic and political power exerted by planning officials on the one hand and the managers of enterprises which are part of nationally important ministries on the other. Thus, the planner is sometimes reduced to a role in which he merely assigns a sector of the city for the development of new industries. In the contest between ministerial priorities and town-planning principles it is almost inevitable that the former takes precedence.

It was suggested earlier that the success of the Soviet style of normative town planning was dependent upon the ability to obtain accurate information with which to formulate planning strategies, the ability to influence decisions so as to fit the prescribed norms and plan guidelines and upon the availability of the financial resources to fulfil planned objectives. From what has been said it follows that information is not always easy to acquire, nor necessarily accurate (Grigor'yeva and Lagushkin, 1976, 86). It has been argued that despite two attempts to reform and strengthen municipal government and its constituent departments, the decision-making environment remains one in which town planners experience difficulty in exercising their legitimate authority. So far as financial resources are concerned, the last reform widened the sources of revenue, and budgets since have increased considerably. But despite some obvious improvements, there remain difficulties concerning revenue generation and allocation which have a bearing on the ability of municipal government to carry out its mandate satisfactorily.

The financial squeeze

Municipal budgets are almost entirely dependent upon the transfer of capital investment and operating funds from higher authorities. These have included proportions of turnover taxes paid by state enterprises, personal income tax and other minor forms of direct taxation (Taubman, 1973, 39). To give cities greater financial autonomy the Council of Ministers in the 1971 decree stated that Republics should give considered attention to the question of bolstering municipal revenues by arranging for:

> ... leaving at the disposal of the district and city Soviet executive committees the revenues obtained additionally during the execution of the budget, and also the excess of revenues over expenditures that is formed at the end of the year through the overfulfilment of revenues or through savings in expenditures.

> ... leaving at the disposal of the district and city Soviet executive committees part of the profits of their subordinate enterprises providing everyday services to the population and enterprises of local industry and the communal economy, and also the transfer to the budgets of the districts and cities of part of the profits of enterprises and economic organizations of republic and province (territory) subordination;

> ... leaving at the disposal of the district and city Soviet executive committees part of the turnover tax on consumer goods manufactured over and above the plan at enterprises of republic and local subordination, and also part of the turnover tax paid into the budgets of the Union republics and derived from the sale of goods produced according to additional assignments from centrally allocated raw and other materials (On measures, 1971, 5).

The years since have witnessed something of a change in the nature of financial problems facing municipal government. To be sure there are still to be found instances of enterprises, departments or ministries, not fulfilling their financial commitments to the municipalities in which they operate (Belchenko, 1974, 16; Azan, 1972, 23). But in the case of non-centralized capital investment allocation a seeming embarrassment of riches has sometimes been created.

Municipal government can in theory regulate enterprise funds for the purpose of developing basic infrastructural services or improving communal and cultural services. As the quotations from the 1971 decree indicate, a share of these funds is to be derived from enterprise profits or turnover taxes resulting from above-plan production. But there is no way in which the amounts involved can be determined in advance. Thus, as was noted at the time of the reform, lack of information as to the scale of revenue virtually precludes the implementation of a rational procedure for incremental improvements in municipal facilities, especially as the nature of the decision-making system tends to militate against municipal over-expenditure (Zamula, 1971, 17). There is also the problems of rising costs and what to do to achieve a balanced budget.

Like municipal governments elsewhere, those in the Soviet Union are caught by the direct-grant arrangements not keeping abreast of real costs. For instance, out of each million roubles invested in a city, something in the order of 10 per cent is turned over to the city Soviet by the ministry concerned to cover costs of basic municipal services. It has been argued that this ought to be increased to 25 per cent to reflect more closely actual expenditures incurred (Rosovsky, 1974, 31). More serious are the consequences of the 1965 economic reform which introduced the concept of profitability as one of the criteria for evaluating enterprise performance. Municipal government operations were not excluded and the need to make a profit has affected the way in which some of them have been managed. The example of public transport illustrates the nature of the problem. In 1970 Moscow's public transport system was two million roubles in deficit (Livshits, 1971, 32). Tram and trolley-bus operations in the country as a whole lost nearly 55 million roubles in 1973. Demands for better service and more extensive systems have pushed capital expenditure up, wages have risen dramatically, but fares have been unchanged for nearly a quarter of a century. The emphasis on profitability has created some situations in which equipment has been permitted to run down, but this can only be a short-term solution to reducing costs of operation (Nedachin, 1974, 11). At some point equipment must be replaced and systems extended, but the problem of rapidly rising operational deficits in public transport certainly has influenced municipal government decision making.

In the course of the five-year-plan period extending from 1976 to 1980 something in the order of 100 billion roubles is to be spent on housing and communal construction (Khodzhayev, 1976, 43). It would appear that as in the past most of those funds will be channelled into city coffers through a process of centralized decision making. Finances will come from the state budget, from state subsidies for particular projects and from ministries which have enterprises in particular cities (Myasnikov, 1977, 8). The 1971 reform certainly has assisted in the quest for greater financial independence for municipal government, but it could not be argued on the basis of available evidence that these new sources now dominate revenue generation (Tsitsin, 1976a, 15; Mikhaylov, 1976, 24). Moreover, the combination of the pressure to make profits and the inability to predetermine a portion of revenue has not made managing municipal affairs any easier. It is not possible to ascertain how an individual city fares in the scramble for the revenue from central government sources but the general situation is probably little different from that described by Taubman (1973, 40) at the turn of the decade:

> City Soviets rely on higher authorities—for advice and consent, and for money, materials and manpower. Yet in the eyes of its superiors, a particular city is only one of many claimants on attention and resources, both of which, in a system characterized by great size and extreme scarcity, are limited.

Summary

The adoption of a grass-roots, democratic organization like the Soviet by a political force like Lenin's Bolshevik faction of the Russian Social Democratic Workers' Party, the distinguishing feature of which was a rigid centralization of decision-making authority, almost inevitably generated some contradictions and tensions. Indeed, the very success of the Bolsheviks in engineering the takeover of the Provisional Government, and ultimately full political power, was in large measure dependent upon the explicit recognition by the membership of the absolute authority of Lenin. It was not a party of consensus. After more than six decades of evolutionary development the concept of centralized decision making remains intact.

Control from above is not incompatible with integrated, harmonious development of the national economy, region and city, provided all participants in the decision-making process observe the same rules or priorities. Indeed, in theory there are some clear-cut advantages and economies compared to a piecemeal approach. But if the participants respond in different ways to the same instruction, or if they do not share the same priorities, in the absence of some overall coordinative body with a measure of real authority, planned economies, presumed integration and rational development became exceedingly elusive goals. It is in this context that the management of urban affairs in general, and town planning in particular, must be set.

In theory, the city Soviet is the final arbiter in urban affairs. In practice, as we have endeavoured to demonstrate, the execution of its mandate is often confounded by the absence of a commonly shared perception of its importance. Inherent in the Soviet socialist system which has evolved are all the necessary ingredients for tensions between ministerial and regional interest groups, between enterprises and Soviets, between enterprise managers and town planners. The town planner is frequently placed in an untenable position insofar as exercising his mandate goes. As a decision-maker his authority is often challenged by vested ministerial interests. To a large extent the degree to which the town-planning process in a particular city is successful or not depends upon the ability of the planner to gain political support, to effect bargains, to arrange compromises. In this regard his function is not so greatly different from his counterpart in the West. What does differentiate his role in the Soviet socialist system is the breadth of his mandate and the absence of competing, formal political forces which could be turned to for support. Soviet town planning is rarely a smooth process, not always even an especially successful one if success be judged solely by the goals the system sets for its town-planning function. But the attempt to bridge the gap between ever shifting ideals and reality does bring real improvements, and it would be a mistake to exaggerate the difficulties and overlook the accomplishments. What we have attempted to do in the discussion of decision making in town planning is highlight some of the contradictions inherent in the Soviet system. A reasonable grasp of the problem facing the town planner in this regard will better enable us to evaluate the Soviet city itself. Before embarking on this task, however, an examination of the pattern and process of city growth during the Soviet period is necessary.

4
Patterns of city growth

Soviet town planning is based on the premise that the tempo and spatial pattern of city growth can be made to comply with normative locational guidelines. As we have argued in the preceding chapter, however, important decisions affecting the city often occur without the town planner's approval, and sometimes even without his prior knowledge. Yet it would be premature to conclude that the conscious direction of urban growth has been entirely confounded by the decision-making process. In this chapter we will first of all briefly review some basic guidelines for locational decision making which can influence the tempo and pattern of city growth. Secondly, the mechanisms which are used to control urbanization will be examined. With the discussion of locational guidelines and control mechanisms as background, the principal temporal and spatial characteristics of city growth then will be evaluated. Finally, the Soviet experience in regulating urbanization and creating a planned settlement system will be assessed.

Locational guidelines and control mechanisms

To the extent that governments influence the location of economic activity, including the location of new towns, they are all confronted with the dilemma of encouraging either national efficiency and growth or regional equity and growth. In the Soviet Union the general guidelines which have ostensibly conditioned locational decision making over the years embrace both objectives (Huzenic, 1977, 263; Rodgers, 1974, 235–6). In the first group are those guidelines seemingly directed toward technical optimization. They include developing regional industrial specialization and promoting regional self-sufficiency, minimizing social costs in the exploitation of resources, and minimizing transport costs in industrial development, usually expressed in terms of locating manufacturing near markets or raw materials. The second group focuses on 'spreading' the benefits of socialism through removing regional inequalities and fostering the urban-industrialization of traditionally backward, largely non-Slavic regions. Eradicating differences between tcwn and countryside, the ideological significance of which we noted earlier, is included in this group as well. Strategic considerations in locational decision making are important, though precisely what impact they have had is impossible to gauge. Indeed, because of the general nature of these guidelines the significance of any single one in locational decision making cannot be established with any real certainty. To be sure, there is the possibility that a particular guideline may be used *ex post facto* to rationalize a decision based on trade-offs between various interest groups. Notwithstanding the difficulty of determining how these guidelines may have shaped the pattern of city growth during the Soviet era, it should be evident that the Soviet decision-making system permits a potentially close fit between a particular locational guideline and actual development. It is the degree of control theoretically possible, rather than the fact of state intervention, which so clearly distinguishes the situation in the Soviet Union from most other industrialized states. This raises the question, precisely what controls does the state have at its disposal to direct urban growth?

Urban growth can be manipulated temporally and spatially by several different means. Given the historic Soviet preoccupation with industrial development, it comes as no great surprise that in a study of the relationship between urbanization and industrialization Lewis and Rowland found a high positive correlation (1969, 791). What is implied by this relationship in terms of the possibilities of manipulating urbanization is important. In a Soviet-type economy industrial investment can be directed to specific regions, or to specific-size cities. At various times since the 1930s precisely these kinds of investment decisions have been made. Of course, the corollary of directing investment in new facilities is restricting expansion of existing ones.

Along with spatial and city-size priorities for the allocation of industrial development and concomitant social-consumption funds, the state has used a system of wage differentials to encourage migration to regions where industrial growth is desired. Regional coefficients have played an important role in promoting migration to Siberia, particularly the eastern and northern regions, and have been in use since the late 1930s. While there is no doubt that they have helped to attract migrants to remote, resource-rich areas, whether such incentives have been compatible with 'stable' city populations is quite another matter.

In addition to these generally positive steps to shape the pattern of city growth, various forms of coercion have been used from time to time. By the late 1930s labour was often assigned to specific projects, there to stay until permission to depart was granted, or until directed elsewhere. It was not until the late 1950s that such administrative controls were eased. Graduates of university and technical-school programmes are still liable to be assigned to a period of employment in a developing region.

The necessary bureaucratic machinery for superintending population movements has been in place since the early 1930s. Without an internal passport or equivalent documentation, movement to cities, or between them, is precluded. All urban inhabitants over 15 years of age are required to have a passport in their possession. Not all citizens have traditionally been allocated passports. Peasants on collective farms, for instance, were 'passportless' until the mid-1970s, at which time they were entitled to apply for one. Clearly, rural-urban migration could be more easily managed if peasants, who until the 1950s comprised the largest single stratum in Soviet society, were required to obtain 'permits' to leave the collective farm. But residence in any city is not assured simply by virtue of possession of a passport. Each urban inhabitant must have a *propiska*, a residence permit the equivalent of a visa, which is entered in the passport and which gives legal recognition of the right to live in a specific city. The *propiska* denotes whether residence is permanent or temporary. In theory, one cannot live in a city without such documentation. In practice, most major cities attract sizeable numbers of 'illegal', unregistered residents. If detected, illegal residents are either prosecuted, 'deported' or both. Registered migrants are normally permitted a three-month temporary residence during which time they must secure a job if they arrived without one in hand. When credentials and employer's recommendations are in order, migrants may then obtain a permanent *propiska*, which allows them to be assigned accommodation. Given the shortage of housing, prolonged waiting times are not unusual (Houston, 1979, 32–44).

In summary, there is an elaborate bureaucratic procedure for acquiring permission to reside permanently in a Soviet city. Though a temporary *propiska* entitles one to continue working in the city, all that can be expected by way of accommodation is a bed in a hotel, hostel, workers' barracks, a friend's apartment, or less commonly, rented space in someone else's home. Little imagination is needed to see how urban growth might be 'administratively' manipulated through discretionary allocation of an internal passport and *propiska*. On the other hand, a lot of imagination has been employed to overcome such institutional barriers to migration. Marriage of convenience between persons holding residence permits and those aspiring to obtain one through a spouse is a common subterfuge.

The growth of cities in the late imperial era

Until the late nineteenth century urban growth in Russia was almost entirely dependent upon in-migration. Many factors were responsible for this state of affairs. Amongst the lower classes, especially the peasants, normal family life in the city was the exception rather than the rule owing to financial constraints or intentionally temporary residence there. Thus, the birth-rate in cities was in a sense artificially held down. And the insalubrious, overcrowded conditions in most cities ensured that the death-rate remained high. Indeed, in contrast with advanced European countries like Great Britain where a surplus of births over deaths in cities, that is, a demographic transition, occurred early on in the nineteenth century, in Russia this phenomenon did not become common until the turn of the century (Weber, 1899). Although a surplus of births over deaths contributed to the rapid urbanization of the early 1900s, it paled in comparison with the sheer weight of humanity which each year descended upon the city from the countryside. The rapidly growing urban economy, offering as it did some hope of employment, and the Stolypin Reform of 1906, which eased the legal restrictions on peasant migration, both served to open the flood gate.

One measure of the tempo of city growth may be obtained by comparing the actual increase in urban population between two dates with what the total would have been if the rate of city growth had simply paralleled that of the population as a whole. This kind of comparison ignores regional variations in birth-rates, the appearance of 'new' cities, and in general the thorny problem of reclassification. Such problems notwithstanding, measuring city growth in this way does provide some useful insights into both temporal and spatial trends.

Between 1897 and 1914 the urban population increased by some four million more people than if the rate of growth had been the same as that of the Empire's total population (Lorimer, 1946, 32–3). By the latter date some 28 million people were living in Russian cities (mostly in European Russia). Since the urban birth-rate was characteristically lower, and the death-rate higher, than in the countryside, the four million additional urban inhabitants understates the scale of in-migration between these two dates. As less than one-fifth of the total population lived in what were classified as urban settlements in 1914, an enormous pool of potential migrants remained.

During the Tsarist era only one national census was ever conducted, and that was in 1897. The first Soviet census took place in 1926. Between these two dates the combined impact of world war, revolution, boundary changes and wholesale emigration make accurate population counts impossible. The population deficit for the period from 1897 to 1926 is reckoned by Lorimer to be in the neighbourhood of 25 to 30 million (1946, 36–9). Even allowing for sizeable error, the scale of the deficit is still a colossal number by any standard. Thus, the population base of the new Soviet socialist state was in total size and ethnic composition rather different from its Tsarist counterpart. It was not until the Second World War that the boundaries and ethnic composition of the population of the USSR once again approximated that of the Russian Empire.

City growth in the inter-war period

According to the census of 1926 there were just over 147 million people living within the new, and truncated, borders of the USSR, 41 million more people than in the same territory in 1897. A shade more than 26 million, or roughly 18 per cent, lived in cities or in an urban-type district (*poselok gorodskogo tipa*), a relative share virtually unchanged from that on the eve of the Great War. What had changed was the constituency of the urban system. More than 60 large agro-industrial centres, which under the Tsarist classification were villages, joined the urban category, while over 100 small, mostly administrative and all non-industrial, places, reverted to rural status. Of course, growth had been inhibited by the outbreak of the World War, and the chaos wrought by revolution and Civil War had even prompted urban-rural migration as we noted in an earlier chapter.

With the introduction of Lenin's New Economic Policy (NEP) in 1921 the national economy stabilized and reconstruction began. Cities once again became potential sources of employment. Rural-urban migration quickened even though not all migrants were able to secure jobs. Unemployment and other difficulties notwithstanding, the 1926 census indicates that 5.6 out of the 26.3 million urban population arrived in the city sometime during the preceding six years (Khorev and Moiseyenko, 1976, 39). The Five Year Plan of 1928, signalling as it did the all-out drive to industrialize, brought about a dramatic up-turn in the rate of urban growth. As the data in Table 1 make plain, the average annual increase of 4.6 per cent in the urban population between 1922 and 1940 has not been equalled since. Not only were huge numbers again descending on the city, but unlike the Tsarist era, most came to stay.

Table 1. Average annual growth of urban population

Period	Average annual increase millions	Average annual increase %
1922–1940	2.4	4.6
1940–1950	0.6	0.95
1950–1960	3.4	4.1
1960–1970	3.2	2.8
1970–1975	3.4	2.4

Source: Khorev and Moiseyenko, 1976, 9.

The Soviet population was enumerated again in 1939, though the complete results of the census were never published. At this time 56 million people lived in cities, an increase of almost 30 million since 1926. Natural increase accounted for approximately 5.5 million of the 30 million. Living conditions in Soviet cities were especially onerous during the early 1930s (Scott, 1942, 65–6). Food rationing was widespread, and although evidence is scanty, most suggests an urban abortion rate much higher than the birth-rate. Indeed, ready availability of abortion, easy divorce and the calamitous consequences of collectivization of agriculture begun in 1929 served to dampen the birth-rate every-where, though the customary rural-urban difference remained intact. The government responded in 1936, (after conducting a census which was never released), by making abortion hard to obtain and divorce more difficult. Reclassification of settlements from rural to urban status accounted for roughly six million of the increase in urban population. Thus, in keeping with the long-standing historical trend, urban growth in the inter-war period was a function of large scale rural-urban migration. More than 18 million people departed the village for the city (Lorimer, 1946, 145–74). But where did they go?

Something of the dimensions and pattern of city growth is conveyed by the data portrayed in Map 7. Both urban and rural population per-centage changes have been compared to the rate of growth of the Soviet population as a whole, and the differences between the population increase which would have occurred if the regional urban and rural rates were the same as that for the total Soviet population are expressed in absolute terms as positive or negative balances. It is clear from Map 7 that urban population gains were greatest in European Russia, specific-ally in the Moscow region, and the Ukraine. And it is equally apparent that rural depopulation in European Russia generally was of sizeable dimension. Nearly 450 centres had been added to the roster of urban places, many of them new towns associated with Stalin's efforts to industrialize the eastern regions. Of the 49 cities tripling their populations between 1926 and 1939, and having at least 50,000 inhabitants in 1939, almost half were located in the Urals, Siberia, the Far East and Central Asia, some indication of the government's success in developing the eastern regions. As war with Germany loomed larger, the drive to the east assumed ever greater importance. The Far East and Central Asia, like the Caucasus, the Crimea and the extreme northwestern parts of Karelia, were distinctive in that both urban and rural sectors increased more rapidly than the rate of increase for the total population. Despite rapid urbanization in the eastern regions, the traditional urban-industrial regions still gained a substantial share of city growth. Of the afore-mentioned group of 49 cities tripling their populations, nearly a third was located in the industrial belt stretching from the Dnepr to the Don river in the South Ukraine. Another half dozen such cities were in the Moscow region. Moscow itself had grown rapidly, even after the enunciation of limits to growth in the 1935 Moscow Plan. With 4.5 million inhabitants in 1939 it had nearly reached the proposed maximum of five million inhabitants (*Narodnoye*, 1976, 27). Had controls not directed some growth into surrounding towns, including the six tripling their populations, Moscow certainly would have experienced an even larger influx.

State policies clearly influenced city growth. The industrialization programme brought into existence many new towns based on iron ore and coal deposits. Indeed, the relationship between industrialization

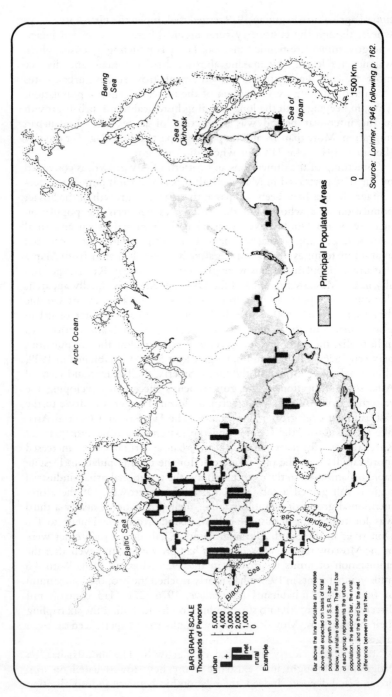

Map 7 USSR —relative population change by study area 1926–39

BAR GRAPH SCALE
Thousands of Persons

urban

5,000
4,000
3,000
2,000
1,000
0

net

+

rural

Example

Bar above the line indicates an increase
above that expected on basis of total
population growth of U.S.S.R.: bar
below, a relative decrease. The first bar
of each group represents the urban
population, the second bar, the rural
population, and the third bar the net
difference between the first two

Principal Populated Areas

Arctic Ocean

Bering Sea

Sea of Okhotsk

Sea of Japan

Baltic Sea

Black Sea

Caspian Sea

0   1500 Km.

Source: Lorimer, 1946, following p. 162.

and urbanization is reflected by the singularly rapid growth of industrial centres. For example, the median rate of population growth amongst industrial cities during this period was 184 per cent, while trade or diversified cities registered a growth rate of just 69 per cent (Harris, 1970, 302).

City growth from 1939 to 1959

The impact of World War II on the Soviet Union and its population is sufficiently well known to require little comment. We need only be reminded of the facts that population losses alone were between 25 and 30 million so that few Soviet families escaped the war untouched by disaster. More than 1,700 cities and 70,000 villages were damaged. In extreme cases, of which there were all too many, city and village alike were literally levelled. In all, about one-sixth of the housing stock was damaged or destroyed (Gendzekhadze, 1976, 42). By the end of the decade a massive programme of reconstruction had not fully repaired the physical destruction. The demographic consequences of the war are visible in the 1970s in the form of the truncated 30 to 39 age group and the unusually large proportion of females aged 60 and over. Psychological scars are not nearly so tangible, but nonetheless are real and enduring.

The war occasioned massive population movements. About 25 million people were evacuated, principally to the Urals, Siberia and Central Asia. Many evacuees settled in the countryside but the city, like the village, was much affected by the sudden influx. In the Kazakh region, for example, the urban population mushroomed during the war years. In 1939 there were 28 cities and 53 urban-type settlements; by 1945 there were 38 and 100 respectively (Khorev and Moiseyenko, 1976, 40–41). The corollary of large population gains in the eastern regions during the war years was retarded growth throughout the occupied part of European Russia. Indeed, absolute population losses occurred in many rural areas and cities. As the data in Table 1 make plain, the 1940s were years of limited urban growth. That which did occur owes much to the border changes the war produced. The incorporation of the Baltic Republics and parts of Poland, Czechoslovakia and Rumania helped to swell the list of urban places. Most of the 314 cities added through border changes were located in these newly acquired territories.

The impact of forced population movement was not entirely ephemeral. As part of the war effort much industry was relocated in the eastern regions, resource exploitation expanded considerably, and both state and collective farm operations were augmented. Thus, at the end of the war a great many jobs remained to be filled. Administrative controls over population migration helped to ensure that an adequate labour supply remained in the eastern regions after the war.

During the inter-censal period 1939 to 1959, the total number of urban places, that is, cities and urban-type districts, increased from 2,762 to 4,619, allowing for territorial gains during the war. The growth in the number of urban places was sizeable, and so too was the increase of 39 million urban inhabitants (*Itogi*, 1, 1972, 61). As the data in Table 1 reveal, it was the 1950s which witnessed the most rapid urbanization. Something of the tempo and spatial pattern of city growth is conveyed by Map 8.

It is readily apparent that all regions garnered more urban inhabitants than would have been the case had city growth simply paralleled the rate of increase of the total population. World war and the drive to industrialize left an indelible stamp on the interior regions of the country during the 1939–1959 period (Harris, 1970, 305–68). As Map 8 indicates, in the Urals, Kazakh and Siberian regions huge increases were registered in the urban sector. The rapid urbanization of the eastern regions was not entirely at the expense of the industrial regions of European Russia as they also experienced a sizeable increase in urban population. For instance, the Centre and Donetsk-Dnepr regions added 3.2 and 2.7 million more to their urban populations than if city growth simply had equalled the growth rate of the total Soviet population. The Volga economic region also underwent something of an urban transformation, in large measure owing to energy-based industrial development during the post-war years.

Between 1939 and 1959 rural-urban migration accounted for roughly 25 of the 39 million increase in urban population. It is apparent from Map 8 that there was a net outflow from the countryside in most regions, though rarely was the dimension of change as great as in the densely populated Centre and South-west economic regions. In only four regions, Uzbek, Kirgiz, Kazakh and Moldavia, did rural population increases exceed the growth rate of total population. Exceptionally high rural birth-rates, especially amongst the indigenous Central Asian peoples, combined with the inertia of the traditional rural life style, helped to stem the drift to the city. In some regions massive rural development projects opened up new lands and created many rural settlements. The most notable example during the period was the Virgin Lands Scheme which brought under the plough nearly 100 million acres, mostly in the Kazakh region. The war resulted in the transfer of many people away from sensitive borders to the interior. For example, many Moldavians were despatched to Siberia and Central Asia. As time passed and restraints on their movement relaxed, they gradually migrated home. Moving to the village rather than the city was easier. Thus, an already high rate of natural increase in the rural sector was boosted further.

In absolute terms the rural population within present-day borders dropped from 130 million in 1939 to just under 109 million in 1959, most of the decrease being accounted for by out-migration. Seven million people lived in settlements reclassified as urban. Only eight million of the increase from 60.4 to 99.9 million urban inhabitants in the

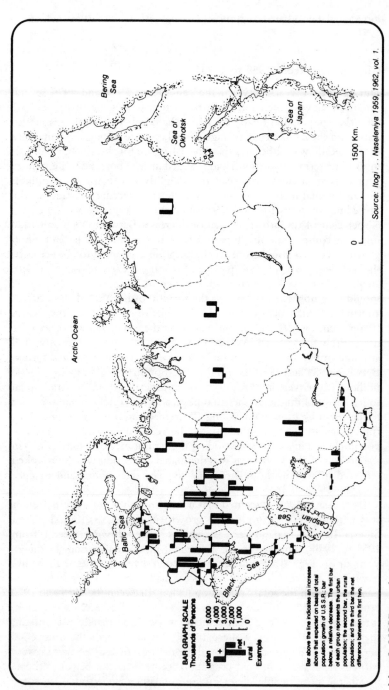

BAR GRAPH SCALE
Thousands of Persons

urban
+
5,000
4,000
3,000
2,000
1,000
net
0
rural
Example

Bar above the line indicates an increase
above that expected on basis of total
population growth of U.S.S.R.; bar
below, a relative decrease. The first bar
of each group represents the urban
population; the second bar, the rural
population; and the third bar the net
difference between the first two.

Arctic Ocean

Bering
Sea

Sea of
Okhotsk

Sea of
Japan

Baltic
Sea

Black Sea

Caspian
Sea

Source: Itogi . . . Naselenya 1959, 1962, vol. 1.

0   1500 Km.

Map 8 USSR—relative population change by study area 1939–59

intercensal period was attributable to natural growth (Perevedentsev, 1971, 1).

City growth from 1959 to 1970

During the 11 years between the censuses of 1959 and 1970 several important developments in the urbanization process occurred. In 1961 the urban population finally overtook the number of rural inhabitants. Although the 2.8 per cent average annual increase during the remainder of the decade was rather less than the 4.1 figure for the 1950s, (Table 1), in absolute terms city growth had changed little. About 3.2 million more people lived in cities each year, only slightly less than the 3.4 million average annual increase registered during the preceding decade. In the preceding intercensal period (1939–1959) rural migrants accounted for 62 per cent of the urban population increase. Between 1959 and 1970 migrants comprised only 46 per cent, or 16.4 million of the 36 million growth in urban population. Reclassification accounted for 14 per cent, slightly less than the 18 per cent in the earlier period. Growth attributable to natural increase jumped from 20 to 40 per cent, but it should be emphasized again that the turmoil of the World War and its aftermath artificially depressed the birth-rate during the 1940s (Perevedentsev, 1971, 1). These changes in the urban growth process are not entirely unexpected. As the urban population grows in relative and absolute importance, the pool of potential rural migrants must shrink. Between 1959 and 1970 the rural population dropped from 109 to 106 million. Moreover, in many parts of European Russia, the traditional source of rural migrants, the rural population is rapidly 'ageing' owing to the out-migration of the young. Therefore, the absolute decline in the rural population in fact understates the real reduction in the pool of potential migrants. Notwithstanding the significance of these changes in the process of city growth, it was the spatial dimension which provoked renewed interest in the relationship between state policy and practice (Shabad, 1977, 173).

By the early 1960s it seemed that urban growth in the eastern regions was faltering. For example, city growth in the Urals, Kazakh, West Siberia, East Siberia and Far East regions slowed down markedly from 1959 to 1970 compared to the preceding intercensal period. In the 20 years up to 1959, 13.3 million more people lived in cities than would have been the case if the urban sector had expanded at a rate commensurate with the total Soviet population. Between the 1959 and 1970 censuses barely 3.8 million were so added. In the Urals economic region, for instance, the 1939–59 'increment' was approximately 5.1 million; for 1959 to 1970 it was a mere 181,000. Even though the intercensal periods are different, urban growth in the eastern regions had slowed. Moreover, as data collected on population registration began to show, in Siberia more people were leaving annually than arriving. In some places an absolute population loss was even recorded in certain of the inter-censal years (Lydolph, 1978, 522). The implications for a balanced programme of regional economic development were a source of growing concern for the planners.

Sluggish city growth in sparsely settled, oft-times labour deficient, eastern regions posed one set of problems. Rapid urbanization in heavily populated, sometimes labour surplus, regions created another set. Given the difficulties entailed in taking up residence in the major European Russian cities, rural-urban migration tended to be oriented to the less urbanized, more accessible regions of the south Ukraine, the North Causasus and Central Asia, none of which are labour deficient (Rybakovskiy, 1973). Out-migration from Siberia, a region of chronic labour shortages, has been similarly directed. Some consequences of these migration flows are displayed by Map 9. City growth in Central Asia has proceeded apace, still in large measure because of an influx of non-indigenous migrants. High rural birth-rates amongst the indigenous Central Asians, combined with strong rural cultural traditions, have resulted in positive changes in the rural population relative to what would be expected if the growth rate simply paralleled the national average. The inertia which has enveloped rural Central Asian society for so long, stifling large-scale indigenous rural-urban migration from a labour surplus region in the process, no doubt will dissipate eventually. But in the meantime Central Asian cities retain a distinctly non-Central Asian ethnic composition. Broadly speaking, the same forces have prevailed in the culturally similar Azerbaydzhan Republic. It too is characterized by a positive 'increment' in the rural sector. In all other regions, the rural population increased much less rapidly than the total Soviet population, and as Map 9 makes plain, European Russia remains the principal source of rural migrants. At the same time it is apparent that the European Russian regions continued to garner a large share of city growth.

In the more relaxed, post-Stalin era, internal migration has increased and more importantly, a growing proportion is unplanned. Perhaps as many as one-third of all moves now occur without the approval, or the knowledge, of officials. Sizeable unplanned migration within a planned economy clearly creates difficulties. That such migration so often has been to labour surplus regions simply makes matters worse. Once the scale of the problem and its consequences began to be appreciated, attempts were made to measure migration flows and to document the reasons for the unplanned components. (Rybakovskiy, 1976, a, b). The volume of research has grown exponentially since the early 1960s. But have the trends set in motion by the relaxation of administrative controls over population movement in the late 1950s been reversed? While the evidence from the 1970s does not provide the basis for conclusive answers, the tempo and spatial dimensions of city growth do provide a few insights on this issue.

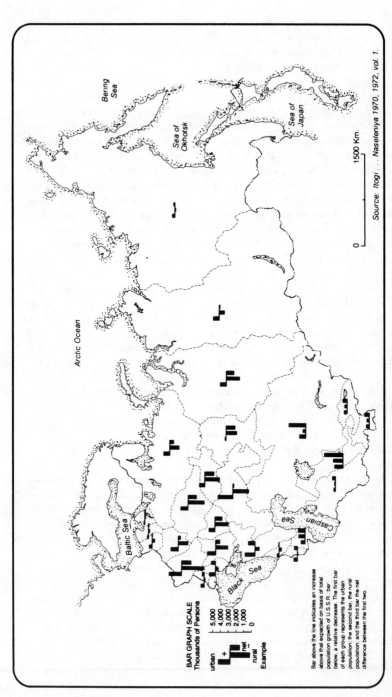

Bar above the line indicates an increase above that expected on basis of total population growth of U.S.S.R.; bar below, a relative decrease. The first bar of each group represents the urban population; the second bar, the rural population; and the third bar the net difference between the first two.

BAR GRAPH SCALE
Thousands of Persons

5,000
4,000
3,000
2,000
1,000
0

urban +

net

rural −

Example

Arctic Ocean

Bering Sea

Sea of Okhotsk

Sea of Japan

Baltic Sea

Black Sea

Caspian Sea

0   1500 Km.

Source: Itogi . . . Naseleniya 1970, 1972, vol. 1.

Map 9 USSR—relative population change by study area 1959–70

The demographic dimensions of city growth in the 1970s

Insofar as the tempo of city growth in the 1970s is concerned, it is apparent from Fig. 3 that there has been no departure from the historic trend of a steady increase in the relative and absolute importance of the urban sector. Close to two-thirds of the total population now live in cities or urban-type districts. While the USSR finally narrowed one long-standing gap between itself and other Western industrialized states, it ought to be remembered that it was only in 1961 that the urban sector overtook the rural, something which happened in most advanced European states a half century or so earlier. But with a steadily shrinking pool of potential rural migrants, and the slowing down of the birth-rate normally associated with urbanization, future city growth seems destined to abate. However, changes in underlying demographic trends could alter such a prognostication.

In general terms there has been a downward trend in both birth and death rates since the turn of the century (Fig. 3). While we have the advantage of hindsight in terms of being able to discern such trends, it is now apparent that the sharp downward turn in the birth-rate which began in the 1950s caught Soviet planners unaware. Official predictions of the total Soviet population made in the late 1950s put the expected 1970 figure at 250 million. In the early 1960s it was estimated to be 248 million (Perevedentsev, 1975, 15). The actual figure was barely 241 million. Such estimates are of considerable importance in a planned economy because from estimated future populations, manpower resources can be calculated and these help shape basic investment decisions as to overall labour-capital ratios. That the expected growth would not materialize was recognized in the 1960s. Sociologists and demographers soon were able to pinpoint many of the social, cultural and economic reasons for the dramatic decline in the crude rate of net natural increase from 17.8 per 1,000 in 1960 to 8.9 per 1,000 in 1969. The fact that abortion was once again made available upon demand in the mid 1950s, after nearly 20 years of restricted access, was of importance in this change in the rate of net natural increase. High rates of abortion, a rapidly increasing rate of divorce, planned deferral of marriage, and a growing tendency to trade off maternal/paternal 'benefits' for those of a material kind, combined during the 1960s with the arrival of the war-reduced age group as a major element in natural reproduction. The birth-rate fell from 24.9 per 1,000 in 1960 to 17.0 in 1969, its lowest point thus far (Fig. 3). Of course, urbanization usually brings about a decline in the birth-rate, but it is of interest that the downturn has been even more precipitous in the rural sector. Since 1960 the birth-rate amongst the urban population has dropped from 21.9 per 1,000 to 15.3 in 1968, its lowest point. Amongst the rural population the drop has been from 27.8 per 1,000 in 1960 to 18.7 in 1969, its lowest point.

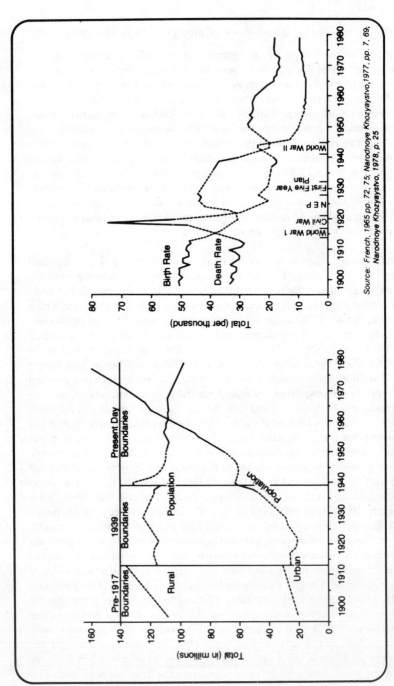

Source: French, 1965 pp. 72, 75, Narodnoye Khozyaystvo, 1977, pp. 7, 69; Narodnoye Khozyaystvo, 1978, p. 25

Fig. 3 Population trends in the USSR 1900–1977

The slight upturn in the birth-rate since 1970 is at least partly related to a structural shift amongst the reproductive age groups. During this decade the post-war baby-boom cohort was entering the reproductive age, while the cohort so severely reduced by the war was phasing out. Thus, there were simply more prospective parents. As well, female fertility is seemingly on the increase, at least to judge by the number of first births by females aged 15 to 19. One observer attributes this phenomenon to the lowering of the draft age and shortening of military service. This has brought more men to civilian status at age 20 instead of 22 as in the past, and more of them are starting families younger than they would have done otherwise (Perevedentsev, 1977a, 2). It remains to be seen whether women will have larger families again. In any event, there will have to be a rather significant increase in the birth-rate before natural growth is much enhanced since the death-rate has been edging upward slowly as well. This development in large measure is attributable to the Soviet population gradually assuming a normal age-sex composition. As the artificially reduced death-rate which the war caused phases out, the death-rate increases. At present it is about 9 per 1,000 and will likely rise to something in the order of 12 or 13. Thus, while the birth-rate has increased during the 1970s, a parallel increase in the death-rate has tended to hold the crude rate of net natural increase to an average of about 9 per 1,000 for the decade.

In the 1980s there will be a steady reduction in the absolute number of people entering the reproductive age group, commensurate with the decline in the birth-rate during the 1960s. Failing a dramatic turn of events, this will further reduce the pool of manpower available to the state.

The problem for the future is that of ensuring an adequate labour supply. Rapid urban-industrialization up to the 1970s drew upon three sources of labour. The first was the large pool of potential rural migrants. The second was the yet not fully exploited reserve of 'socially un-productive' females. In the main this group comprised housewives who did not work for the state but occupied themselves in domestic chores. In the countryside especially, they looked after the personal plot and livestock holdings. Able-bodied pensioners, who in labour deficient regions like Siberia, could be enticed back into full or part-time labour, were the third source. By the early 1970s all three sources had been almost fully tapped. It is no longer possible to foster indiscriminately rural-urban migration. In the still under-capitalized Soviet agriculture, labour is needed. In fact, in marginal, but still important, agricultural regions there is a severe labour shortage. The youth in such regions, of course, are often most anxious to depart because of the consequences of marginality in yields in terms of income and general amenities. Thus, even with 25 per cent of the labour force still in agriculture, there is no large surplus pool of labour to sustain rapid urban-industrialization. The 1970s have seen most of the realizable female labour from the 'socially unproductive' category brought into the state's employ. And employing pensioners is clearly a short-term, stop-gap measure to offset acute regional labour shortages.

With the prospect of a marked slow-down in the growth of the labour force, the state has two options, neither of which is new. The first is to call for higher levels of labour productivity, to which the Soviet work-force is increasingly indifferent. It is now recognized as well that monetary incentives are no longer the simple answer to flagging pro-duction either. Remuneration has to be coupled with better quality consumer goods, recreational and cultural facilities; in general, with the possibility of realizing a better quality of life. For an increasingly urbanized society, the quality and level of consumer and cultural facilities in cities play an important part in this equation, as we shall see in a later chapter. The second option is long term and simply involves stimulating the birth-rate. While there has been prolonged public discussion of the ways such an objective might be achieved, nothing of real substance has yet been done to alter dramatically the usual benefits. Given the past trend to smaller families in cities, indeed, the trend toward instability in the family as reflected in the fast rising divorce rate (332 per 1,000 marriages in 1976 up from 228 in 1960) there seems little prospect for a substantial increase in the labour supply from a higher birth-rate.

Birth-rates not only differ between city and countryside, but within the urban and rural sectors there are wide deviations from the national average. In the ensuing chapters we will deal with the consequences for the Soviet city of such demographic variations. At this juncture we need only highlight the general nature of the differences which impinge on urban growth in general and Soviet town planning in particular.

In the main, those cities with the most stringent controls over in-migration are least influenced by natural growth. Many suffer from a distinctly ageing population, a phenomenon which not only affects labour recruitment but also the provision of facilities for the citizenry. New towns, particularly in regions like Siberia where wage coefficients play a part in inducing migration, are demographically young. While labour recruitment may or may not be a serious problem, the provision of consumer and cultural facilities is often inadequate to meet the demo-graphically-biased demand. In short, demographic differences do exist between Soviet cities, and the normative planning process has not always permitted sufficient flexibility to compensate for this phenomenon. We earlier referred to the relatively high birth-rates of the indigenous rural Central Asians. As the data in Table 2 indicate, there are differences between Republics in terms of birth-rates. Since the death-rate is far less variable, the crude rate of net natural increase varies markedly from one Republic to another. Obviously, there is an ethnic component in the variations in crude rate of net natural increase. Insofar as the future growth of the labour supply goes, indeed, insofar as the future rural-urban migration process is concerned, the traditional reliance on the Slavic component of the population must diminish. This has some potentially far-reaching implications for the ethnic balance of cities in the non-Slavic regions especially. Having now outlined some of the demographic forces influencing urban growth in the 1970s, we now turn to a consideration of the spatial dimensions of the process.

Table 2. Birth, death and crude net natural increase rates 1970–77 (per 1,000 population)

| Republic | 1970 | | | 1977 | | |
	Birth	Death	CNNI*	Birth	Death	CNNI
RSFSR	14.6	8.7	5.9	15.8	10.2	5.6
Ukraine	15.2	8.9	6.3	14.7	10.5	4.2
Belorussia	16.2	7.6	8.6	15.8	9.0	6.8
Latvia	14.5	11.2	3.3	13.6	12.2	1.4
Lithuania	17.6	8.9	8.7	15.5	9.8	5.7
Estonia	15.8	11.1	4.7	15.1	11.8	3.3
Moldavia	19.4	7.4	12.0	20.3	9.6	10.7
Georgia	19.2	7.3	11.9	17.8	8.0	9.8
Armenia	22.1	5.1	17.0	22.5	5.4	17.1
Azerbaydzhan	29.2	6.7	22.5	25.2	6.7	18.5
Kazakh	23.4	6.0	17.4	23.9	7.2	16.7
Uzbek	33.6	5.5	28.1	33.7	7.1	26.6
Turkmen	35.2	6.6	28.6	34.2	7.7	26.5
Kirgiz	30.5	7.4	23.1	30.2	8.2	22.0
Tadzhik	34.8	6.4	28.4	36.5	8.8	27.7
USSR	17.4	8.2	9.2	18.1	9.6	8.5

Source: *Narodnoye Khozyaystvo*, 1978, 25.
* CNNI—Crude Net Natural Increase

Patterns of city growth in the 1970s

Between 1970 and 1979 the Soviet population increased from 241.7 million to 262.4, an overall increment of just a shade less than 9 per cent. Although we only have preliminary census returns for 1979, it is probable that the official estimate for 17 January 1979 is not too wide of the mark (On the preliminary results, 1979, 1). During this period the urban population rose from 136.0 to 163.6 million, while the rural population declined from 105.7 to 98.8 million. Compared to the preceding intercensal period which spanned 11 years these changes over just nine years are certainly noteworthy. Whereas the 1959 to 1970 increase in the urban population was 36 million, only 27.6 million more people lived in cities in 1979 as compared with 1970. The comparable absolute declines in the rural sector were 3.1 and 6.9 million respectively.

The precise contributions to urban growth of migration, natural increase and reclassification are not yet available. However, the preliminary results of the census indicate that natural increase accounted for about 12 of the 27.6 million increase in urban population, or about 43 per cent. Reclassification has apparently been averaging about 350,000 to 450,000 annually during the 1970s (Lydolph, 1978, 535). This is broadly in step with the 450,000 annual addition to the urban population resulting from reclassification during the 1959 to 1970 intercensal period (Perevedentsev, 1971, 1). Taking the upper figure of 450,000 this means that about 15 per cent of the intercensal urban growth is accounted for by changes from rural to urban status. Growth owing to migration is therefore likely to be about 42 per cent, or on average about 1.3 million per annum. The share attributable to natural increase is in keeping with the post-World War II trend. But where has urban growth occurred? To shed some light on this question the increase in urban and rural sectors from 1970 to 1977, relative to the growth of the total population, once again has been computed for the 26 regions depicted in Map 10.

Whereas from 1959 to 1970 city growth in the eastern regions seemed to falter, the evidence from the 1970s suggests a different trend. Part of the relative decline of the eastern regions from 1959 to 1970, most especially of the Urals, West and East Siberia, was related to the net out-migration of more than 1.8 million people. Over half of this net loss was accounted for by the Urals alone (Kurman, 1976, 134). Out-migration seems to have tempered somewhat in the 1970s, though in the absence of detailed statistics on regional migration balances this judgment is conjectural. Such a trend, however, would be in keeping with increases in regional wage coefficients for Siberia and the Far East which were introduced in the late 1960s and reckoned at the time to be having an immediate positive impact on migration patterns (Perevedentsev, 1971, 6). As well, the initiation of the massive Baykal-Amur railroad construction project has drawn a substantial labour force into Eastern Siberia and the Far East (Zhelezko, et al., 1976, 75–6). As the data in Map 10 indicate, the Urals, Siberia and Kazakh regions still do not stand out in terms of urban growth. However, city growth in the Urals, which had dropped sharply during the 1960s, has picked up again. From 1959 to 1970 the region gained 181,000 more urban inhabitants than it would have if the rate of city growth had equalled the national average. From 1970 to 1977 the 'increment' was a shade over 417,000.

The Centre region, focused on Moscow, traditionally has experienced the largest increase in urban population. What is of interest in terms of the 1970s is the fact that this region is no longer pre-eminent. From 1970 to 1977 the Volga, Southwest and Uzbek regions have all added more people to their urban populations, relative to the national average growth rate, than did the Centre. Taking this trend at face value would suggest that state policies have been directing growth away from the traditional

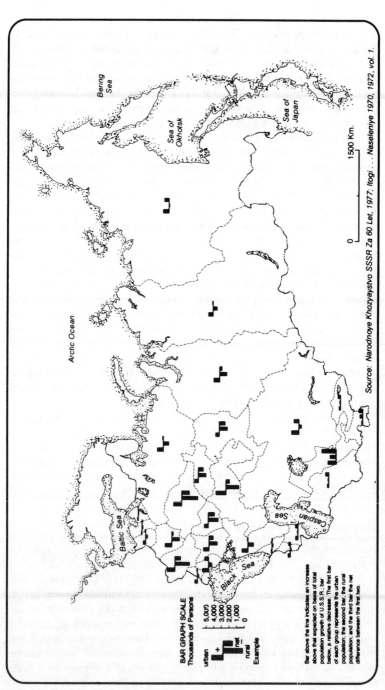

Map 10 USSR—relative population change by study area 1970–77

Bering Sea

Sea of Okhotsk

Sea of Japan

Arctic Ocean

Baltic Sea

Caspian Sea

Black Sea

BAR GRAPH SCALE
Thousands of Persons

5,000
4,000
3,000
2,000
1,000
0

urban +

net

rural −

Example

Bar above the line indicates an increase above that expected on basis of total population growth of U.S.S.R. bar below, a relative decrease. The first bar of each group represents the urban population; the second bar, the rural population; and the third bar the net difference between the first two.

0   1500 Km.

Source: Narodnoye Khozyaystvo SSSR Za 60 Let, 1977; Itogi . . . Naseleniye 1970, 1972, vol. 1.

urban-industrial regions of European Russia, primarily the Centre and Donetsk-Dnepr regions. But what has been happening is far from satisfactory. In the case of the Uzbek region, for instance, urbanization is having little impact on the pool of surplus labour in the countryside. The indigenous rural population is still little inclined to migrate to the city, while the amenable climate and relative ease of access draw migrants from cities in labour deficient regions like Siberia. To a lesser extent the Southwest region suffers from the same problems.

In the predominantly Islamic regions of Uzbek, Tadzhik, Turkmen, Kirgiz and Azerbaydzhan, both rural and urban populations showed positive changes relative to the rate of growth of the total population. In 1977 these regions were, with the exception of Azerbaydzhan, predominately rural. And even in Azerbaydzhan the rural population comprised 48 per cent of the total population of 5.8 million. All other regions experienced negative relative population changes in the rural sector.

Marked regional variations in the level of urbanization have persisted to the present day. As Map 11 indicates, the most intensely urbanized regions are in the west, central and eastern parts of the USSR. With the exception of Armenia, where about 64 per cent of the population is classified as urban, all of the 'southern' regions, including Moldavia and the Southwest region in the Ukraine, are still predominantly rural. In the Central Asian regions of Uzbek, Kirgiz and Tadzhik, the urban population makes up less than 40 per cent of the total. In frontier regions where resource exploitation has been the principal stimulus to settlement, the urban share predominates. The Urals, West Siberia, East Siberia and the Far East generally fall into this category. There the urban components range from 68 to 76 per cent.

Cities of different sizes obviously grow at different rates, though in the Soviet Union the policy of directing growth into the smaller and medium-size cities has been part of a long-standing effort to forestall the emergence of urban agglomerations. We need to examine this facet of the urbanization process before beginning an assessment of the Soviet experience in creating planned settlement systems.

City growth by city size

For more than four decades the notion of an optimal city size was widely accepted as an essential element in Soviet policy, though what was to be the optimum size was far from consistent (Strongina, 1974, 139–40). Early schemes for the Soviet socialist city limited the population to 50,000 or 60,000. This was large enough to make provision of the necessary goods and services economic, yet small enough to permit a sense of community and a communal, socialist ethos to be created and maintained—admirable objectives but soon confounded. Industrialization brought about a seemingly unending circular and cumulative process of urban growth. Unable to hold city growth in check, ideas about what

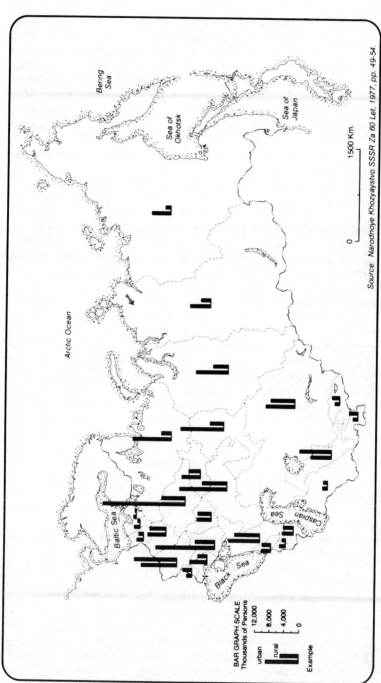

Map 11 Urban and rural population by study areas 1977

constituted the optimum size began to change. By the mid-1950s the most frequently cited figures ranged between 150,000 and 200,000 a rather pragmatic accommodation with the reality of urbanization but also reflective of changing notions about the nature of urban economies. By the 1960s the optimal size had been bumped into the 200,000 to 300,000 range (Murav'yev and Uspenskiy, 1974, 90–91). Notwithstanding the inflation in theoretical optimum city size, the actual pace of urban growth far outstripped it. By the beginning of the 1960s the validity of the concept was being challenged openly (Pchelintsev, 1966–7, 15–23). Events since have put paid to its utility in town-planning theory and practice.

It is apparent from Table 3 that the five city-size classes up to 50,000 inhabitants have been steadily reduced in relative importance since 1926. At that time 48 per cent of the Soviet urban population lived in cities with 50,000 or fewer inhabitants. By 1977 less than one-third did. It is also clear that during the 1970s city growth in both relative and absolute terms was greatest amongst the largest city-size category (over 500,000). Symptomatic of the changes which are in motion is the rapid escalation in the number of cities with more than one million inhabitants. In 1959 there were still only three; Moscow, Leningrad and Kiev. By 1970 seven more had been added to the roster. In 1979 there were 18 'million' cities (See Map 1, page 3). Six more had in excess of 900,000 inhabitants. Given recent rates of urban growth, it is only a matter of a year or so before they too will join the 'million' city category (On the preliminary results, 1979, 4).

There is, of course, nothing magic about one million. However, the trends underlying these differential urban growth rates are important. Despite a flood of decrees establishing limits to city size, the maintenance of the system of internal passports and *propiski*, and the very real need for planners to predict city populations accurately, urban growth, and particularly that of the larger centres has occurred at unprecedented, and invariably unplanned, rates (Gokhberg, 1974, 129–35). Long-standing legislation directing ministries to locate new facilities in small cities has not changed the trend (Loginov and Lyubovnyy, 1975, 47–9). Nor has a host of other measures.

In the 1970s the larger cities have grown more rapidly than the exceedingly fast growth rate they registered in the 1960s (Kochetkov, 1975, 24). Of the many reasons for this phenomenon one is of particular importance.

As we noted earlier, there are a number of locational guidelines which ostensibly condition decision making. But with ministries, departments and enterprises increasingly preoccupied with efficiency in the allocation of financial resources, linked closely to the issue of profitability as introduced by the 1965 economic reform, there can be little doubt that the financial benefits accruing from the loosely defined concept of external economies put a premium on urban locations,

Table 3. Urban population, by settlement size groups, 1926–77

Settlement size (000's)	1926 M	%	1939 M	%	Population 1959 M	%	1970 M	%	1975 M	%	1977 M	%
less than 3	1.2	(4.6)	0.9	(1.5)	1.6	(1.6)	2.1	(1.5)	2.0	(1.3)		
3–5	1.3	(4.9)	2.1	(3.5)	3.6	(3.6)	4.1	(3.0)	4.1	(2.7)		
5–10	2.7	(10.3)	5.3	(8.8)	9.2	(9.2)	10.0	(7.4)	10.7	(7.0)	48.7	(30.5)
10–20	3.5	(13.3)	6.9	(11.4)	11.2	(11.2)	12.7	(9.3)	13.7	(8.9)		
20–50	4.0	(15.2)	9.7	(16.0)	14.8	(14.8)	18.5	(13.6)	19.5	(12.7)		
50–100	4.1	(15.6)	7.0	(11.6)	11.0	(11.0)	13.0	(9.6)	15.4	(10.1)	15.3	(9.6)
100–150	5.4	(20.5)	15.7	(26.0)	24.4	(24.4)	38.3	(28.2)	43.1	(28.2)	46.8	(29.3)
over 500	4.1	(15.6)	12.8	(21.2)	24.2	(24.2)	37.3	(27.4)	44.6	(29.1)	48.8	(30.6)
Total	26.3	(100)	60.4	(100)	100.0	(100)	136.0	(100)	153.1	(100)	159.6	(100)

Source: Lydolph, 1978, 535; French, 1979, 77; *Narodnoye Khozyaystvo*, 1977, 7, 59–68.

Table 3. Urban population, by settlement size groups, 1926–77

Settlement size (000's)	1926 M	%	1939 M	%	Population 1959 M	%	1970 M	%	1975 M	%	1977 M	%
less than 3	1.2	(4.6)	0.9	(1.5)	1.6	(1.6)	2.1	(1.5)	2.0	(1.3)		
3–5	1.3	(4.9)	2.1	(3.5)	3.6	(3.6)	4.1	(3.0)	4.1	(2.7)		
5–10	2.7	(10.3)	5.3	(8.8)	9.2	(9.2)	10.0	(7.4)	10.7	(7.0)	48.7	(30.5)
10–20	3.5	(13.3)	6.9	(11.4)	11.2	(11.2)	12.7	(9.3)	13.7	(8.9)		
20–50	4.0	(15.2)	9.7	(16.0)	14.8	(14.8)	18.5	(13.6)	19.5	(12.7)		
50–100	4.1	(15.6)	7.0	(11.6)	11.0	(11.0)	13.0	(9.6)	15.4	(10.1)	15.3	(9.6)
100–150	5.4	(20.5)	15.7	(26.0)	24.4	(24.4)	38.3	(28.2)	43.1	(28.2)	46.8	(29.3)
over 500	4.1	(15.6)	12.8	(21.2)	24.2	(24.2)	37.3	(27.4)	44.6	(29.1)	48.8	(30.6)
Total	26.3	(100)	60.4	(100)	100.0	(100)	136.0	(100)	153.1	(100)	159.6	(100)

Source: Lydolph, 1978, 535; French, 1979, 77; *Narodnoye Khozyaystvo*, 1977, 7, 59–68.

without railroad access, and almost by definition devoid of much industry (Harris, 1970, 401–11). Harris's pioneering study has stimulated Soviet research along similar lines, but as yet there has been no analysis of equivalent temporal and spatial scale. Some characteristics of the evolving Soviet urban system have prompted suggestions that it '. . . is converging toward a hierarchy similar to that of the United States' (Adams, 1977, 313). But such judgments are still highly conjectural. We might ask at this point, what are the trends in the evolution of the Soviet urban system?

During the past half dozen years or so there has been a concentrated effort to turn the attention of the town planner away from the city to the problems of the city system or agglomeration (Kogan, 1976, 20–23; Strongina, 1970, 24–54). The notion of an optimal-size city is now generally acknowledged as bankrupt if only because the criteria for the location of enterprises fly in the face of town-planning principles and policies aimed at fixing population at a particular size (Murav'yev and Uspenskiy, 1974, 73; Strongina, 1974, 139; Khorev, 1972, 153–4). Traditionally, town planners have had jurisdiction only within the borders of the city. Thus, when policies have been enforced within the city, outlying settlements have been the recipients of much new investment. New investment produces jobs, and jobs urban growth. Very frequently the towns selected for such investment are part of existing, or nascent, agglomerations. Thus, while controls over population movement restrict entry to the major cities, satellite communities are experiencing explosive growth. Even in the case of Moscow where planning authority does extend well beyond the 'official' city border, the growth rate of urban settlements subordinate to the Moscow City Soviet is, for some observers, alarmingly high. Between 1959 and 1975 the population of Moscow itself increased by 26 per cent. But the population of the subordinate urban settlements increased 4.7 times during the same time span (Khorev and Moiseyenko, 1976, 48). The same phenomenon is occurring in many other places, but often without the equivalent jurisdictional authority of the central city Soviet. An examination of where such growth is occurring is instructive.

The distribution of cities with more than 100,000 inhabitants, ranked according to their annual growth rate from 1970 to 1977, is portrayed in Map 12. Belorussia, the western part of the Ukraine and the region around Tashkent in Central Asia clearly stand out by virtue of the concentration of cities with annual growth rates in excess of 4 per cent. Generally speaking, cities in the long-established industrial regions, like the Centre, Donetsk-Dnepr and Urals, registered moderate growth rates by comparison. But even acknowledging more restrained growth rates does not take away from the principal message which the map conveys. Urban growth in the 1970s is still spatially clustered. Clearly, the recent attempt to turn the attention of the town planner away from the city to the urban agglomeration is absolutely essential if the evolving urban system is to be at all amenable to manipulation through state policy

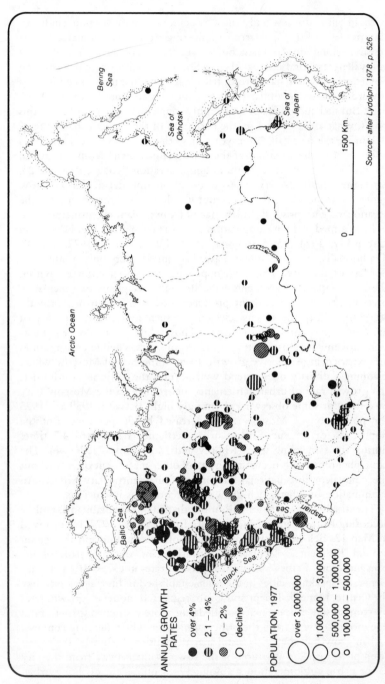

ANNUAL GROWTH RATES

- over 4%
- 2.1 – 4%
- 0 – 2%
- decline

POPULATION, 1977

- over 3,000,000
- 1,000,000 – 3,000,000
- 500,000 – 1,000,000
- 100,000 – 500,000

Map 12 Annual growth rates of cities with population of more than 100,000 in 1970–77

Bering Sea

Sea of Okhotsk

Sea of Japan

1500 Km

0

Arctic Ocean

Baltic Sea

Caspian Sea

Black Sea

(Svetlichnyy, 1974, 142–4; Sharov, *et al.*, 1973, 116; Dryavnev, 1974, 6–7; Lappo, 1974, 531–42; Tsitsin, 1977, 12).

At least 70 major urban agglomerations are now identifiable. It is probable that one-half of the Soviet urban popu!ace now lives in agglomerations focused on cities with more than 100,000 inhabitants (Listengurt, 1975, 564). While obviously an integral part of the Soviet urban scene, agglomerations are as yet divorced from the day-to-day jurisdiction of town planners, and until recently did not figure significantly in overall urban planning strategies (Kubal'chich and Lyubovnyy, 1976, 239–50; Litovka, 1976, 50). The concept of planning for urban systems has now taken root, but has not yet borne fruit in terms of juridically-based planning regions throughout the country (Sharov, *et al.*, 1973, 112–18).

A 1970 survey sheds some light on the dimensions of the task. Only about one third of the 75 major agglomerations had been subjected to even initial stages of regulation (Map 13). Most have continued to expand unchecked. Part of the difficulty in coming to grips quickly with the task of the planned development of the urban system is that there is mixed opinion as to the consequences of agglomerations (Vishnevskiy, 1972). Provided massive conurbations can be avoided, some authorities like the economist and demographer V. Perevedentsev view agglomerations very positively. Demonstrably higher labour productivity and returns on investment figure prominently in the arguments for allowing urban agglomeration to continue with minimal interference from planners (Perevedentsev, 1971, 4). The other viewpoint, held for instance by the geographer B. Khorev, is that such a process is counter-productive in the long-run and contrary to basic principles of Soviet socialist urban development (Chinn, 1977, 35–42).

Summary

The Soviet experience in regulating city growth does not lend itself to easy generalization. It is apparent that during the Stalin era, when tight controls were maintained over population movement, ideal and reality tended to be reasonably congruent. But those were years of forced industrialization and World War, and determining how much of the reworked pattern of urban growth is attributable to endogenous policy or exogenous forces is impossible to gauge. In any event, urban development in the eastern regions proceeded at a rapid pace. The subsequent relaxation of controls and the growing preoccupation with efficient allocation of resources has brought forth urban growth trends which are not in accord with original principles.

The general locational guidelines enumerated at the beginning of the chapter reflect the basic objectives of the Soviet socialist system. But events since the 1920s have made egalitarian locational concepts difficult to apply in practice. The preoccupation since the 1965 economic reform

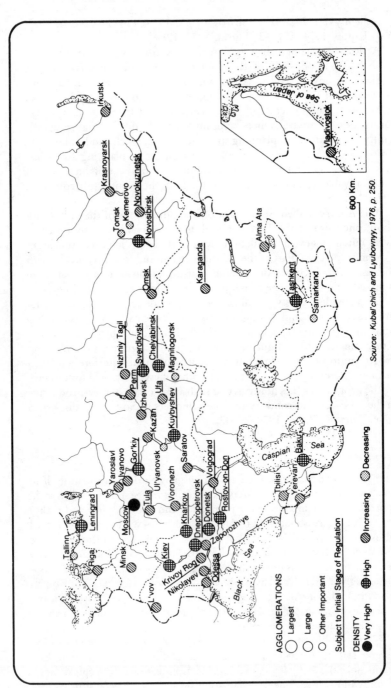

Map 13 Urban agglomerations

AGGLOMERATIONS

○ Largest
○ Large
○ Other Important

_____ Subject to Initial Stage of Regulation

DENSITY

● Very High   ⊕ High   ◍ Increasing   ◍ Decreasing

Source: Kubal'chich and Lyubovnyy, 1976, p. 250.

with efficiency, return on investment and profitability has made the external economies offered by the large cities especially attractive. Thus, enterprises have been located in major centres whenever possible, and often as close to them as possible when restrictions on entry have been successfully enforced by planners. The consequences have been pointed out. The largest cities are growing the most rapidly and agglomerations are now the dominant feature of the Soviet urban system. The concept of the optimal city size has been largely rejected because of the reality of the urbanization process. But planners are still handicapped because of the lack of any juridically based planning regions to deal with the agglomeration process. Moreover, it has only been in recent years that a strategy for planning a unified settlement system has been given much attention. In short, there is much still to do in the task of working out the theoretical and practical basis for creating a unified settlement system. Meanwhile, labour problems in major cities are exacerbated by the continued influx of enterprises and by the restrictions on in-migration and the resultant demographic ageing of the populations. On a national level, differences in the level of urbanization persist.

In the final analysis, the success of the Soviet socialist city will be judged not so much by the aggregate dimensions of city growth but by the quality of life offered its inhabitants. Having now got some appreciation of the antecedents and evolution of town-planning principles, the decision-making environment within which town planners operate, and the urban system within which the majority of Soviet citizens now live, there remains the task of examining the internal structure of the Soviet city and evaluating what it is like as a place to live.

5

The spatial organization of the Soviet city

For nearly half a century a normative style of town planning has been followed in the attempt to create an efficient and equitable spatial organization of the Soviet city. While the task of translating general planning principles into the myriad minimum standards, or norms, which guide town planners on a day-to-day basis is relatively straight-forward, enforcement of these norms often is not. As we demonstrated in an earlier chapter, the role of the town planner and city Soviet in the decision-making process is frequently ambiguous, often ignored. Thus, the planner's access to information, his ability to influence events and the finances available have been such as to produce some gaps between principle and practice, between ideal and reality. The questions addressed in this chapter are, where do ideals and reality diverge, why, and how efficient and equitable is the spatial organization of the contemporary Soviet city?

In an attempt to provide some answers, five facets of the spatial organization of the Soviet city will be examined: industrial location and land-use zoning; the allocation and organization of housing; transportation and the journey to work; the provision of items of collective consumption; and the role of the central city. There are other common elements to theoretical formulations of the spatial organization of the Soviet city (Belousov, 1976, 10). However, these five facets are of acknowledged importance in the literature, and their examination ought to enable us to establish the extent to which town-planning practice relates to theory.

It was emphasized in the Introduction that not all Soviet cities are products of the same mould. The application of standard norms, to say nothing of industrialized building techniques and consequent limited architectural variation, has homogenized parts of all Soviet cities. However, the stamp of uniformity has been applied to many cities with markedly different architectural and planning legacies, ethnic compositions and physical environments. In short, despite popular images to the contrary, there still are regional variations in the urban milieu, a feature some architectural efforts of late have attempted to sustain. The fact that Moscow has figured so prominently so often in discussions of the Soviet city no doubt has also contributed to the somewhat stereotyped image. In all respects but size Moscow does indeed serve as a model for Soviet town planning. But it should be obvious that what is done there does not necessarily find expression in lesser cities throughout the country. Thus, in evaluating Soviet town planning in practice, it is imperative that examples be drawn from as reasonably representative a cross-section of cities as is possible.

Moscow (8.0 million), of course, cannot be ignored, and developments there certainly will be included in the ensuing discussion. But in terms of town-planning history, its legacy is markedly different from Leningrad (4.6 million), which, created *de novo* by Peter I, emerged as the classic planned city of the eighteenth century. The character of its central area vividly testifies both to the achievements of that era and Soviet efforts at preservation of historic architectural ensembles. Ethnicity, among other attributes, sets Central Asian cities like Tashkent (1.8 million) apart from the major centres of European Russia. Brought into the Russian Empire only in the latter half of the nineteenth century, its built environment reflects three epochs: the traditional, pre-Russian quarter—still dominated by the indigenous Uzbek people; the central 'colonial' Russian outpost, which stands in relation to the old quarter much as New Delhi does to Delhi; and the Soviet transformation of the old quarter, central city and suburb—a transformation which has not always reflected architecturally very much of the indigenous culture. Smaller industrial centres like Vladimir (0.3 million) and Pskov (0.18 million) often have rather different problems than the major centres, and where data permit the discussion will turn to developments in smaller, old industrial centres like these. Outwardly at least the hundreds of new towns created during the Soviet era stand in sharp contrast to such established places. Bratsk (0.21 million) and Ust-Ilimsk (0.053 million) are representative of the post-World War II drive to industrialize the eastern regions. Located in a frontier environment in Eastern Siberia, they afford tangible evidence of recent new town-planning successes and failures. These seven cities will appear frequently in the pages of this chapter and the one following. In examining the spatial organization and quality of life in the Soviet city, space, if not data deficiencies, precludes using all seven cities as examples for each topic. And, of course, the examples brought to bear in the argument will not be restricted to just these particular places. However, by consciously focusing attention on large and small, old and new, and Slavic and non-Slavic cities, perhaps something more of the range of planning problems, achievements and the diversity of urban environments in the USSR will be conveyed than through the customary devotion to Moscow or, by contrast, through an entirely eclectic array of examples.

Industrial location and land-use zoning

A minimal expenditure of time in journeying to work has been a

fundamental consideration in planning the Soviet city from the beginning. This facet of spatial organization was given most tangible expression in Miliutin's application of the linear-city idea to the plans for
Magnitogorsk and Stalingrad. The close proximity of the residential and
industrial zones is readily apparent from Map 6, page 25. Although
the linear-city concept was essentially still-born, the application of the
principle of minimal journey to work in the development of Soviet
cities meant that industrial location would have to be strictly controlled
if environmental problems were to be avoided. Thus, the general principle of a minimal journey to work is directly related to the principle
of strict separation of non-conforming urban land uses, most especially
industry and housing. As a first priority, existing noxious industries were
to be closed down or relocated. Thereafter, all non-conforming land
uses were to be sorted out. So far as the location of industry was concerned, within each city an industrial zone (or zones) was to be
designated.

In separating industry from residential areas three methods are available. Noxious and/or outmoded industrial facilities can simply be closed.
Relocation of necessary, and viable, operations may be undertaken. Most
commonly this entails decentralizing central-city factories to the periphery, or in some urban regions to specific satellite centres. New industry
may be restricted to specified city areas. Directing new, or relocating
enterprises to locations outside the city limits is a quite recent endeavour,
though it is in keeping with the long-standing objective of controlling
urbanization through spatially manipulating the principal engine of
growth, industry. But this is dependent upon the existence of a regionally
based, rather than just city based, planning authority. Only a few cities
currently have such an administrative system, Moscow and Leningrad
being the two main examples. Given the history of forced industrialization in the Soviet Union, it comes as no surprise that closures and even
production-disrupting relocations have not always been easily realized.
But before examining industrial location in the contemporary Soviet
city, it would be appropriate to get some understanding of industrial
location in the Tsarist era in order to judge better the task confronting
Soviet planners.

Up until the middle of the nineteenth century, Tsarist zoning regulations had managed to keep noxious industry at bay. In St Petersburg,
for instance, the impact of the 1833 legislation on the distribution of
noxious industry at mid-century is quite apparent from Map 14. The
rapid urban-industrialization of the late nineteenth century, however,
put paid to the effectiveness of urban land-use zoning regulations, and
the scramble for sites within the heavily built-up area soon transformed
the conditions of labour and life (Bater, 1976, 308–82). It is apparent
from Map 15, that most central-city areas had some industry in 1913,
and it was frequently of a non-conforming kind. Conditions in the capital
were typical of cities throughout the Empire as long-standing zoning

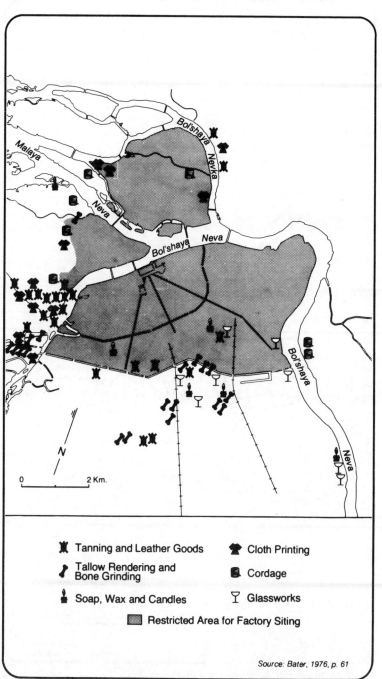

Map 14 Restrictive zoning of industry—St Petersburg 1852

Legend:

- Tanning and Leather Goods
- Tallow Rendering and Bone Grinding
- Soap, Wax and Candles
- Cloth Printing
- Cordage
- Glassworks
- Restricted Area for Factory Siting

0   2 Km.

N

Source: Bater, 1976, p. 61

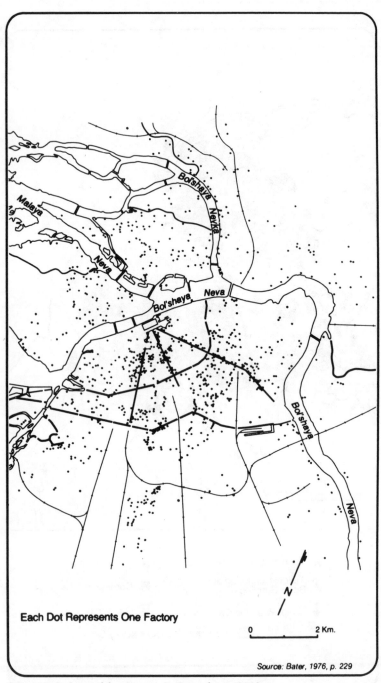

Each Dot Represents One Factory

0   2 Km.

Source: Bater, 1976, p. 229

Map 15 Industrial location—St Petersburg 1913

and architectural restrictions collapsed in the face of unprecedented industrialization. Thus, the task facing the Soviet town planner was much complicated by the fact that few cities had a rational distribution of industry at the time of the revolution. Correcting past breaches of zoning regulations was going to be a huge undertaking. Inasmuch as town planning in Moscow has tended to serve as a model, it is worth examining the achievements there before considering the situation in less well planned cities.

Although it is not especially evident from the schematic portrayal of the evolution of industry in Moscow (Map 16), the 1935 General Plan, which affirmed the general principles for town planning, did bring a measure of organization to industrial location in the capital. Previously industry had developed more or less at will, (though often oriented to major transport arteries) and basic municipal services were usually inadequate. The 1935 Plan delimited several industrial districts, especially on the eastern and southeastern flanks of the city. And hardly too soon, for the First Five Year Plan (1928–32) had witnessed an intensive programme to develop the metal-working, engineering, machinery and electrical industries in the city. In the mid-1930s it is probable that the majority of Moscow's near 800 industrial enterprises did not conform to this *ex post facto* zoning exercise. But at least a rational basis for siting new or relocated establishments was laid (Gokhberg, 1973, 12).

The 1935 General Plan had a formal life of 25 years. However, a new General Plan spanning a similar period was not ratified until 1971. Upon adoption it was back-dated to 1961. Between 1935 and 1970 Moscow's population roughly doubled while the city's area tripled, the largest extension of boundaries occurring in 1967 when the area was bumped from 356 square kilometres to 886. Despite attempts to limit growth, which in the context of industrial development was supposed to be restricted to city-serving enterprise, countervailing forces won out. Strict regulation of in-migration and legislation to direct industry into smaller centres and the eastern regions have been partly confounded, This is because of the combined impacts of forced industrialization, World War, reconstruction requirements and, as the industrial structure has evolved toward a higher technological level, by the external economies which the existing industrial base, urban infrastructure and burgeoning scientific, research and administrative sectors offer. It is hardly surprising that there are now nearly 1,400 industrial enterprises in Moscow and that the largest share serves a national market. There is no question but that the restrictions set down in the 1930s have prevented the growth of some industry in the capital, and for that matter in other major industrial centres, but the spillover into the surrounding settlements, both planned and unplanned, has created an agglomeration and exacerbated the traditional urban labour shortage (Hamilton, 1976, 26–7). With a growing proportion of its population on pension, a crude rate of net natural increase of less than three per 1,000 over the last decade, and

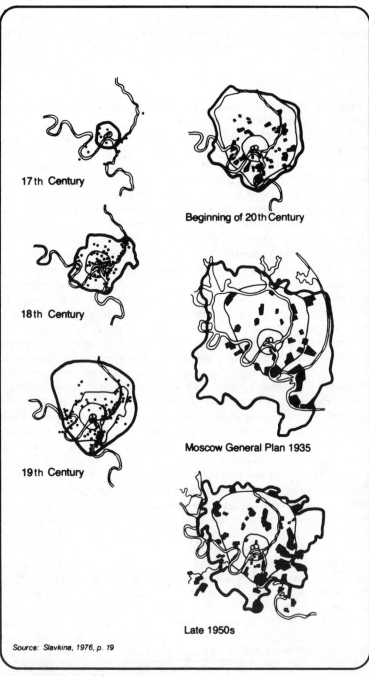

17th Century

Beginning of 20th Century

18th Century

19th Century

Moscow General Plan 1935

Late 1950s

Source: Slavkina, 1976, p. 19

Map 16 Industrial location—Moscow

restrictions on in-migration, the labour deficit in Moscow grows more serious despite much effort to substitute capital for labour in the productive process. At present the labour deficit is in the order of 500,000 individuals, most of which is offset by commuters from centres outside the city boundary (Gokhberg, 1973, 13; *Moskva*, 1976, 7). Not all commuters work in factories of course. Still, despite a relative decline in importance, manufacturing continues to account for about 30 per cent of all jobs in Moscow and it is beyond doubt that a sizeable share of the daily commuting population ends up at a factory gate. It is apparent that despite restrictions industrial growth has been considerable since the 1930s. But to what extent does industrial location at present conform to existing zoning requirements?

Despite the strictures laid down by the 1935 General Plan it really had little impact on the location of existing industries, many of which clearly constituted non-conforming land uses. Most of the land-use conflicts were in the central city, but some were created by the steady outward extension of city boundaries. In an era of forced industrialization non-conforming industrial land use did not rank high on the list of immediate priorities. However, during the past two decades there has been considerable effort to bring industrial location practice in line with principle. In the central core and inner industrial ring much industry pre-dates the Soviet period. Relocation of factories from this central core to peripheral industrial regions has been very considerable. Common as well is the closure of out-moded, noxious industrial enterprises. It is certainly possible yet to smell, if not to see, some obviously non-conforming industrial operations in the inner core and adjacent inner industrial ring, but this legacy of the past is fading. Still, it would be incorrect to suggest that relocation and closure have fundamentally restructured the distribution of industry in Moscow. The vast majority of the approximately one million industrial jobs are still concentrated in the inner industrial ring. But as Litovka observes, 'nearly three-quarters of industrial enterprises are located outside of production zones. The greater part of these enterprises are combined with residential buildings or are situated among residential districts, which impedes their territorial development' (1976, 73). And with such an admixture there remain numerous violations of zoning regulations. The dimension of this problem is outlined by Gokhberg who notes that 'over 510 enterprises are located in the residential built-up district and in green areas without the observance of normative sanitary breaks' (1973, 13). Though there is no indication of just how serious these breaches of planning principle are, the fact that upward of a third of all industrial establishments were in that category in the early 1970s is itself rather telling. Clearly, interests of national industrial development preclude any draconian moves to interrupt industrial production through a massive programme of plant closure and relocation. Progress is steady, if belated. But we are here discussing Moscow, the model Soviet city.

It stands to reason that if in excess of one-third of the industrial enterprises in Moscow contravene basic zoning regulations, then the situation in other established industrial centres is not likely to be better, and in all probability is likely to be rather worse. Certainly the impression conveyed by the literature is that in many cities industrial location is still not adequately controlled (Yaralov, 1975, 24). This is particularly the case in the new towns in resource frontiers where the relentless pressures to develop production facilities override the niceties of town-planning principles (Beshkiltsev, 1974, 14; P'yankov, 1978, 2). Established procedures, or more correctly their absence, have resulted in many new town environments in which industry and housing are not properly separated. As numerous Soviet observers have commented, this perhaps would be understandable if the city in question had been created during the early years of the drive to industrialize. What is difficult to rationalize is the continuation of such practices. A recent discussion of new towns in the eastern regions offers a case in point. It was noted that in the city of Komsomolsk in the Far East region, a city spawned by the forced industrialization of the 1930s, 'the lack of coordination has allowed enterprises to be scattered haphazardly throughout the city: some have been sited in the city centre even recently' (Perevedentsev, 1977b, 11). New towns of more recent vintage like Bratsk reveal the consequences of a somewhat similar kind of decision making. While conceived as an integrated industrial complex based on the huge hydro-electric power generating capacity of the Bratsk power station, in execution several physically removed urban settlements associated with the endeavours of particular ministries have been created (Bater, 1977b). Thus, not only is industry cheek-by-jowl with housing in some of these settlements, all inhabitants are disadvantaged by the distances separating the constituent parts of what is otherwise a single administrative entity. Such examples of 'departmentalist' mentality in urban development are scarcely yet past history, as later discussion will verify.

We earlier emphasized the inability of the town planner always to control events ostensibly within his jurisdiction. This certainly applies to industrial location and zoning as the following observation by the chairman of the Sterlitamak (0.22 million) city Soviet executive committee makes plain:

> when the question of building new chemical enterprises in the northern outskirts of the city was being decided, we demanded that a three-kilometre sanitary buffer zone be created between the city's industrial and residential sections. No one objected to this, but economic managers later intruded into this zone without permission, and they are continuing to use this territory to expand their facilities (Mullagalyamov, 1977, 8).

This clear-cut transgression in a small town in the Bashkir region is by no means the rule, but it is sufficiently common as to point up some clear-cut problems.

The relationship between industry and housing is also affected by the fact that ministries are still involved in providing accommodation for their own enterprises' employees, for reasons pointed out in the preceding chapter. Thus, '... industrial and residential areas remain awkwardly interlarded' as the situation in Donetsk, an industrial centre of one million inhabitants in the southeast Ukraine, was recently described (Kishkan, 1977, 6). Part of the difficulty of bringing about a rational land-use configuration results from the fact that few city Soviets control much of the industry found within their jurisdiction. Even in Moscow, where the long-standing objective of turning industry oriented to the local market over to the city Soviet has gone as far as anywhere, barely one-fifth of the near 1,400 industrial enterprises are directly controlled by the city Soviet (Kulikova, 1976, 12). Having to influence decisions taken by a multitude of organizations controlling the remaining industrial establishments does not augur well for integrated planning. In cities where the Soviets are less influential, and have the activities of an even smaller share of industry under their thumb, the task of ensuring compliance with zoning regulations is indeed a difficult one. While it is apparent that the principle of a strict separation of industry from housing has not yet been fully realized, we might well inquire, just how well planned are the industrial zones themselves?

Assuming that a city has a general plan relevant to present planning requirements does not ensure that the layout and development of industrial zones proceed in a rational and efficient manner (Bocharov, 1975, 44–6). The problem has been summed up as follows:

> The State Civil Construction Committee directs the drafting of general plans. However, it still has no special subdivision responsible for the level of the final work-up of a city's industrial areas and their interconnection with its residential zones. Therefore, it is no surprise that industrial zones which occupy 30 per cent to 40 per cent of all urban land, are not planned in detail and that projects done by city-planning, territorial and branch institutes do little to coordinate these zones (Bocharov and Lyubovnyy, 1976b, 8).

> Having no uniform planning document for such zones, the city Soviet executive committees are compelled to agree to the 'piecemeal' siting of enterprises within them. This gives rise to the 'patchwork' arrangement that is clearly evident in a number of cities (Libkind, 1975, 8).

Thus 'the city planner's role in shaping a city's industrial zone', in the opinion of Yu. Bukreyev, director of the State Institute for City Planning, 'usually reduces to that of assigning a sector' (1972, 20). This is scarcely satisfactory for it contradicts the whole notion of planning the city as an integrated system. When anywhere between 30 and 100 organizations can be involved in developing urban industrial zones, the potential for waste is considerable. Very frequently basic municipal services are built by the ministry wishing to get an industrial enterprise into operation quickly. Instead of centralized, regional heat networks serving industrial establishments, a multitude of energy-wasteful and pollution-prone boilers appear. Until quite recently nearly 50 organizations owned and administered parts of the water supply system in Komsomolsk (Perevedentsev, 1977b, 11). And so on it goes—a quite general picture of inadequately developed, maladministered urban-industrial zones. Or at least that was the situation until fairly recently.

The quest for efficiency began in earnest in the 1960s and is reflected in the 1965 economic reform and subsequent measures. Resource use—including the use of land in cities—has come under close scrutiny. What has happened in industrial zones is symptomatic of a rather larger problem about which more will be said at a later point. Each year thousands of hectares are assigned by city Soviets to industrial enterprises and associated facilities (Libkind, 1975, 8). Norms are used to determine how much land should be turned over to particular industrial enterprises, dependent of course on both present and estimated future requirements. Delays in building productive facilities, overestimation of future needs, perhaps even over-generous norms—all have given rise to underutilization of land in industrial zones. And when eventually the industrial zone becomes built-up, the piecemeal approach already described results in measurable, unnecessary costs.

In response to this situation the formation of industrial clusters or centres, which are akin to industrial parks or estates, has been promoted actively (Berezin, 1973, 19–24). Both centre and estate incorporate a unified approach to the provision of municipal services, transportation routes and so forth. However, in the Soviet context considerable emphasis is put on locating functionally linked industries together in a single cluster. For example, among the city-serving branches of industry, those involved in food production (meat packing, dairy, baking enterprises and the like) comprise a logical grouping. During the 1970s several hundred plans for industrial centres have been adopted, a great many centres are now under construction or in operation. The advantages are obvious. Estimates of savings indicate that the development of industrial centres reduces enterprise construction costs by 3–10 per cent, operating expenditures by 10–15 per cent, personnel by 10–20 per cent, length of utility lines by 15–20 per cent, and of growing significance, required land by 10 per cent (Gokhberg, 1973, 17). Overall, urban industry is reckoned to occupy, on a per capita basis, about 50 per cent more land in major Soviet cities than in American (Lyubovnyy and Savelyev, 1977, 8). The iron and steel, woodworking, chemicals and food-processing factories have the highest ratios of land area to workforce. It has been suggested that planners need to pay particular attention to the use of space by these industries (Gornostayeva, 1979, 11–12). Industrial land use would be of less concern if it were not that much industrial land in Soviet cities is not used at all for the purpose intended. Once allocated there is no effective way of penalizing non-use (Balezin,

1963, 1970). From the standpoint of the ministry or enterprise there is every reason not to relinquish a legal claim to a valuable, but free, resource.

Recent measures to create industrial centres are attempts to utilize industrial land more rationally. Most success has been registered in situations where an industrial zone is being developed *de novo* and where there is a single administrative organization coordinating both the planning and construction. Imposing a plan on an existing industrial region would help shape future development but is unlikely to alter dramatically the existing pattern with its built-in spatial inefficiencies. Thus far few cities have a single authority responsible for infrastructure. Consequently '... individual facilities are, as a rule, built by different construction organizations', and in the opinion of A. Drobnys, chairman of the Lithuanian Republic State Planning Committee, it remains '... virtually impossible to coordinate their actions' (1978, 13), *Plus ça change* ... ?

To summarize briefly, it is apparent that ideal and reality in the context of industrial location and land-use zoning diverge in many Soviet cities. Even in Moscow there remain some obvious inconsistencies. Notwithstanding the legacy of the imperial era, entrenched institutional and decision-making procedures have been considerable barriers to rationalizing land uses. Industrial location problems are being addressed, most recently through the drive to develop industrial centres or clusters within industrial zones. Soviet calculations show that industrial centres are clearly superior to the customary individualized approach to industrial development on the part of particular ministries. But for the most part, the higher costs fall on the city not the ministry or enterprise. As elsewhere, persuading decision-makers of the need to recognize social and opportunity costs of their actions, and to modify their behaviour accordingly, is difficult.

The allocation and organization of housing

Providing each person with an equitable share of items of personal and collective consumption is a fundamental tenet of Soviet town planning. Few would dispute the importance of adequate housing in this context. It is thus of considerable significance that between 1960 and 1975 in excess of two-thirds of the total population has been allocated improved accommodation (Rodin, 1977, 2). Yet in retrospect probably nowhere else has the difference between principle and practice been as pronounced for so long than in the provision of housing (Barry, 1969; DiMaio, 1974; Morton, 1974). It is necessary to understand something of the development and scale of the housing problem before attempting to assess the recent efforts to rectify it.

The emergence of a Soviet housing crisis

An urban housing crisis had loomed, arrived and deepened during the last years of the imperial era. In Chapter 2 we attempted to illustrate the degree of overcrowding with some comparative data on the numbers of occupants per apartment in several European and Russian cities. What those data and other statistics on the levels of death and disease revealed was a rapidly deteriorating urban environment. City and state governments alike were engaged in a rearguard action to put matters right. But for every step forward, ever greater demands were generated by the human tide which swept into the cities each year with greater force. The dismal state of labour and life in Russian cities certainly played some part in the events of 1917, though precisely what cannot be reckoned. It was only prudent for the new Soviet government to tackle immediately the serious problems of the city. In the early years the task was eased somewhat by the urban-rural migration set in motion by the chaotic state of the national economy. Legislating equality, however, began within months.

In August 1918 a major initiative was taken. Urban real estate was municipalized, which meant in practice that all dwellings, except for small single-family houses, came under the jurisdiction of the city Soviet. The process of reallocation had begun. As many existing buildings had been designed to suit the middle and upper classes, reallocation of housing space necessitated multiple occupancy of apartments and hence sharing of kitchens, bathrooms and toilets. Conflicts over shared facilities obviously ensued, but the overall situation was nonetheless a marked improvement. It is difficult to gauge the scale of the reallocative process, but in Moscow alone some 500,000 people were rehoused in less than half a dozen years. Rehousing brought the share of the capital's population living in rooms with more than two people down from more than three-fifths in 1912 to less than 37 per cent in 1923 (Blumenfeld, 1942, 49).

The basis for assigning urban housing was formally established in 1922 (Jacobs, 1975, 67). At that time it was decreed that the All-Union minimum sanitary allocation, or norm, would be nine square metres of living space per person. By living space was meant the living room, dining room, bedrooms and so forth, exclusive of the area devoted to corridors, closets, kitchen, bathroom etc. (Broner, 1966). As the average amount of living space per urban inhabitant at this time was only about six square metres, the statutory minimum for many people became the maximum assignable. Exceptions were made for certain categories of the workforce. Professionals such as architects who regularly worked at home were sometimes permitted an additional nine square metres. And, of course, high ranking positions in party, government, administration of the economy, the arts and so forth frequently brought above-norm housing allocation perquisites. For the masses of workers, however, even the statutory minimum of nine square metres of living space per capita was to recede slowly as a realistic expectation. Put simply, part of the price paid in the quest for rapid industrialization during the Stalin era was consumer well-being. All items of personal and collective consumption were relegated to a low priority. When the minimal expenditures on new housing are set against the phrenetic tempo of urbanization during the 1930s and post-World War II era, the inevitability of a crisis in adequately housing the urban population becomes clear.

From 1918 to 1950 about 350 million square metres of housing were built by the state, or with state assistance, throughout the country (excluding the collective farms) (*Narodnoye*, 1977, 492). State assistance could take the form of mortgages to individuals to assist in the construction of privately-owned dwellings or to legally incorporated cooperatives. Private and cooperative house and apartment construction did help augment the housing stock a little, at least until the late 1930s when even stricter regulations were imposed on the former while cooperatively-owned apartments were 'de-legalized' and taken over by the state. However, not all house construction occurred in the cities, and when the huge scale of post-war reconstruction is taken into account, it becomes apparent that the net addition to the urban housing stock was less than the figure initially suggests. In short, there were more people occupying the available urban housing stock in 1950 than in 1918. By 1950 the average amount of living space per person was less than four square metres—less than one half the sanitary minimum established in 1922 (Sosnovy, 1954, 269). In many cities a family per room had become the rule rather than the exception. A housing crisis was at hand.

Yet the crisis was not everywhere of the same dimension. Sosnovy has calculated living space per person for a selection of Soviet cities and these data help shed some light on the extent of regional disparities (Table 4). It is apparent that between 1926 and 1955 the ratio of living space per person decidedly worsened in each of the selected cities. Overcrowding was especially acute in Central Asian cities like Alma-Ata or Frunze, and in fast growing Siberian cities like Novosibirsk, but nowhere was the situation tolerable, and certainly not in Moscow which ranked well behind a number of otherwise lesser cities. Disparities, of course, existed within cities as well as between them. We have already noted the differential basis for allocating space to the population. Thus, the kind of buildings put up by the state reflected both the need to economize on housing space and the need to maintain the existing system of differential housing allocations.

The need to economize on space was manifested in the construction of apartment blocks in which communal use of facilities was a major design consideration. In the 1930s and 1940s three and four-bedroom apartments were still being designed and built despite the changing demographic structure of the average family. In other words, although families were usually smaller, apartments were being built too large to

Table 4. Living space per capita selected cities 1926 and 1956

City	1926 Living space (sq. metres)	1956 Living space (sq. metres)
Moscow	5.7	4.8
Leningrad	8.7	5.2
Kiev	7.2	5.1
Baku	5.1	4.8
Kharkov	5.7	4.9
Gorkiy	5.2	4.4
Tashkent	4.8	4.0
Kuybyshev	5.4	3.9
Novosibirsk	4.1	3.8
Sverdlovsk	4.9	4.5
Minsk	5.9	4.1
Odessa	7.4	5.8
Tbilisi	6.8	5.5
Chelyabinsk	4.5	4.0
Kazan	5.6	4.0
Dnepropetrovsk	5.8	5.0
Omsk	4.8	4.0
Rostov-on-Don	5.5	5.2
Saratov	5.4	4.4
Alma-Ata	4.6	3.7
Frunze	4.0	3.8

Source: Sosnovy, 1959, 5–6.

accommodate them on a one family per apartment basis. Certainly one factor in the reluctance to design self-contained apartments better suited to the smaller family was the higher cost of providing more facilities per unit of floor space. Yet when a sample survey of Moscow families in 1940 revealed that nearly three-fifths of the families comprised three or fewer members, the demand for smaller-scale units was clearly there (Blumenfeld, 1948, 28). The point is, for economic reasons apartment design frequently precluded single-family occupancy. Thus, families of up to three, and sometimes more, members were expected to live in a quasi-communal fashion. For example, a three-bedroom apartment could have three families. Kitchens might be designed with three cooking stoves and so forth, but all other facilities were to be shared. Something of the consequences of the differential, indeed, preferential, procedures for allocating housing is indicated by the data in Table 5. Apparently Group B apartments were the most common, while Group C reflected an emergency type of accommodation, by which is presumably meant that the assignment of such apartment space to so many people was to be a temporary phenomenon. Group A apartment designs, however, were for privileged members of society. While only a relatively small

Table 5. Differential housing space allocations by apartment design

Number of persons per apartment	Apartment area (sq. metres)	Useful space per person (sq. metres)	Living space per person (sq. metres)
Group A			
4	63	15.5	10.2
3	52	17.3	11.4
2	47	23.5	15.5
Group B			
4	36	9.0	5.9
3	31	10.3	6.8
2	25	12.5	8.3
Group C			
4	31	7.8	5.1
3	25	8.3	5.5
2	19	9.5	6.3

Source: Based on Blumenfeld, 1948, 29.

number were to be built, it is abundantly clear that elites were going to be comparatively well off according to these particular design specifications (Blumenfeld, 1948, 29). In terms of living space, which Soviet calculations reckon to be about two-thirds of useful space, the elite assigned to apartments in Group A are roughly two to two and a half times better off than those in Group B or C apartments (Frolic, 1964, 305; *Narodnoye*, 1977, 501). Not only were the apartments larger, but they included more facilities. How general such apartment differentials were is impossible to say. However, it does seem reasonable that such considerations played a part in housing design and construction throughout the country since the design component of the building industry tended to be highly centralized and the models available rather limited. It is worth noting as well that in designing apartments in the Group B and C categories the statutory sanitary minimum of nine square metres of living space was not used as the common denominator. It is possible, however, that for an apartment building including all three categories, the norm might be realized. However, apartment buildings were often built without such an admixture. To the extent that such apartment buildings catered to elites only, the urban landscape was obviously differentiated by strata of society, albeit at a micro-level. Whether such apartment buildings were built in clusters or on certain streets cannot be determined with any certainty. There is, however, the intuitive feeling that this did occur, thereby effecting a measure of residential segregation during the Stalin era.

In examining Table 4, it is well to remember that the per capita living-space data for selected Soviet cities are just averages. Clearly a privileged few had far more than the average, but a great many more people had even less. Housing was in a state of crisis in the early 1950s. It took the death of Stalin in 1953 before a re-examination of priorities occurred. Consumer well-being did not displace industrialization as a national priority, but it did at least receive a larger share of the available resources.

Social justice and housing

The industrialization of housing construction, including prefabrication, and more recently module units, ushered in a period of enormous progress in housing. There has been justifiable pride in achievement since. Most large centres now give plentiful visual evidence of the transformation. As we noted earlier, fully two-thirds of the population were rehoused between 1960 and 1975, during which time some 1.55 billion square metres of new housing were put up. We might briefly examine the organization of this housing within cities before probing the actual dimensions of this rather remarkable achievement.

The *mikrorayon* emerged as the basic building block in Soviet town planning in the post-war period. Indeed, it is reckoned that half the urban population now lives in *mikrorayon* (Dementyeva, 1974, 16). Comprising a set of smaller housing units or living complexes (traditionally referred to as a super block or a *kvartal'*), the *mikrorayon* usually has somewhere between 8,000 and 12,000 residents—and a long list of appropriate norms to go with them. The *mikrorayons* are then aggregated to comprise what is frequently labelled a residential complex. Something of the population and spatial dimensions of this system are indicated by the following figures. Five to eight living complexes, each with a population of 1,000–1,500 and a radius of perhaps 50 to 100 metres, comprise a *mikrorayon*. Four to five *mikrorayons*, each with a population of between 8,000 and 12,000 inhabitants and a radius of between 300–400 metres, comprise a residential complex (Gradov, 1973, 343). One variant of this type of hierarchical system is portrayed in Map 17. Ample green space, perimeter thoroughfares with public transport facilities, day-care, educational and health services—all are common denominators of long standing in the planning of residential areas. Certainly in theory there is a logical progression of facilities such that all the day-to-day requirements can be met with a short pedestrian journey. Higher-order goods and services are located strategically within the *mikrorayon* and residential complexes, with only infrequent journeys to the central city expected, and then more for the purpose of mass culture than personal consumption. By so structuring the housing and consumer and cultural-services components of the urban system waste is minimized, efficiency maximized. Of course much depends upon successfully integrating the activities of a variety of actors on the urban

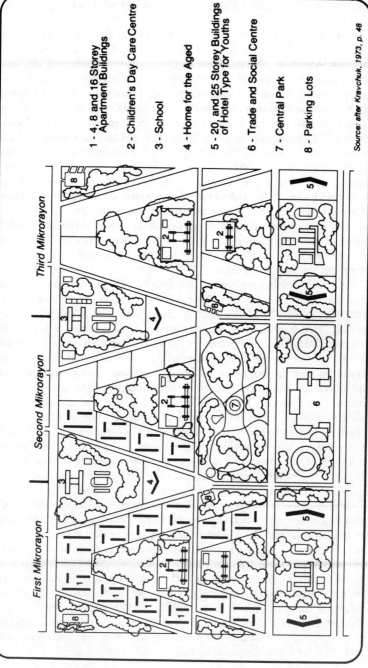

1 - 4, 8 and 16 Storey
Apartment Buildings

2 - Children's Day Care Centre

3 - School

4 - Home for the Aged

5 - 20, and 25 Storey Buildings
of Hotel Type for Youths

6 - Trade and Social Centre

7 - Central Park

8 - Parking Lots

Source: after Kravchuk, 1973, p. 48

First Mikrorayon   Second Mikrorayon   Third Mikrorayon

Map 17 Residential complex

scene. In this context the coordinative abilities of the town planner already have been called into question. But just who can engage in the construction of housing?

In keeping with the spirit of the late 1950s, the potential contribution of cooperatively-owned housing in alleviating the housing crisis was acknowledged. In 1962 cooperative apartment ownership was legalized once more. Since then the construction of housing by such means has grown quickly. Housing cooperatives are restricted to 60 participants in Moscow and Leningrad, 48 in Republic capitals and other large cities. The state will provide loans to cover 40 per cent of the cost of construction (Gendzekhadze, 1976, 44–5). It is not too surprising that the construction of housing by such means has been developed most fully in the larger cities. In Moscow, for example, it is estimated that 11 per cent of all housing put up in 1973 was in the form of cooperatives (Gendzekhadze, 1976, 5). And each year the proportion steadily increases. Throughout the urban sector as a whole, however, the current share is only about 5 per cent. While still small its impact is felt in a variety of ways. At present some 25,000 cooperatives accommodate 2.2 million people (Pudikov, 1977b, 2). How they are accommodated, and who they are, are important issues.

As a rule, cooperative housing tends to be of higher quality than that available in the state sector. Moreover, given the opportunity, most cooperative members have built apartments as large as the regulations permit. Hence, the occupants tend to be more generously housed in a qualitatively better environment. As the cooperatives' success depends as much upon the ability to get things done in the bewildering bureaucratic maze as it does upon having the requisite down-payment, the membership is frequently less than representative of the whole societal strata. To the extent that differentiation of cooperative members from society at large occurs, then a form of residential segregation is being created. The fact that in some cities the movement has been resisted vigorously simply means that where it does occur it is at a level rather in excess of what the national averages might suggest (Pudikov, 1977a, 17). It is not possible to determine if cooperative apartments are segregated spatially within cities, but clearly this may occur.

While cooperatives were prohibited from the late 1930s until 1962, private ownership of detached, usually wooden, homes has been permitted throughout the Soviet period, though under various pressures at various times. There are restrictions on construction of new dwellings of this kind in most regional capitals and major centres, but their role is still far from being eclipsed. Indeed, loans of up to 1,500 roubles have been recently authorized by the government for the purpose of private house construction in cities (Loans, 1977, 28). While the amount is small, the fact that there is some government support is significant. Certainly the construction of such accommodation will continue in the least well endowed urban places and in the process help to perpetuate their 'wooden' fabric. While about one-quarter of the urban housing stock is of this type, it is not evenly distributed (*Narodnoye*, 1977, 498). As with so many other urban attributes it varies by region and city size. In this instance, however, the share correlates positively the more remote the region, the smaller the urban place. It scarcely needs emphasizing that urban housing schemes such as that envisaged in Map 17 do not include the customary wooden, detached, minimally serviced and low-density private housing sector.

The state sector obviously has outstripped the expansion of both the cooperative and private sectors in absolute volume of housing erected. Between 1965 and 1977 the floor space almost doubled. As much old, usually inner-city housing, has been redeveloped in the process, the actual level of construction exceeds the net gain registered. It has been without doubt a phenomenal achievement, and fully testifies to the capabilities of the state once objectives are set. To be sure, the annual and five-year quotas for additions to the housing stock are rarely fulfilled, but that does not take away from the real gains registered. But there are problems in organizing construction, in integrating plans, in developing residential areas according to norms, indeed, in meeting long-standing norms for adequately housing the population, and it is to some of those features of the housing scene that we now turn.

The state sector accounted for about 70 per cent of the 1977 total urban housing stock of two billion square metres of useful space (*Narodnoye*, 1978, 415). But state control does not mean unified control. In Chapter 3 it was observed that despite numerous attempts to bring housing under the jurisdiction of the city Soviet, the realization of this objective was constantly stymied by the self-interest of the multitude of enterprises, departments and ministries which controlled two-thirds of the state's share of the housing stock in 1971. Given the growing labour shortage, ministries are understandably reluctant to relinquish control over such a traditionally important factor in attracting labour as housing. The creation of a single administrative authority over housing has made some progress, but usually in cities like Moscow, Leningrad or Kiev, where planning is well articulated, and where the city Soviet does have political power. Elsewhere progress is slow. Indeed, between 1971 and 1975 Union and Union-Republic ministries and departments had control over roughly three-fifths of the total fund of state finances for investment in housing construction (Mil'ner, 1978, 20). So much for turning funds and control over to city Soviets.

The consequences of the continuation of a departmentalist approach to housing development are several. In the first instance, ancillary facilities still tend to get short shrift—a point developed later. Secondly, the spatial integration of all housing-construction activities becomes more difficult the more actors involved. Thirdly, national goals and removing regional disparities are less easy to achieve when the funds available are expended to meet ministerial objectives and needs. But to what extent is the distribution of housing equitable, indeed, has the norm of nine square metres of living space per capita been reached?

Table 6. Urban housing stock by republic 1977

Republic	Living space per person (m²)
RSFSR	8.1
Ukraine	8.7
Belorussia	8.0
Moldavia	7.3
Lithuania	8.5
Latvia	10.0
Estonia	10.1
Georgia	9.0
Azerbaydzhan	6.5
Armenia	7.0
Kazakh	7.1
Uzbek	6.0
Kirgiz	6.3
Tadzhik	6.1
Turkmen	6.7

Source: *Narodnoye Khozyaystvo*, 1977, 43, 497; *Narodnoye Khozyaystvo*, 1978, 417.

In 1970 living space per capita was 7.5 square metres: seven years later it was eight (*Narodnoye*, 1977, 7, 496). Compared to the situation in 1950 there has been a dramatic improvement, especially when the rapid growth in the urban population and the aforementioned demolition of existing, inadequate stock are taken into consideration. Still, the statutory sanitary minimum is not yet satisfied for the urban population as a whole. As the data in Table 6 reveal, however, there are some exceptions at a gross regional scale. By 1977 two Republics, Latvia and Estonia, had exceeded the nine square metres of living space which has served as the basic norm for more than half a century, while the Republic of Georgia had equalled it. Although several other Republics had more than eight square metres of living space per capita, Central Asian Republics in particular still fall far short of the norm, a situation exacerbated by the demographic trends discussed earlier. These figures, of course, mask the disparities which still exist within Republics. Mil'ner and Gilinskaya's analysis of the RSFSR, the Russian Federative Soviet Socialist Republic, indicates that in 1974 the differential between maximum and minimum regional per capita figures was in excess of five square metres (1975, 60). Put simply, the eastern regions of the RSFSR, Middle Asia and parts of the Caucasus lag behind the core regions of

European Russia and the Baltic Republics. A finer edge can be put on this point by once again examining the housing situation in selected Soviet cities.

Table 7. Housing stock in selected Soviet cities

	Population (thousands)			Living space per person (m²)		
	1971	1974	1977	1971	1974	1977
Moscow	7172	7632	7819	9.5	10.0	10.3
Leningrad	4002	4311	4425	8.3	8.7	9.1
Kiev	1693	1947	2079	8.8	9.0	9.1
Baku	1291	1383	1435	7.1	7.0	7.2
Kharkov	1248	1357	1405	8.2	8.6	8.9
Gorkiy	1189	1283	1319	7.5	7.7	8.0
Tashkent	1424	1595	1689	5.6	5.8	6.3
Kuybyshev	1069	1164	1204	7.2	7.4	7.7
Novosibirsk	1180	1265	1304	7.3	7.8	8.0
Sverdlovsk	1048	1147	1187	7.8	7.9	8.2
Minsk	955	1147	1231	7.4	7.8	8.0
Odessa	913	1002	1039	7.7	7.7	7.8
Tbilisi	907	1006	1042	7.5	7.8	8.1
Donetsk	891	950	984	9.2	9.3	9.4
Chelyabinsk	891	969	1007	8.0	8.2	8.4
Kazan	885	946	970	6.6	6.9	7.3
Dnepropetrovsk	882	958	995	8.0	8.3	8.7
Perm	863	939	972	7.4	7.5	7.7
Omsk	850	968	1026	7.3	7.4	7.5
Volgograd	834	900	931	7.9	8.1	8.2
Rostov-on-Don	808	888	921	7.5	7.6	7.9
Yerevan	791	899	956	6.5	6.6	6.8
Saratov	773	834	856	7.3	7.6	7.8
Alma-Ata	753	836	871	7.2	7.6	7.8
Riga	743	796	816	9.4	9.5	9.7
Frunze	442	486	511	6.3	6.6	6.7
Dushanbe	388	436	460	6.2	6.5	6.5

Source: *Narodnoye Khozyaystvo*, 1975, 589; *Narodnoye Khozyaystvo*, 1977, 59–68, 500–1; *Narodnoye Khozyaystvo*, 1978, 419–20.

From the data presented in Table 7 it is at once apparent that the 1970s have witnessed a progressive improvement in the living space available to the inhabitants of the selected cities. Only Dushanbe has not improved one year to the next, despite the fact that population growth between 1974 and 1977 slowed down quite markedly when compared with the growth from 1971 to 1974. The traditional pattern of regional disparity persists as the cities of Middle Asia and Siberia still fall notably short of the nine square metres of living space sanitary norm.

The problem of providing adequate housing in the industrializing frontier regions remains a particularly serious obstacle to rational regional economic development strategy. In the city of Ust-Ilimsk, for example, the per capita living space averaged just slightly more than five square metres for the near 50,000 inhabitants in 1976 (*Stroyka*, 1976, 3). Dormitory living continues to be an integral part of life for many inhabitants of new cities like Ust-Ilimsk, and is regarded as one of the principal reasons for the extremely high rates of labour turnover. But it is by no means restricted to new towns. Well over three million people live in dormitories throughout the Soviet Union, the overwhelming majority in the so-called 'corridor' type which afford no privacy (Pavlov, 1977, 6). These, like most apartment buildings, are usually owned and managed by ministries. Where the state fails to house the population adequately, private initiative manifests itself in a variety of ways. In frontier settlements like Ust-Ilimsk, Bratsk or Krasnoyarsk construction personnel frequently build their own homes, not always with the requisite official sanction (Matvechuk, 1971, 44–6). If permitted, settlements appear for which no services are provided other than electric power and for which there has been no provision in the general plan. The settlement of Padunskiy in the Bratsk administrative area is a good example. If not permitted, the houses are sometimes bulldozed, as has occurred in Ust-Ilimsk (Chernichenko, 1977, 16). More common still is renting of beds in private apartments. Such *ugol*, or literally corner living, is all too common in Siberian new towns, and is reminiscent of the division of available space in the overcrowded cities of Tsarist Russia. The analogy cannot be taken too far, but it is of interest that the same phenomenon exists in the 1970s and is described by the same word.

The data on per capita living space in Soviet cities does suggest that overcrowding continues to be a major social problem, a theme to be developed in the ensuing chapter. While congestion in housing and high population densities do not necessarily go hand in hand, at the present time there is reason to link the two insofar as Soviet cities are concerned. Over the past few years the average number of storeys per apartment block has increased noticeably. In 1963, for instance, new apartment buildings averaged 5.1 storeys; in 1971 the average was 7.8 (Bulgakov, 1973, 391). At present it is probably in excess of ten storeys since twelve storeys is the intended minimum for major cities. Even the skyline of new towns like Ust-Ilimsk is dominated by nine and fourteen-storeyed buildings (*Stroyka*, 1976, 3). The result of building up—from centre to periphery—has been to increase population densities toward the periphery. In most large cities some progress has been made in redeveloping the customarily overcrowded housing stock of the central city. But even there high-rise replaces low-rise substandard accommodation. The actual numbers of residents declines, but large numbers still continue to live in the central city. In the absence of detailed census material for city census tracts and the dearth of pertinent Soviet studies, it is impossible to generalize with any certainty about the aggregate population densities in Soviet cities or about density gradients (Khanin, 1971, 1976; Gurevich, 1967; Pen'kov, 1971; Il'in, 1972; Sevost'yanov, 1972). It has been argued, however, that a density gradient from centre to periphery does not exist in Soviet cities, thereby distinguishing it from its Western counterpart (French, 1979, 88–9). Such conjecture tends to be reinforced by the visual impact of multi-storeyed apartments which so frequently signal arrival at one of the major urban centres. But the majority of Soviet cities probably still have at least as much of the periphery made up of extensive land using privately-owned, wooden detached housing as they do multi-storeyed *mikrorayons* (Gornostayeva, 1979, 10). Insofar as the one known density gradient actually calculated and published is concerned, there most certainly is a gradient in population density from centre to periphery. The calculations are for Moscow and although the data only go up to 1963 the pattern is still of interest (Fig. 4). It is apparent that central Moscow population densities have been steadily lowered since 1954 while on the periphery densities are increasing. The decentralization of some central-city residents to new *mikrorayons* on the periphery has been carried out more extensively in Moscow than in most other cities. After all, it is a model, but as in most things the rest of the urban system is usually some way behind. What one can conclude is that by comparison with say London or Chicago (Fig. 4), in the early 1960s population density in Moscow was substantially greater, that it declined toward the periphery, but owing to vast differences in land-use practices, transport modes and so on, it was much higher everywhere than was evident in either of these two Western cities.

There is no need to dwell long on the matter of housing quality. Rising expectations in the Soviet Union have ensured that what would have been luxuries twenty years ago are now taken for granted and subject to vitriolic criticism if not of the quality expected. Again the issue is not simply aggregate levels of provision but whether equal accessibility is everywhere possible. Clearly from the data provided in Tables 6 and 7 this is unlikely to be the case. The little other evidence available is corroborative. In the above-mentioned study of Mil'ner and Gilinskaya (1975, 60) it was noted that in the eastern regions of the RSFSR barely 50 per cent of housing is connected to water, sewer or central-heating networks. In the west, essentially European Russia, the equivalent percentages were 70, 66 and 70. Moreover, the figures cited apparently refer only to the state housing stock and it will be recalled that this accounts for about 70 per cent of the total, the balance being privately or cooperatively owned. Again, as a rule, the smaller and more remote the urban place the greater the share of private housing and invariably the lower the level of municipal service provision. To be sure, most detached private dwellings have electricity, but few are connected to water or sewage systems. Thus, when the privately owned

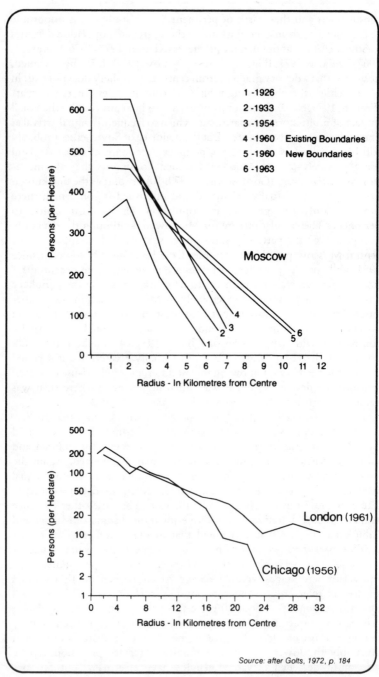

Fig. 4 Population density gradients, Moscow, Chicago and London

Source: after Golts, 1972, p. 184

housing stock is taken into account, the overall level of services must be lowered.

If by social justice in housing we mean the equitable allocation of available living space it may be fairly said that the situation in the Soviet Union is far better than in most countries. But the average allocation remains small, the quality of that living space is still below that common in western Europe and North America and the differential allocative procedures that give housing perks to privileged elites remain intact. Moreover, the recent upsurge in cooperative apartment ownership could well establish a trend toward greater residential homogeneity, albeit at a micro-scale, than the customary egalitarian admixture the typical *mikrorayon* produces. The fact that representatives of the various strata of Soviet society live in a particular *mikrorayon*, indeed, in the same apartment building, does not necessarily result in social interaction between members of those various strata. In short, there is some way to go still before the goal of social justice in housing is fully realized.

Given the state of housing a mere quarter of a century ago, the subsequent massive urbanization and the problem in coordinating the construction of housing, the state has indeed registered remarkable achievements. By the same token, practice has some way to go to catch up to principle. Nonetheless, in the past few years there has been a move to have the basic norm increased from nine to twelve to fifteen square metres (Kravchuk, 1973, 1). Whether expressed in useful-space or in living-space terms, a real challenge has been set the coordinative abilities of planners. To bring the reality of the housing scene closer to the ideal is dependent more upon ironing out administrative tangles than anything else.

Transport and the journey to work

Thus far we have dealt with the seemingly separate issues of industrial location and land-use zoning and housing. They are, of course, related, the most tangible expression of the spatial efficiency of that relationship being the time taken journeying to work. The basic planning principle is that the journey to work should be minimized and that spatial mobility in general should be public-transport based. We will consider principle and practice in general terms first and then examine the journey to work in specific urban contexts.

The link between public-transport based mobility, the journey to work and the efficient spatial organization of the city has long been acknowledged as of fundamental importance in Soviet town planning (Fedutinov, 1968; Belousov, 1973). Early concepts like the linear city stressed the advantage of proximity of workplace and residence, though the two were to be separated by a buffer zone (Miliutin, 1974). Recent interest in the basic idea of the linear city has been justified largely on the grounds that it does offer scope for bringing journeys to work within the realm of established norms (Starr, 1971, 171; Kravchuk, 1973, 49; Yaralov, 1975, 24). It follows then that journey-to-work norms are not now being met, and that this somehow reflects on both public transport and the efficiency of the spatial organization of the contemporary city.

In 1970 nearly 37 billion people travelled on urban tram, bus, trolley-bus and metro systems. By 1977 traffic volume exceeded 48 billion (*Narodnoye*, 1978, 325, 330–32). While decisions to embark on the construction of underground networks receive considerable publicity, as do the seven systems presently operational, above-ground public transport still accounts for well over 90 per cent of the traffic. Though traffic has increased substantially so have the costs of operation. Salaries especially have risen sharply, and with more sophisticated equipment, maintenance costs are naturally higher. With a seemingly immutable fare structure, the net result is an annual operational deficit, the size of which is of much concern in the current era of emphasis on cost efficiency and profitability. How well these increasingly expensive transport systems serve the public is difficult to ascertain for several reasons.

In the first place, there have been criticisms of irrational location of employment nodes—industrial, commercial or administrative—in relation to the probable place of residence of workforces (Kochetkov, 1975, 25). Whereas the development of the *mikrorayon* is premised on at least a sizeable proportion of the potential workforce being employed nearby, the tenor of much recent criticism is that this has not generally worked out in practice and with the increasing redevelopment of central cities, which includes the dispersal of population and industry, the problem is getting worse (Gol'ts, 1972, 172). According to Litovka, 'sociological studies in Leningrad reveal that no more than 15 per cent of the employed population work close to their place of residence' (1976, 47). What constitutes close is not specified, but the consequences of such a situation, produced by the enormous scale of rehousing and the fact that in most families there is more than one wage earner and rarely a common place of work, are obvious. The greater the volume of 'unplanned' cross-city journeys, the more overloaded public-transport facilities become. In the second place, the usual lag between the construction of housing and provision of services has been everywhere exacerbated by 'unplanned' population growth. The growing volume of commuters from outlying centres simply makes matters worse (Gokhberg, 1976, 51). In short, for any particular city any of these factors, and no doubt others as well, adversely affect public-transport operations. Available evidence suggests that there is not necessarily a close correlation between city size and time taken journeying to work though as a rule this would be the case. The exceptions most often occur in the extremely fast-growing industrial centres of small to medium size, that is, of less than one-quarter million inhabitants, where such facilities are extremely primitive (Gol'ts, 1972, 172).

In general, public transport and rational planning of employment nodes and residential areas should permit a norm of a 40-minute journey to work to obtain in the case of large cities (say one half million or more) (Baranov, 1973, 90; *Planirovka*, 1965, 18). For smaller centres, about 25 minutes is the usual norm (Gol'ts, 1972, 167). Owing to a lack of integrated urban development, travel times have increased over the last decade. In the mid-1960s Moscovites were reckoned to spend about 37 minutes on the journey to work. Recent evidence suggests that one hour would be a more realistic, if not conservative, estimate. Indeed, a survey conducted in a new residential complex showed that just over half of the respondents spent between two and three hours on the return trip. For inhabitants of outlying residential complexes, up to four hours can be consumed getting to and from the workplace (Matveyev, 1972, 17). Although throughout the country increased distances in the journey to work have been noted (Baranov, 1973, 90), theoretically this should be offset by technological improvements and resultant speedier service. But two factors militate against this being the normal course of events. Firstly, the financial squeeze has made new technology very difficult to introduce, especially in light of the rapid escalation in operational costs. Secondly, even a passing acquaintance with the reality of Soviet cities is sufficient to bring out the fact that the introduction of technologically improved rolling stock could be handicapped by the state of city roads. This point is frequently made by Soviet observers and in so doing specific situations are cited. In the article by Baranov (1973, 91) it is noted that only 40 per cent of streets in Gorkiy, Kuybyshev and Novosibirsk are hard-surfaced. The data may well refer to the state of affairs in the late 1960s, but the fact that each of these cities has more than a million inhabitants says a great deal about what the comparable shares might be in small and medium-size cities at present (Loginov and Lyubovnyy, 1975, 49; Khodatayev, 1973, 227). The above-mentioned figures pertaining to travel times in Moscow, the city where planning has been most effective, also intimate the probable state of affairs in other large and not-so-large cities, where planning has been demonstrably less effective. For most large industrial centres journeys to work are certainly close to one hour on average. In Donetsk, for example, the norm for journeying to work is 45 minutes. Apparently it would be necessary to double the average speed of public transport for the norm to be met, something not possible owing to the poor state of roads, intersections etc. Judging from the data provided, the journey to work is perhaps in the range of 90 minutes, not 45 (Kishkan, 1977, 6). There is no question that norms are not yet being realized on any very large scale and this fact goes a long way to explaining the recent, insistent emphasis on the need for planners to integrate better the urban development process so that workplace and residence give rise to more rational journey-to-work times (Kravchuk, 1973, 15). The growing evidence accumulated by sociologists showing the negative effect of prolonged, and especially modal split, journeys on labour productivity gives an added sense of urgency to the issue (Kabakova, 1973, 81–2).

In the absence of any kind of systematic data base for journey-to-work times throughout the country, we are dependent upon the occasional survey in which this facet of urban life is detailed. To help put the foregoing general discussion into sharper perspective, we will examine journey-to-work characteristics of several Siberian new towns.

Prolonged journeys to work have been demonstrated to have a bearing on labour productivity and, indeed, seem as well to figure in the high rates of labour turnover which have come to characterize so many Soviet cities. In the building of new towns there is clearly an opportunity to put principle into practice, to create a spatially efficient urban form. In a sample survey of some 10,500 workers in four Siberian new towns in the early 1970s data on journey-to-work times and general patterns of movement permit some evaluation of the achievement in this regard. The four eastern Siberian cities are Angarsk, Shelekhov, Bratsk and Ust-Ilimsk, which at the time of the survey had populations of about 200,000, 25,000, 150,000 and 20,000 respectively. Angarsk and Shelekhov are located near Irkutsk, while Bratsk and Ust-Ilimsk are about 500 kilometres north.

On the whole journey-to-work times are clearly well within the established norm of about 25 minutes, though it should be emphasized that the sample is drawn from cities of different sizes and may be biased downward somewhat by the inclusion of Ust-Ilimsk and Shelekhov.

Table 8. Journey to work by age group Siberian new towns*

| | Average time (minutes) | | |
Age group	All workers	Men	Women
16–20	25.2	25.3	24.5
20–30	24.3	25.0	23.2
30–40	23.0	23.5	22.0
40–50	22.8	23.2	21.5
over 50	22.0	23.0	20.0

Source: Zagaynova, 1974, 34.
* Angarsk, Shelekhov, Bratsk, Ust-Ilimsk.

Insofar as can be determined, the data in Table 8 have not been weighted to account for such differences. The somewhat greater travel times for the younger age groups generally reflect the fact that dormitory, or rented beds or rooms in someone else's apartment or private house, are the usual form of accommodation. Recently-arrived young workers often are obliged to take the least accessible accommodation, while the opposite tends to hold amongst the older age groups.

Table 9. Journey to work by place of work and place of residence Siberian new towns*

Place of work	Central city	Place of residence Periphery residential complex	Residential complex under construction
Central region	16	40	45
Peripheral regions	42	23	30

Source: Zagaynova, 1974, 37.
* Angarsk, Shelekhov, Bratsk, Ust-Ilimsk.

Of particular interest in this survey are the data which differentiate journey-to-work times according to the relative location of place of work and residence. As Table 9 shows, age-group averages mask some considerable deviations when cross-town journeys are necessitated. Inasmuch as we are dealing with new towns, the fact that substantial numbers of workers are daily obliged to travel across the city to get to work suggests that in *mikrorayons* and residential complexes there is less than a perfect match between jobs and people. In established cities redevelopment of the inner city core has resulted in people and jobs both being decentralized, generating irrational journeys to work in the process. But in new towns the appearance of such trips must be attributed mainly to the absence of an integrated approach to urban development. In the case of Bratsk specifically, the situation is sometimes extreme. As was pointed out at an earlier juncture, Bratsk comprises half a dozen physically separated residential areas. Most have sprung up in association with major industrial enterprises. Except Padunskiy, the original dam builders' settlement which does not have much of a local employment base. As a result many inhabitants travel daily to other settlements in the administrative system. As inter-settlement public transport is not intended to expedite large-scale movements of workers, the journey to work for such people is at least one hour. Part of the problem in Bratsk is the departmentalist approach to urban development; perhaps as much at fault though is the fact that such services rarely equal the prescribed norms (Bater, 1977b).

Viewed historically, journey-to-work times have steadily edged up-ward, a fact linked to the growth of the large city and agglomeration, and to the massive post-war programme of rehousing the population. Longer travel times are arguably the logical outcome of better housing conditions. Faced with the prospect of a longer journey to work in return for better accommodation, the average Soviet citizen makes a perfectly rational choice. Flat fares tend to reinforce such decisions. And, after all, while labour productivity may be reduced because of longer journeys and split modes, it is usually the state not the individual concerned who loses out. By focusing attention on journey-to-work time, the planner is able to present a seemingly strong argument in support of the need for greater control over the location of housing and jobs. Whether enterprise or individual will be persuaded by its logic is still a moot point.

What happens in the city and what happens outside it are not un-related; however, there is a jurisdictional impasse at the present time. Planning urban transport to accommodate trips by city dwellers is made all the more complex in many urban centres by the growing volume of commuters. Some 500,000 daily commuters pour into Moscow, while perhaps as many as 100,000 leave the city to work in outlying enterprises (Glushkova and Kopilov, 1976, 267). The volume of commuters tends to correlate positively with size of city. Overall the number is enormous, and growing (Fuchs and Demko, 1978; Kogan, 1976). Assuming com-muters to constitute anyone crossing an administrative boundary in journeying to work, ten million people so qualified in 1970. Aside from the social costs of the phenomenon, discussed in the next chapter, there are obviously some negative consequences for an intra-urban transport system developed primarily on the basis of the needs of the urban population.

A growing number of Soviet urbanites avoid the trials and tribulations of public transport by using their own automobile. Use of privately-owned cars has grown rapidly during the 1970s owing to the decision to build more cars and to sell a larger proportion to the population. Conventional wisdom regards this move by the central authorities as one intended to spur labour productivity by holding forth the possibility of private-car ownership as a carrot to initiative. It is doubtful whether productivity has increased as a result. What is beyond doubt, however, is the growing traffic congestion fed in part by a privileged segment of society using private means of conveyance in the journey to work. In 1976 there were roughly nine privately owned automobiles per 1,000 population, a miniscule number compared to the ratios of between 200 and 400 in advanced European countries and the United States (Efimov and Mikerin, 1976, 34; Khodatayev, 1973, 213). It takes little imagination to envision the impact of the privatization of travel on cities designed and built according to the premise that spatial mobility would always be public-transport based. To be sure, norms for parking spaces per 1,000 population in *mikrorayons* have been steadily augmented, and some allowances for parking in central cities have been made, but norms are rarely met and parking is still a low priority in central-city planning (Dubinsky, 1972, 24). Thus, otherwise well designed *mikrorayons* are being visually blemished by shanty-town garages and car parking, storage and repair taking place in space designed primarily for pedestrian purposes. Egalitarian town-planning principles and private automobile ownership are not necessarily incompatible, but in the context of the Soviet city they are unlikely co-habiters. Facilitating the journey to work

or leisure time activities for the few, car ownership creates dispropor-
tionate social costs for the majority.

Consumer and cultural services

The spatial allocation of consumer and cultural services was to be
governed by the principle of equal accessibility. The adoption of a
normative approach to the overall provision of items of collective consumption was intended to ensure equibility within, and amongst, cities
(Gradov, 1973). For the most part, norms pertaining to items of collective consumption are expressed in terms of per capita ratios. For instance,
35 seats per 1,000 residents for cafeterias and 15 for coffee bars and
restaurants are standard. Aggregate figures are sometimes cited, particularly in the case of the *mikrorayon* (Otdel'nov, 1975, 23; Selivanov and
Gel'perin, 1970, 166). But whether the evaluation of norm fulfilment
proceeds on a per capita basis for the total urban population, for a specific
city, or for a particular *mikrorayon*, it ought to be remembered that the
question of accessibility to facilities is as important as the overall level
of provision. We might appropriately begin the discussion by considering first the question of the level of provision. Disparities, and reasons
for them, will then be examined.

In a recent assessment of the social and economic aspects of town
planning Kochetkov (1975, 26) noted that in the majority of cities
established norms are far from being met. Schools, shopping facilities,
restaurants, cultural facilities—all are less than two-thirds, and in some
cases less than one-half, the prescribed levels. Gradov (1973, 323) has
contended that, in general, consumer and cultural services are only about
70 per cent fulfilled. There are essentially two ways of viewing this state
of affairs. One presumes that the norms set were unrealistically high
—perhaps a conscious decision taken in the hope of stimulating greater
effort and hence more rapidly improving consumer well-being. The
other, less charitable, view is that the norms represent minimum levels,
but not yet satisfied. Most non-Soviet analyses subscribe to the latter
view, but judging from the literature of the 1970s so too do most Soviet
observers. There is no reason not to accept the suggestion that the level
of provision of items of collective consumption falls short of the basic
requirements of the population (Ofer, 1973, 150). While all cities are
affected it is obvious that some are rather worse off than others.

Moscow's population is by Soviet standards extremely well provi-
sioned. But even in the capital construction of consumer and cultural
facilities can lag behind demand (Denisov, 1978, 1). However, the
inconvenience is usually only a temporary one, something which cannot
be said for many other of the largest cities. In places like Rostov-on-
Don, for example, the discrepancy between what should be provided
for the million or so inhabitants and what is provided, remains substantial. For whatever reason, construction of consumer and cultural

services cannot be managed in such a way as to come on stream as new housing is opened (Efimov, 1977, 3). In Sverdlovsk, another million city in the Urals, the '... disproportion between the steadily multiplying might of the industrial giants and the constantly lagging growth of cultural and consumer-service enterprises not only is not being reduced but at times shows a tendency to increase' (Manyukhin, 1977, 9). 'Significantly lagging behind the tempo of housing construction is the building of schools, *detskiy sad*, hospitals and other cultural-service enterprises' is the recent judgment of the situation in Novosibirsk (1.3 million) (Astaf'yeva-Dlugach, 1976, 3). In general, the probability of a disparity between the level of actual provision of items of collective consumption increases the smaller the city and the more remote its location. The following description of Angarsk (0.24 million), a new town in Eastern Siberia, emphasizes the general point, if in somewhat extreme terms.

> If you walk through the new micro boroughs of Angarsk, you can't help noticing the absence, in places where the plans envisage them, of shopping centres, consumer-service buildings, movie houses and theatres. In the past, when the city was small and the USSR Ministry of the Petroleum-Refining and Petrochemical Industry was the only organization doing construction work, its funds were used to build institutions of this kind. But then Angarsk became a multibranch centre. One would have thought that now the appropriate non-industrial departments would strengthen the bases of social, consumer-service and cultural-enlightenment institutions. What has been done for the development of Angarsk by, for instance, the republic Ministries of Consumer Services and of Culture and the Russian Republic State Committee on Cinematography? Virtually nothing. They have not allocated a single rouble from their centralized capital investments for the expansion of the network of institutions under their jurisdiction. The Russian Republic Ministry of Trade has declined all responsibility for serving the residents of Angarsk; this job is handled only by the workers' supply administration for the construction workers, who constitute a tiny share of the population. For this reason, there are gaping holes in the rows of new apartment buildings (Brovkin and Yermolayev, 1978, 11).

Judging by some recent reports the problems encountered in Angarsk continue to plague new construction throughout the eastern regions. The situation in Neryungri, an industrial centre of several thousand inhabitants in the southern Yakutsk territorial production complex in the Far East is rather typical. It was decreed a city in 1975 at which time it comprised several workers' settlements associated with the construction of the Baykal-Amur railway. An idealized general plan was soon adopted, but it bore little relationship to the real pattern of settlement. What is more, it does not yet seem to serve as an effective guide for development. As in the past each enterprise looks after some of the basic requirements of its own workforce, the principal focus of attention being housing, though recreational, cultural, sanitoria and holiday facilities are sometimes brought under ministerial jurisdiction as well. For the rest the inhabitants simply make do (P'yankov, 1978, 2). In Tynda, a city of 22,000 in the same region, which also owes its existence to the railway construction project, the same situation prevails. Elevated to city status in 1975, the year-old complex of workers' settlements was presented with a general plan which prescribed centralized municipal services and integrated development of housing and collective consumption facilities. The inability of the city Soviet to ensure adequate financing means that '... the current five-year plan does not include enough schools, child-care institutions, stores and public catering establishments and makes no provisions for a hotel, youth centre or sports complex.' (Pekarsky, 1977, 16). The regional disparity that was shown to exist in terms of housing also exists in the context of collective consumption facilities. But it is worth noting that the degree of regional difference in consumer and cultural services between core area and periphery, between large city and small, is rather greater than in the case of housing.

Differences in the level of provision of items of collective consumption obviously occur within cities as well. A cross-town journey may be a major inconvenience but it is better than no service at all. About half the urban population now lives in *mikrorayons*, as we noted earlier. While ideally they are planned and built in an integrated fashion, this is not borne out in reality, and therefore residence in a *mikrorayon* is no guarantee of access to consumer and cultural services (Dementyeva, 1974, 16; Gradov, 1973, 347). Indeed, if relocation from a central-city location is involved, there is every chance that access to services will be less. Complaints about inadequate, primitive or non-existent communal and cultural services in new suburbs are common (Dementyeva, 1974, 17; Rosovsky, 1974, 31; Kruglyak and Dal, 1972, 25–6). Goods being retailed from the backs of trucks in Togliatti, the new town on the Volga, or converted dump trucks serving as public transport in Bratsk, cannot, however, be taken as representative (City under construction, 1973, 25; Levikov and Moyev, 1972, 15). These and similar tales usually refer to cities where industrialization has proceeded at a phenomenal pace, required a huge influx of labour and in the process totally outstripped the capacity of all concerned to provide even basic facilities—let alone those of a consumer goods or cultural kind (Peri, 1971, 27–9; Mel'nikov, 1974, 9–10). But the reasons for the gap between principle and practice go beyond the simple fact that many cities are developing at an exceedingly rapid rate. In a great many cases coordinative abilities of planners, inadequate finances and the norms themselves may be individually or collectively responsible.

So far as the norms are concerned, several points can be made concerning their inappropriateness for many planning situations. 'While a great deal of attention has focused on the spatial aspect of the location of service establishments,' Pokshishevskiy notes that, 'the recipients of services have generally been treated as an undifferentiated homogeneous mass settled uniformly, say, within the built-up area of a city' (1975, 353). In terms of demographic profiles Soviet cities are no different than Western urban centres in having a characteristically younger population in the new *mikrorayons* or suburbs than in the central city. The extremes are not as great since, in contrast to American cities, for example, the central parts of Soviet cities still have a substantial residential population, but differences there are nonetheless. Hence, allocation of items of collective consumption like schools or hospitals on a per capita basis can lead to imbalances between supply and demand. Lando has also noted that per capita norms usually prescribe upper and lower limits. Since existing facilities are sometimes ignored in the process of spatial allocation, this simply makes possible discrepancies even more pronounced. Thus, '... the average level of availability of cultural-domestic enterprises in different micro-regions is not comparable and does not take into account the demographic structure of the population which has come about in the residential region.' (Lando, 1971, 3). Clearly the disparities which result within the city from the application of standard norms to a differentiated mass of potential consumers are susceptible to even greater distortion at a regional level given the enormous differences in crude rates of net natural increase we earlier described.

The seeming inability of the normative approach to discriminate effectively between different demographic profiles is especially injurious in the high birth-rate, non-Slavic regions and in the newly developed frontier regions. Vladimir (0.29 million), an historic industrial centre east of Moscow has a birth-rate probably one-third or less than that of Bratsk. Though the latter city is predominantly Slavic as well, its 214,000 population has an average age of about 28 years. On the basis of existing norms, Vladimir would be entitled to nearly 50 per cent more spaces in schools, hospitals, restaurants and so forth than Bratsk. Although '... the number of places in schools, children's combines, clubs and hospitals in Bratsk is close to or exceeds official norms, ... the schools there operate in three shifts per day, there is not enough kindergarten space, and the hospitals are overcrowded' (Myasnikov, 1977, 8). In Central Asian cities the indigenous population is a distinct minority but still those who do live in the city have special needs, if only in terms of housing. Until recently standardized, mass-produced apartments did not easily accommodate families with five, six or seven children (Broner, 1973). However, such demographic realities are now being acknowledged in apartment design in the new *mikrorayon* of Kal'kauz in Tashkent (Strin'kovskiy, 1978, 2). The fact that standard norms do not sufficiently take into account demographic and regional differences is of course recognized. But use of norms based on national averages is likely to continue for some time. Norms have become entrenched features of a highly bureaucratized process of decision making, a state of inertia encouraged by the realization that to introduce changes would more than likely strain even more a limited pool of financial resources.

The below-norm level of consumer and cultural services in most cities is closely linked to the multitude of sources of funding, the lack of influence the city Soviet and planners have over these sources and the fact that the monies which should be provided cities often are not. It has been reckoned that one-time capital investments in housing really demand an additional 55 per cent for the construction of consumer and cultural enterprises (Khafizov, 1978, 7). Rarely is such a ratio ever realized. Ministries are regularly castigated for failing to comply with their legal, if not moral, responsibilities for worker welfare (Osipenkov, 1978, 14). With the best intentions and up-to-date plans, little can be done without the necessary finances. Not only does the lack of some form of administrative control over financial affairs complicate town planning, by definition regional disparities become more entrenched. The problem has been summarized as follows:

> At present only a small portion of allocations for housing construction and the construction and operation of cultural and service establishments are planned on a direct territorial basis (through the budgets of local Soviets). Thus, in 1971–1975 the Union and Union-republic ministries and departments controlled approximately 60 per cent of investments in housing construction, 70 per cent of investments in the construction of children's pre-school institutions and from 40 per cent to 45 per cent of investments in the construction of hospitals and polyclinics in the Russian Republic. Ministries and departments distribute such money by territories without coordinating their efforts among themselves and without adequately taking the needs of individual regions into account. Since construction costs in the country's eastern regions are higher, the ministries and departments have no interest in making full use of the money that is allocated to them for housing and social and cultural construction in the territories of new development. Because of departmental fragmentation, the tremendous amount of money that the state appropriates for improving the working people's living conditions is spent irrationally.
>
> At present, comprehensive planning of living standards is done only for the Union republics. Plans for improving the living standard in individual districts, provinces, territories and autonomous republics are mere compilations of the plans of individual ministries and departments. Hence planning agencies have no means of determining beforehand and actively affecting the relative living standards of various regions (Mil'ner, 1978, 20).

To some extent disparities in items of collective consumption amongst cities within the same region can be overcome through journeying to the places where needed items or services are available. Apparently more than ten million people avail themselves of service establishments in other cities each day (Pokshishevskiy, 1974, 356). To the extent that these trips are generated because of the below-norm, or straight absence of, consumer and cultural services that ought to be in place in the home town, then the waste is twofold. First, because of the unnecessary journey and cost in terms of time and money. Second, because the additional demand on existing facilities is 'above plan' and most probably disadvantages those for whom the service was intended. Disparities within the city do not create such heavy individual losses in terms of time and money, but collectively the spatial inefficiencies of increased cross-town journeys are considerable for consumer and state alike.

Clearly, the obvious gap between ideal and reality in the provision of items of collective consumption is sizeable, and potentially much exaggerated depending upon where one lives in a city, where that city is located and how large or how small is the population. A society showing all the signs of an insatiable rising expectation in terms of consumer and cultural services is not likely to tolerate such discrepancies indefinitely. They much influence the quality of life available in Soviet cities, and these perceived differences already have triggered substantial unplanned internal migration.

The city centre—functions and future

During the debate over the future Soviet socialist city in the 1920s the notion that there would be no distinguishable centre was embraced by those proposing a radical departure from the past, and indeed contemporary, trends. The 1935 Moscow Plan, however, established the guiding principle which was certainly a pragmatic accommodation with reality. There would be a city centre and it was to become the nucleus of urban social and political life. By means of unified and uniform architectural ensembles, thoroughfares and squares, the city centre was to cater to massive public demonstrations (Bunin, 1943; Byulinkin *et al.*, 1962; Barkhin, 1974). As we remarked in Chapter 2, the design problem was one of striking a reasonable balance between occasional public functions and the ordinary day-to-day purposes these same thoroughfares, squares and buildings had to serve. With the emphasis on the cultural and political uses of the central city, the usual central-city functions were downgraded (Baranov, 1964; Bocharov and Kudryavtsev, 1972). The result was the conscious decentralization of administrative and distributive services into fully developed secondary centres. That Soviet central cities do differ in several ways from say cities of western Europe or North America is evident upon first setting foot in one. Some of these distinctive features we have already noted, but we will briefly review them before putting forward some evidence to support the argument that past trends are changing.

Unlike Western cities, the central core still has a substantial residential, as opposed to day-time, population, as the comparative density gradients presented for Moscow, London and Chicago made plain. While densities are generally declining, there is no intention of turning the core over to non-residential uses. Like Western cities, during the day there is a substantial net inflow of workers, including a good number still employed in industry.

The most striking feature of Soviet central-city areas is the comparative paucity of shops of one kind or another. While the Nevskiy Prospect in Leningrad and Gorkiy Street in Moscow stand out in terms of pedestrian traffic, neither street presently embraces anything like the array of consumer and cultural service enterprises which existed prior to the revolution. Some specialized shops are still located on or near to these historic arteries, but many more have since been located in new *mikrorayons*. In short, the usual association of central-city location and specialized shopping does not strictly obtain in Soviet cities for reasons already made clear. Those facilities located in the central city, moreover, tend to occupy ground floor and mezzanine only. Multi-storey shopping complexes are anomalies. Indeed, the famous GUM in Moscow and the *Gostinny Dvor* in Leningrad are hold-overs from the Tsarist era. Such bazaar-like complexes exist in other cities as well, but rarely in such grand architectural style.

Similarly, dense concentrations of administrative activities are not characteristic features of the core. While Moscow boasts of central government and state planning functions, the various bureaucracies are scattered throughout the core and even beyond. This partly results from the swift transfer of government from Petrograd to Moscow in 1918, a time when government agencies were located wherever possible. Since then the policy of decentralization has prevented any significant concentration. Aside from the Kremlin complex, the closest counterpart to concentrated, and literally built-up, offices are those of the state planning agency (GOSPLAN) which runs behind Karl Marx Prospect almost to Gorkiy Street. Government bureaucracy is pervasive, but its physical manifestations certainly do not overwhelm the senses when in the central city.

While the central city boasts a fair complement of industry, it is more often factory rather than workshop. Indeed, the concentrations of specialized workshops which characterized the central parts of cities like St Petersburg and Moscow at the turn of the century have virtually disappeared. Even the plethora of small printing and publishing enterprises, so much a part still of the central core of Western cities, has been greatly diminished as centralization and scale economies have been institutionalized. Traditional handicraft functions still survive in the streets around the central market in the old quarter of Tashkent, for example, but these are rather distinctive anomalies. The workshop/handicraft function very largely has been supplanted by mass production and state-run and state located small-scale repair outlets.

The cultural and symbolic roles assigned the Soviet central city are clearly distinctive. Red Square, the Kremlin and Lenin's Mausoleum in Moscow have a special symbolism, of course, but the function is not unique. The regular use of central squares and thoroughfares for mass demonstrations is an important facet of orchestrated public participation in formal and informal events alike. The evening mass promenade to the central city following the May day celebration is representative of the latter, while the November 7 mobilization of the masses epitomizes the former. What goes on in Moscow receives most attention, but on a more modest scale the scene is enacted in large and small cities throughout the country. Cultural facilities like theatres, both pre-Soviet and Soviet, are centrally focused, though again the concentration is by no means exclusive as the decentralization of Soviet theatres to secondary centres has occurred. Generally speaking, however, for many forms of 'passive' culture for the masses—museums, theatres, parks and gardens —the central core acts as a magnet. In a great many instances what is seen, or sat in, is the legacy of the past, a legacy which reflects a different economic system, one which put a premium on centrality through the market mechanism. What has emerged in the Soviet central city by way of economic, bureaucratic, cultural or consumer activity is there because of a normative planning system in which land 'values' traditionally have played no part. It is precisely the consequences of this system, seen most clearly in the central city, which are now being called into question. We earlier noted that land-use allocation procedures have given a somewhat patchy quality to the urban landscape. Substantial areas remain underutilized, in some cases unused entirely, after having been allocated to potential users on the basis of some expectation of need and according to prescribed norms (Litovka, 1976, 79). However, once having been allocated land, the user is under no great pressures to develop it. Land, even in the central city, has not always been used intensively. But the situation is fast changing. Why?

Resource-allocation procedures have been the subject of intensive debate over the past few years for the same reasons as have prompted similar discussions elsewhere—a growing appreciation of the scarcity of natural resources and the recognition that economy in their extraction and consumption is overdue (Gabyshev, 1969, 17–23). The situation in the Soviet Union is complicated, according to some observers, by the fact that until very recently no charge was made for most resources —they were simply allocated to legitimate users on the basis of presumed requirements or prescribed norms. The consensus among Soviet writers now is that this approach works against rational resource-development practice. But what has been done to change the terms of reference in decision making?

A number of resources now bear direct or indirect charges, a situation in marked contrast to that say 25 years ago. Again the major stimulus in this development was the 1965 economic reform and the use of profitability as one measure of economic performance, for it was soon recognized that efficiency in resource use would not be encouraged if resources continued to be allocated free of charge. In the use of natural resources like land and water the response has been much less direct—and less effective. In the first place, legislative invocation for more careful husbandry was introduced for land management in 1968 and water in 1971. In both sets of legislation the possibility of initiating charges was not taken up despite some vigorous argument to the contrary during public discussion of the draft legislation. The basic problem, of course, is that land and water have not been produced by human effort and, hence, in the predominant (but not necessarily correct) Soviet interpretation of Marx's labour theory of value they cannot be charged for (Sheynin, 1977, 2). Still, it is accepted that water resources and land both have differential utilities: yield and location being but two determinants in the case of agricultural land use (Paskhaver, 1972). What has resulted is a series of exceedingly ingenious attempts to establish a set of quantitative but usually non-price values or weights which reflect, amongst other things, scarcity, accessibility, and difficulty of development related to the use of a particular resource, which can be used in the decision-making process (Oziranskiy and Cherkasskaya, 1968, 67–75).

It is against this general background of creating what in effect are surrogates for market-determined prices that the debate over urban land-use allocation procedures must be seen. In the last four or five years there has been growing recognition of the inadequacies of the land-use allocation procedures within cities and the resultant less than efficient spatial organization of the built environment (Gornostayeva, 1974, 10). There is also a growing recognition that the procedures must be tightened up, which demands more than simply a firmer grip on decision making. It implies changes in fundamental principles, and if carried out even in part, portends some interesting developments in form and function of the Soviet city.

In virtually every serious assessment of Soviet town planning over the past half-dozen years the question of how better to allocate urban land uses has arisen. The high proportion of one-storeyed structures is regarded as wasteful of land. According to Bocharov and Lyubovnyy, for example, single-storey buildings occupy 75, 67, 57 and 55 per cent of city land in Arkhangelsk, Kuybyshev, Gorkiy and Novosibirsk respectively (1976a, 78). Above-norm use of land by industry also has been singled out, but transport, trade and other sectors of the urban economy have not been spared criticism either (Polyak, 1974, 17; Baranov, 1973, 76–7; Yanovskiy, 1973, 29–30; Ovesyan, 1974, 68–75).

In a detailed survey of land-use characteristics of 180 cities, Kudryavtsev (1971) concluded that the normative approach was simply not working adequately. The reason for this judgment was directly tied to economic considerations. Put simply, extensive land use in the central city or suburb brought with it much higher costs for services and added to the overall operational and maintenance costs of the urban system. In Kudryavtsev's opinion, part of the problem of insufficiently intensive land use stems from the absence of a general plan to guide city growth in the past and a shortage of professional architect/planners to see to its implementation (1971, 22–6). The present state of the general plan we will deal with in a moment, but what of the immediate need to bring greater awareness of the costs of inefficient land use to the attention of those directly involved in land development?

Kabakova in a fascinating study published in 1973 offers one solution. Noting that in East European countries there has been less reluctance to tackle directly the problem of land rent, she embarks on a detailed examination of irrational urban land uses which have been created through the use of norms. To counteract this tendency a methodology is formulated and its application demonstrated for five cities. The approach involves the assignment of values for some 15 variables which fall into two groups—those of an engineering-construction kind and those of a socio-economic nature. The methodology also entails a regionalization of the city based on a wide range of criteria, including accessibility, level of consumer and cultural services, quality of housing and the like. All told, there is a high degree of subjective interpretation and arbitrarily assigned values. What is created is something approaching a land-value surface for the cities in question. As the graphs in Figs 5–7 clearly indicate, in Moscow, Leningrad and Yerevan the core area has an assigned 'land value' three to four times greater than peripheral locations. The purpose of the whole exercise is to establish a mechanism for more effective discrimination in the land-use allocation process. The relative merit of Kabakova's approach is really beside the point. Its significance lies in the attempt to create a surrogate for market-determined land value and to introduce the consequences of that into the decision-making process. The sentiment is shared by numerous Soviet observers, including Loyter, an outspoken proponent of the need for some means of charging for natural resources. In a recent article in the journal *Gorodskoye Khozyaystvo Moskvy* he turns his attention to the issue of economic evaluation of urban land and suggests charging rents based on the economic characteristics of the user (Loyter, 1975, 27). His suggestion is more direct than others in the same journal, but certainly in step with them (Sheynin, 1976; Silant'yeva, 1975; Polyak, 1974; Segedinov, 1972).

A great deal of effort therefore is being directed toward changing prevailing principles in land-use allocation. There is too a concerted effort simply to use land more intensively. The pressure to build upwards is having results. As we have noted, the average number of storeys per apartment block has increased noticeably over the last few years. Apartments of 15 to 20 storeys are desired and continued construction of five-storey walk-ups condemned (Silant'yeva, 1975, 33; Bulgakov, 1973, 391). Within the central city, the Soviet equivalent of skyscrapers is rapidly changing the skyline.

Insofar as central-city land use is concerned, there are several recent trends which are directly related to a concern with spatial efficiency.

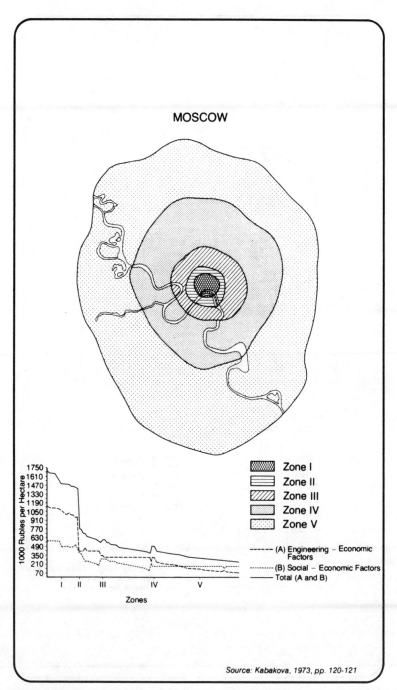

Fig. 5 Land value surface—Moscow

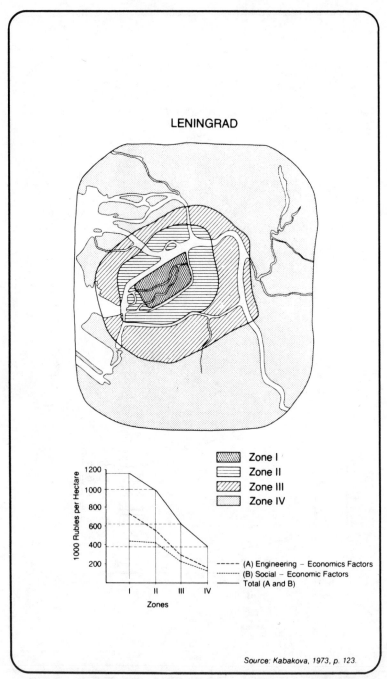

LENINGRAD

1200
1000
800
600
400
200

1000 Rubles per Hectare

Zones
I II III IV

Zone I
Zone II
Zone III
Zone IV

----- (A) Engineering – Economics Factors
········· (B) Social – Economic Factors
——— Total (A and B)

Source: Kabakova, 1973, p. 123.

Fig. 6 Land value surface—Leningrad

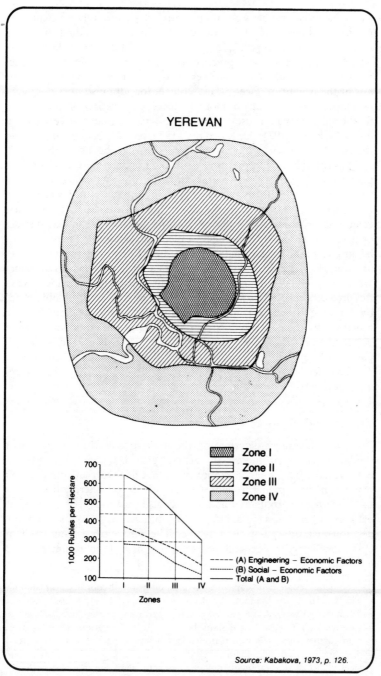

YEREVAN

Zone I
Zone II
Zone III
Zone IV

(A) Engineering – Economic Factors
(B) Social – Economic Factors
Total (A and B)

1000 Rubles per Hectare

Zones

Source: Kabakova, 1973, p. 126.

Fig. 7 Land value surface—Yerevan

There has been emphasis on using central-city land more efficiently by putting a whole array of functions underground—including those of a retail kind (Gerasimov, 1975, 139; Segedinov, 1972, 21–5; Kabakova, 1970, 30–33). Even the traditional practice of decentralizing administrative functions is being questioned. A number of observers have commented on the loss of the benefit of 'face-to-face' contact for administrators now geographically remote one from another; indeed, even the lack of convenience for the public in making use of typically dispersed administrative services is noted (Sokolov, 1971, 32; Kabakova, 1973, 85). The call is for deriving the potential benefits from external economies at the intra-urban level.

The central business districts of cities like London, New York or Paris play no small part in the dynamics of national growth since they serve a unique role as incubators of ideas. Trading in intelligence is facilitated by concentration, something which is not peculiar to any particular economic or political ideology. Thus, in the Soviet context, decades of decentralization are now being called into question. There will not be an overnight transformation to be sure. But just as the advantages of groupings of linked industries in the equivalent of industrial estates are recognized, and adjustments to the planning process made, so too the pressures to use central city land more intensively by building up, by building down, are apparent. Planned clusters of administrative functions are the next logical step. Convenience and efficiency go hand in hand. As yet there is nothing particularly convenient, and not much particularly spatially efficient about the layout of the Soviet central city. To the extent that it becomes more so, some of its distinctive features inevitably will be muted in the process.

The general plan—an assessment

The basic document determining the ultimate spatial organization of the Soviet city is, in theory, the general plan. But as we have stressed in Chapter 3, what goes on in the city cannot be divorced from decision making at the regional, republic or national level. Therein lies one of the fundamental problems, for as we have argued throughout, the tension between urban and sectoral interests constitutes a major weakness in the decision-making system as a whole. The difficulties encountered in operationalizing the general plan recently have been summarized as follows:

> Soviet cities are handicapped by overlapping and ill-coordinated planning. The USSR State Planning Committee's Council for the Utilization of Productive Forces draws up long-range territorial plans; the USSR State Construction Committee designs borough layouts; various state agencies compile their own economic plans; and architectural planners draw up general plans for urban development. Each of these documents deals with only one facet of urban development; not one of them treats the city as an integral unit.

The long-range territorial plans and borough layouts only set basic guidelines for a city's evolution. Borough layouts bear no relation to basic administration or long-range planning.

The so-called general plans for urban development, which are usually drawn up by architectural organizations, deal primarily with construction plans. While they are legally binding on all organizations engaged in urban construction, they deal only tangentially with the social and economic aspects of urban development. Moreover, general plans do not accomplish even their limited purpose—actual urban growth commonly exceeds plan estimates, sometimes tripling or quadrupling them. The frequency with which the plans are revised attests to their inefficacy: Since the war, 370 of the 720 general plans drawn up for Russian Republic cities have been either radically revised or entirely reworked. Novokuznetsk has had eight general plans, Volgograd six and Kharkov three.

As for the economic plans drawn up by territorial units—republics, provinces and territories—they are comprehensive enough to have an effect on all social and economic processes within the given territory. But where cities are concerned, only those whose administrative agencies are equal in status to province agencies—and so far this means only Moscow and Leningrad—are empowered to draw up plans containing indices affecting more than just the local economy.

It is true that now every city formulates its own summary plan for the development of the urban economy and social and cultural construction. But while this plan includes the entire range of indices for enterprises and institutions subordinate to the city Soviet, for departmental enterprises it contains only operations indices. This means that there is unified planning of the functioning of the urban economy but not of its development. In large cities in particular, Union and republic departments have long since become multibranch complexes that construct social and cultural as well as production facilities. In other words, a growing sector of the urban economy is only partially under the jurisdiction of city authorities (Dmitriyev, 1976, 12).

Thus, as was stressed in Chapter 3, the city Soviet is not yet 'master of its own house' (Ivanova, 1973, 26–8). The consequences are now apparent so far as the planning of the Soviet city is concerned. Lacking control means that the spatial organization of the city is less efficient than it might be. To validate the general plan in theory is simple enough. In practice, a multiplicity of ownership of essential facilities renders having reality conform to the general plan exceedingly difficult. Even the 1971 reform of municipal government is not necessarily a solution:

> Ministries and departments, seeking to fulful their branch plans as fast as possible, build not only production facilities but also housing, nurseries, kindergartens, recreational facilities, 'their own' educational institutions, etc. The result is a burgeoning sector that is not subordinate to city agencies but is developing under many different branch programs. Even in Moscow and Leningrad 30 per cent to 40 per cent of the housing stock does not belong to the local Soviets. For Russian Republic cities and workers' settlements as a whole, only 35.3 per cent of the publicly owned housing stock is under the jurisdiction of local Soviets. Before Leningrad drafted its comprehensive

plan of economic and social development for 1976–1980, the 'branch' sector accounted for 22 per cent of all hospital beds, 35 per cent of the physicians, 36 per cent of the places in day nurseries, 47 per cent of the seats in movie theatres and 51 per cent of the hotel rooms. The situation is similar in all major cities.

The new USSR Constitution (Art. 147) gives the local Soviets the right to control and coordinate the activity of *all* enterprises, institutions and organizations on the Soviets' territories (regardless of departmental subordination) in the fields of conservation, construction, use of labour resources, production of consumer goods and the provision of social, cultural, consumer and other services. Many urban problems can be solved only by including the city in the system of national-economic planning as an independent entity. When this is done, branch and territorial interests will be combined on an equal basis, binding on 'both parties'. Partial measures are not enough. Take the system of 'single client, single contractor, single designer.' First of all, from the standpoint of the strategy of planning urban development it changes nothing, since all its does is ensure a single line in implementing assignments already adopted for the city. Second, the system of pro rata participation is voluntary. In other words, what we have here is a tactical instrument that does not ensure integral city planning and integral management of urban development (Mezhevich, 1978, 15).

To date this rather harsh judgment of the 1971 reform seems vindicated by events. Progress is slow, problems persist.

Summary

In attempting to come to grips with the spatial organization of the Soviet city we have concentrated on five specific dimensions. In some instances the gap between ideal and reality remains sizeable, but it is clear that there are established goals toward which the whole system is gradually being moved. Still it is a fact that after several decades of promoting egalitarian principles for the spatial organization of the built environment, an egalitarian spatial organization has not yet been achieved. Disparities persist, both within cities and between cities in various regions. The application of a non-discriminatory normative planning process must assume a share of the responsibility. As much at fault, of course, is the decision-making system itself for cities still have too little autonomy in practice.

Disparities are particularly acute in the realm of the provision of items of collective consumption. To rectify these departures from principle and at the same time make the urban system more efficient is a daunting task. Still there is no shortage of ideas as to what to do; indeed, the underlying problems have been publicized perceptively, in some cases for decades. It remains to put principle more completely into practice, while at the same time striving for greater equality and more efficient spatial organization of the Soviet city. And efficiency needs to be as much planned for the consumer of goods and services as it does for the producer. Having now got some appreciation of where ideal and reality diverge, and why, there remains the task of assessing what these differences mean in terms of the quality of life offered by the Soviet city.

6

Life in the Soviet city

The central question addressed in this chapter is simply, what is life like in the Soviet city at the present stage of development? We can give free rein to the imagination when speculating what the successes and failures of Soviet town planning might mean in terms of the conditions of daily life and labour. However, a real dearth of information seriously limits the possible lines of inquiry. Thus, the discussion here will focus on just three rather broad features of Soviet city life: the pattern of daily activity; some social and environmental costs related to town-planning practice: and the role of social planning as an ameliorative force in urban development.

The spate of time-budget studies since the late 1950s permits an evaluation of many features of daily life in different parts of the country. As we shall see, the nature of the data base is not what might be desired. Still, it is adequate for the purpose of establishing general patterns of activity and the recent trends in the use of time. Evaluating the social and environmental costs associated with town-planning practice is a rather indirect, and admittedly somewhat subjective, business. Despite the problems in establishing social and environmental costs, the topic is important and deserves consideration. The kinds of problems which are involved in such an assessment may be highlighted by reference to the issue of urban environmental quality. To Western eyes, and some Soviet ones as well, Soviet urban architecture often seems drab, even oppressive. Yet the same architecture could well create entirely the opposite impression in the mind of a recent migrant from the country-side. Obviously perceptions are value-laden. But personal opinion, rather than surveyed opinion of a sample population about whose potential biases we might be expected to know something, comprises the main body of information on the quality of the urban environment. In short, even if adequate definitions of urban environmental quality were available, most relevant data to measure it are not. In attempting to assess the quality of the urban environment, we will focus on water, air and noise pollution and the maintenance of public space. The failure of the town planner to fulfil the norms for the provision of items of collective consumption and housing will be discussed in terms of the apparent social costs. On the other hand, the very success of authorities in manipulating population movements has produced some unforeseen social problems and these will be examined as well. The chapter will conclude with an examination of the origin, implementation and success thus far of the social-planning movement, which during the last decade has helped to bring the reality of the Soviet city a little closer to the ideal. As in the preceding chapter, examples will be selected to reflect conditions in large and small, old and new and Slavic and non-Slavic cities.

Patterns of daily life

To the extent that people have some choice in the allocation of their time, time-budget surveys can reveal a great deal about a particular society's values and life-style preferences. Time budgets therefore have some clear ideological connotations. In the Soviet Union the use of free time is regarded as being linked, ideologically, to the labour theory of value (Netsenko, 1975; Wiles, 1977, 566). Thus, it comes as no surprise that the human use of time was the subject of intensive study during the early years of the Soviet era.

The first time-budget survey occurred in 1922 as part of a broader examination of conditions of life and labour amongst various groups of Soviet workers. Later time-budget studies focused more directly on the issue of how economies in the organization of time might be of direct benefit to the state. However, all of the early time-budget surveys shared four general objectives: to delineate the conditions of labour and life of the population; to assist in finding ways of improving the organization, management and productivity of work; to facilitate upgrading the skill, education and cultural level of the population; and to chart the changes in all facets of life produced by the transition from the pre-revolutionary era to Soviet socialism (Zuzanek, 1980, 8–9; Kolpakov and Patrushev, 1971, 8–9).

During the early years of the Stalin era the legitimacy of time-budget research, as with most other forms of social inquiry, began to be questioned. Restrictions were soon imposed. Controversial topics like the dimensions of, and reasons for, criminality and suicide under the conditions of Soviet socialism were amongst the first lines of social inquiry to be prohibited by the authorities. In 1936 time-budget studies came into official disfavour and were banned altogether. More than two decades were to pass before studies of the human use of time were again legitimized (Zuzanek, 1980, 29–30).

Concern over the amount of non-productive time spent at work seems to have prompted the resumption of time-budget research in the late 1950s. From 1958 until 1968 something in the order of 100 surveys were undertaken. Not only were large numbers of studies conducted, some improvements in methodology were being registered as well. Up until the late 1950s the use of time was divided into three basic categories, work, rest and sleep. This classification had been established in the research directed by the eminent Soviet economist S. G. Strumilin in the years from 1922 to 1924. In 1960 it was decided that in future a bi-modal classification would be used. This entailed separating work time from non-work. Since then the major categories used in time-budget surveys have been work and time related to work, household obligations, personal needs and free time (Zuzanek, 1980, 37–42). Thus, despite the relatively recent emergence of sociology as a recognized field of study, there is a sizeable body of time-budget research. Unfortunately, this research, like sociology in general, has been handicapped by too few improvements in methodology and of greater importance, by inconsistent use of established research procedures (Rutkevich, 1977, 14).

Generalizing from the existing time-budget literature poses some problems. In the published studies there is often no clear indication of sampling procedures, categories of activities sometimes differ, and the duration of the survey, the time of the year and the methods used to record time spent in various pursuits are often inconsistent as well. Notwithstanding the seriousness of these and other shortcomings, time-budget data do provide some unique insights into the conditions of labour and life in Soviet cities (Trufanov, 1977). We shall be using some data for six cities in the early 1960s as an initial point of reference. Information for selected Soviet cities for the early 1970s then will be presented for some of the major categories of activity. By using the least controversial elements of the available time-budget data, it ought to be possible to establish trends in the use of time.

Table 10. Time budgets of male workers (average number of hours per day over a seven-day period)

Activity	Pskov	Ivanovo	Gorkiy	Rostov-on-Don	Sverd-lovsk	Krasno-yarsk
Work and time related to work	7.6	7.1	7.3	6.9	7.1	7.5
Household obligations	1.4	2.0	1.8	2.2	2.0	1.8
Personal needs	9.3	9.6	9.5	9.3	9.3	8.5
Free time	4.9	5.0	5.1	5.3	5.0	5.8
Non-work related travel	0.8	0.3	0.3	0.3	0.4	0.4
Not specified	—	—	—	—	0.2	—
Total	24	24	24	24	24	24

Source: Kolpakov and Patrushev, 1972, 83

*Date of survey and number of respondents: Pskov, 1965, 1097; Ivanovo, 1963, 74; Gorkiy, 1963, 238; Rostov-on-Don, 1963, 51; Sverdlovsk, 1963, 99; Krasnoyarsk, 1963, 595.

The time budgets of male and female workers in six cities are presented in Tables 10 and 11 respectively. With the exception of Pskov all of the data are for a weekday in 1963. The Pskov study was undertaken in 1965 as the Soviet contribution to an international survey of the human use of time (Szalai, 1972). Not only is the number of respondents much larger than in any of the 1963 studies, it embraced a more representative population in terms of occupation. The timing of the survey also differed in Pskov as it was conducted in the autumn (October and November), while the others reflect patterns of activity in the spring and early summer (May and June). Pskov's population was 115,000 in 1965. The other cities had populations in excess of one-half million. The Pskov data are by far the best available for the 1960s. But if the restricted nature of the other studies is kept in mind, we still can make some useful generalizations about the rhythm of daily life in six industrial cities which may be taken as representative of the European Russian, Urals and Siberian regions.

It is apparent from Table 10 that male workers put in roughtly 50 hours per week in work and work-related activity (including the journey to and from work). In mid-1960s the legal work week was reduced to 41 hours, but those hours were still spread over six working days. While the work-related activity pushed the average work week well above the legal limit for male industrial workers, and in the case of Pskov for workers in other sectors of the economy as well, most observers reckon that the reported work hours were underestimated. Overtime, moonlighting, volunteer work and labour in garden plots,

Table 11. Time budgets of female workers (average number of hours per day over a seven-day period)

Activity	Pskov	Ivanovo	Gorkiy	Rostov-on-Don	Sverd-lovsk	Krasno-yarsk
Work and time related to work	6.9	7.3	7.1	6.8	7.0	7.4
Household obligations	4.1	4.1	4.5	4.3	4.7	4.2
Personal needs	9.2	9.2	8.8	9.2	8.8	8.2
Free time	3.0	2.8	3.2	3.1	3.0	3.8
Non-work related travel	0.8	0.5	0.4	0.6	0.4	0.4
Not specified	—	0.1	—	—	0.1	—
Total	24	24	24	24	24	24

Source: Kolpakov and Patrushev, 1971, 83

* Date of survey and number of respondents: Pskov, 1965, 1574; Ivanovo, 1963, 170; Gorkiy, 1963, 297; Rostov-on-Don, 1963, 104; Sverdlovsk, 1963, 182; Krasnoyarsk, 1963, 364.

the produce from which was sold to supplement income—all were regularly underestimated or simply not reported (Zuzanek, 1980, 76). And, of course, the more responsible the position held, the greater the likelihood of above-norm work hours. In short, Soviet male, mainly industrial, workers spent a sizeable proportion of the available time budget on the job. But as we have already indicated elsewhere, there is no necessary correlation between hours at work and labour productivity. Indeed, the problem of low labour productivity continues to be a major reason for conducting time-budget studies.

The minor variations in the work and work-related activity by city cannot be attributed to any specific set of factors, though it is likely that they are more related to the particular occupations of the sampled population than they are to fundamentally different conditions of employment in a particular city. In the case of coal miners, for instance, there was usually a substantially longer time spent journeying to work than was the case for employees of machine construction plants (Kolpakov and Patrushev, 1971, 111).

Amongst female employees of industrial establishments (and a wider range of occupations in Pskov) the number of hours spent in work and work-related activity was marginally less than for males (Tables 10 and 11). Insofar as the six cities are concerned, there was no evidence that women consistently worked fewer hours in the factory however. This was the case in Pskov, Gorkiy and Sverdlovsk, but in Ivanovo and Krasnoyarsk women put in longer hours on the job. In Rostov-on-Don there was no difference (Kolpakov and Patrushev, 1971, 83). In any event, the fact that women did have such a substantial share of available time taken up in work and work-related activity had important ramifications for the balance of their time budget.

The male worker in Pskov put in substantially less time in household obligations than did his counterpart in the other industrial cities, or so it seems at first glance. However, as a sizeable proportion of the male contribution to household obligations entails working in the garden and vegetable plot, the difference is more apparent than real because the survey in Pskov was conducted in October and November when the time commitment is clearly much less than in the late spring and early summer when the other time-budget studies were carried out. In the household-obligations category of activity, it is the difference between males and females, rather than amongst cities, which is of paramount importance.

Not only do Soviet women living in cities work nearly as long in the factory as men, their contribution to household chores is between two and three times as great. As a rule, the more educated the respondents the greater is the male contribution to household duties. But since a number of surveys have shown that the imbalance between male and female is greatest amongst the young marrieds, there does not appear to be any major alteration in the traditional pattern of sex roles (Gordon and Klopov, 1972). For this particular sample population in the mid-1960s, an average of 30.1 hours were taken up in household obligations each week. For the male sample the equivalent time commitment averaged just 13 hours. As we shall see later on, gaps between town-planning principles and practice are partly responsible for the large share of available time taken up in household duties by women, but responsible as well are prevailing male attitudes to domestic chores and the limited availability of labour-saving devices for the home. The preparation of meals and shopping accounted for almost half of the time spent in the household-obligation category.

The consequences of the disproportionately greater amount of time working wives commit to domestic chores is evident from an examination of the amount of time allocated to personal needs and free time by men and women in our six selected cities. In every case sleep, eating and personal hygiene comprise a larger share of the male's time-budget than they do of the female's. In the main, both male and female spent about the same time in eating and in personal hygiene, thus the deficit was in terms of the hours of sleep. How less sleep might affect labour productivity amongst working wives is an interesting but as yet not clarified issue. In every case the sampled male population had more free time available. But this does not mean that these hours were perceived as leisure time, that is, entirely discretionary. Approximately one-fifth of this 'free' time was committed to study and organized socio-political activities. As elsewhere, upward mobility at work is frequently dependent upon acquiring more advanced training. The possibilities for working wives in this regard are clearly impaired to the extent that they have substantially less free time in which to fulfil the prerequisite courses of study (Zuzanek, 1980, 80–81).

Non-work-related travel requires no elaboration other than to highlight the fact that in the mid-1960s the possibilities of workers using privately-owned automobiles for such purposes were extremely limited. What the 1970s have brought by way of change in time-budget, related matters is the topic to which we now turn.

The transition from a six to a five-day work week occurred in 1967. As the legal limit of the work week itself was not changed, this simply meant that more hours were spent on the job each working day. The rhythm of daily life obviously was altered in the process. One of the principal intentions of the reform was to provide Soviet workers with more free time. But how has this worked out in practice, and with what consequences?

We can provide some answers to the first part of the question by referring to some time-budget data pertaining to sample populations in Riga and a group of other Latvian cities. While other equally comprehensive time budget studies have been conducted in the 1970s, to date this is the only one known to have been published (Geydane, 1976). While there were some procedural and classificatory differences between this study and those already cited, the data do provide an adequate basis for drawing some general conclusions concerning recent trends. The Latvian survey involved the recording of more than 4,000 time budgets of 'socially productive' men and women in both urban and rural locations for both summer and winter seasons. The data which we will present are the averages of these two periods for the urban male and female sample populations.

One of the first impressions conveyed by the data in Tables 12 and 13 is that compared to the situation in the mid-1960s very little had changed.

Table 12. Time budgets of female workers Latvia 1972 (average number of hours per day over a seven-day week)

Activity	Riga	Other Latvian urban centres
Work and time related to work	7.0	7.1
Household obligations	3.7	4.1
Personal needs	9.8	9.4
Free time	3.5	3.4
Total	24	24

Source: Geydane, 1976, 64.

Table 13. Time budgets of male workers Latvia 1972 (average number of hours per day over a seven-day week)

Activity	Riga	Other Latvian urban centres
Work and time related to work	7.3	7.9
Household obligations	1.8	1.9
Personal needs	9.7	9.7
Free time	5.2	4.5
Total	24	24

Source: Geydane, 1976, 64.

The categories of activity are fewer for the Latvian data, but the overall pattern of time allocations is broadly in line for particular activities. Given that there was no reduction in the legal work week this perhaps is expected. But despite considerable effort to encourage male participation in household chores, the data seem to indicate that very limited, if any, progress was made. While there is no available body of data for the late 1970s equivalent to that for Latvia in 1972, the few observations which have been made do not indicate any change in behaviour pattern. Thus, women's earnings continue to be an essential component in urban household budgets, but the very fact that women both work full time and assume the major burden of domestic duties skews their daily time budget in a manner that has been regarded as inequitable for a long time. The only positive development in this context is that there appears to have been a slight reduction in the average number of hours spent in household chores each day. Working females in Riga spent almost 26 hours in this activity each week, whereas their counterparts in our survey of the mid-1960s situation spent an average of 30.1 hours. In the smaller, other Latvian urban centres women put in more hours, 28.7, but still less than the earlier figure. Before examining some of the apparent social consequences of this broad, and continuing, difference in involvement in household duties between males and females, there are some other features of the Latvian data which merit discussion.

In Riga both males and females spent about 50 per cent longer in the journey to and from work than did the respondents living in the much smaller urban centres. But the latter group had more time allocated to work and work-related activity, the principal reason being that longer hours were put in on the job. Why this should be the case is not made clear, but differences in industrial and occupational structures may well have played some part.

Within the category of free time, the number of hours given up for study and organized socio-political activity was somewhat less amongst the Latvian urban population than seemed to be the general pattern in the mid-1960s. Males in Riga spent the most time in such pursuits—but this amounted to barely one half-hour each day, or about 10 per cent of their free time. The mid-1960s surveys indicated that such activity usually accounted for about one-fifth of the free time of urban males and females. There was not any appreciable differences in the total amount of free time available between these two dates (Tables 10, 11, 12, and 13). But how was the rest of the free time used?

The international survey of the use of time conducted in 1965 showed that in capitalist countries most free time was devoted to mass forms of leisure and recreation. Television viewing, for example, figures prominently in this largely passive category of free time activity. In socialist countries the proportion of free time taken up this way was less, but only marginally so. In the study of Pskov, however, only three-fifths of free time was spent participating in mass forms of leisure and recreation instead of three-quarters or more. In the Latvian study roughly the same proportion of free time was also used in this manner, though amongst females the proportion was slightly higher and amongst males somewhat lower, the very opposite of the male–female pattern in Pskov a few years earlier. Thus, evidence from Latvia suggests that the Soviet urban population still puts more 'free' time into study, organized socio-political activity and various forms of physical activity than is characteristic of some other socialist and capitalist societies. But these are the trends from a Republic which has one of the highest material standards of living in the USSR. Though fragmentary in nature, information on the use of free time in some Siberian new towns and several cities in the Moscow region will help to provide a somewhat broader perspective.

A survey conducted in the early 1970s amongst factory workers in Bratsk and Sheleklov indicated that free time was dominated by essentially passive activities like reading, watching television or going to the cinema. Moreover, amongst the younger males, who comprised the bulk of the labour force, passive forms of leisure activity were frequently of a negative, anti-social kind. Card playing and drinking, for example, were particularly difficult to combat despite the existence of organized sports activities, houses of culture and clubs of one kind or another (Romanenko, 1974, 90–96). In the context of Siberian new towns, however, recreational and cultural facilities often have been inadequate in number owing to the imbalanced development of the urban economy (Levitskaya, 1971, 148–53). Amongst the young, unmarried workers, dormitory accommodation is customary. The relatively low proportion of free time allocated to study and organized socio-political activity amongst this group perhaps is related to living conditions in these facilities. A study of dormitory life in several towns in the Moscow region would seem to bear out such a possibility.

According to the questionnaire survey of the residents of a number of large workers' dormitories, between 4.5 and 6.5 hours of free time were available each day. Most of this time was spent in the dormitory itself and was not put to what was considered to be socially productive purposes. Indeed, heavy drinking was common and, worse, widely accepted as the norm. Since the majority of dormitory residents had a general or specialized secondary education and since more than half were Party members or belonged to the Young Communist League, the prevailing pattern of leisure-time activity was of particular concern. Once again the lack of adequate recreational facilities was noted (Lozbyakov, 1979, 14). What these comments on dormitory residents reveal most clearly is the simple, but important point, that different social groups have different leisure habits. Thus, although the data for Latvian cities provide some useful insights, the patterns in the use of time are not necessarily valid for all groups of Soviet urban society.

The shift from a six-day work week to five days was particularly important in terms of providing longer, more useful, blocks of free time. With Saturday and Sunday the common off-days, there is far greater scope for using leisure time effectively. The only complication in planning weekend activities for married men and women with children is that Saturday is still a schoolday. There is growing pressure to put the school week on a five-day schedule as well. But with the creation of more useful blocks of free time, the state will be expected to accommodate the growing demand for leisure and recreational pursuits. The weekend exodus to the countryside, for example, not only requires adequate public transport, it brings along the demand for more and better recreational facilities. So far, the record of the planners in meeting this fast rising demand is not satisfactory (Shaw, 1979, 139–40). As with most other facets of consumerism, rising expectations are rarely easy to satisfy.

Continuity and change in the time budgets of Soviet urban inhabitants certainly say something about life-style preferences. Though we have been limited in our inquiry by the dearth of recent, published, time-budget data, that which we have presented for Latvian cities in 1972 is probably, on balance, reasonably representative of the pattern of daily life amongst married workers in the larger Slavic and Baltic cities. Unfortunately there are no known studies of a comparable kind which have been published for Caucasian and Central Asian cities. Given that the conditions of urban life in Latvia are high by Soviet standards, in many respects they represent a stage of urban development to which all regions aspire. In this sense at least, the pattern of daily life there in 1972 may have much more relevance to Soviet urban society in general today than otherwise would be the case. Having now established the general pattern of daily life and the recent trends in the use of time, we can now turn our attention to some of the apparent social costs of town-planning practice.

Social costs and the Soviet city

The question addressed in this section is simply, what are some of the social and environmental costs associated with town-planning practice? Clearly, this sort of inquiry can seldom prove any simple, direct causal relationships. This is even more likely to be the case in the context of the Soviet city given the problems in acquiring data. What we will do first of all is consider selected areas of town-planning jurisdiction, expand somewhat on what has been said already about what the gaps between principle and practice mean in terms of day-to-day life, and offer some suggestions as to the apparent social costs. The themes are: the provision of consumer services and the time budgets of married working women; the availability of housing; and the quality of the built environment. To conclude the discussion, we will examine the relationship between the successful implementation of restrictions on population movement and the distribution of criminality.

Consumer services

Between the mid-1960s and the early 1970s, the number of hours spent by working women each week in household obligations declined slightly —if we assume that our time-budget data are reasonably representative of the general situation. Given that the availability of labour-saving household appliances has such an important influence on the time spent in household duties, the fact that they have become much more widespread since the mid-1960s would tend to bear out such a trend. For example, in 1965 only 11 per cent of Soviet families had a refrigerator; by 1977 nearly three-quarters did. For washing machines the respective shares were 21 and 69 per cent. Despite improvements of this kind it is reckoned that only about 15 per cent of housework is as yet mechanized, while in the United States the corresponding figure is 80 per cent (Shelokov, 1978, 12). The number of household appliances tends to correlate positively with the size of the city. Thus, in our Latvian sample working women outside Riga spent more time in household obligations. Still, the combination of more appliances and a growing proportion of the population living in new apartments with all the basic facilities has meant that in general less time is now spent on housework. However, shopping continues to account for a sizeable proportion of the time allocated to domestic duties. In this context we can see how town-planning practice has not yet brought about a reduction in the amount of time spent buying groceries and other household items commensurate with that spent doing housework.

One of the basic tenets of Soviet town-planning theory is that day-to-day needs ought to be possible to satisfy by a short pedestrian journey to the appropriate local establishment. But as we have demonstrated in the preceding chapter, the overall level of provision of items of collective consumption is much less than the established norms. In the first place then, there is frequently an inadequate range of shops in the local area. Secondly, the practice of locating the existing specialized, retail outlets on the ground floor of apartment blocks means that within any single neighbourhood complex there is a rather dispersed pattern of shop locations. Thus, instead of being able to purchase most items in either a single large retail outlet, or in a cluster of shops, several shorter journeys are required. Given the harsh winters in many parts of the country, greater spatial clustering would be distinct advantage if only because it would reduce the time spent outside. While self-service is becoming more common, a great many retail outlets still require extensive queueing, and hence wasted time. Thirdly, if journeys to some distant shops are required the frequent bottlenecks in the distribution of goods to retail outlets mean that there is no guarantee of being able to obtain the desired products. In short, shopping is made inefficient because of the inadequate number of retail outlets, their distribution and the manner of doing business. The same general criticisms may be directed at the provision of other items of collective consumption, even day-care facilities and kindergartens. For example, seldom do the closing times of these sorts of institutions put the needs of working mothers ahead of the desired working hours of the staff (Perevedentsev, 1975, 29). Aside from the longer-term possibilities of changing stereotyped sex roles, which have resulted in inequalities between husband and wife in respect of assuming household obligations, the burden on working women could be eased through a more efficient spatial allocation of items of collective consumption at levels stipulated by the existing norms.

The consequences of working women in effect doing two full-time jobs are varied, but probably the most often suggested social cost is that of a reduced birth-rate and the trend toward smaller families (Perevedentsev, 1975, 30; Kostin, 1978, 2). Obviously an inordinately large portion of the time-budget spent on household chores is not the only reason for the falling birth-rate. Indeed, there is no guarantee that a dramatic improvement in the provision of items of collective consumption, and hence reduction in hours spent in household obligations, would reverse the trend. Urbanization produces many different currents of change within a society—demands for more education, a higher material standard of living, more leisure time and so on. Amongst some demographers, however, the notion that improvements in the provision of consumer services would result in a higher birth-rate is almost an article of faith. In the words of V. Perevedentsev, one of the leading demographic authorities, 'An improvement of . . . [the service] . . . sphere of our everyday life should have a marked and favourable effect on family life and on all our demographic problems: divorce, number of children, their upbringing' (1975, 29). To the extent that this assumption is correct, then there are significant social costs related to the town planners' failure to fulfil the norms for the various items of collective consumption.

The social costs of the housing shortage

Imputing some demographic benefits to improved consumer services may be rather tenuous. However, in the context of housing the social costs and possible demographic consequences appear to be a little more tangible. In the preceding chapters we have described the emergence of a housing crisis during the Tsarist era and examined some of the main reasons for its continuation under the conditions of Soviet socialism. In recent years enormous progress has been registered in improving the quantity and quality of housing for Soviet urban inhabitants. But the long-standing norm of nine square metres of living space has not yet been fulfilled and we should now examine some of the social costs attributable to the housing shortage.

As we have intimated already, factors other than poor consumer services and resultant heavy time commitments to household obligations have a bearing on the trend toward fewer children in each family. Sociological research has documented the obvious connection between the rising rate of divorce and a falling birth-rate (Galetskaya, 1974, 1). But what are the reasons for more divorces?

Sociological surveys during the last decade or so have shown that of the many factors which figure in the decision to seek a divorce, inadequate housing frequently plays a prominent part. For instance, in a recent study conducted in Volgograd and Astrakhan provinces, fully 25 per cent of the respondents who were petitioning for a divorce gave as one reason for doing so, 'We didn't have a place to live' (Drobotov,

1979, 13). For newlyweds, the acquisition of their own apartment is a first, but frequently unrealized, priority. Thus, newly-married couples renting space in private apartments, living separately in factory dormitories or living with relatives is a regular occurrence in Soviet cities. The difficulties of such a situation are compounded if there is a child. Thus, aside from any other reason for postponing having a family, the need to secure accommodation can be a major factor in the decision.

The demographic consequences of inadequate housing may be viewed as one social cost, high rates of labour turnover are certainly another. Serious problems of labour productivity have prompted innumerable surveys of reasons for workers leaving their job for positions elsewhere. Whether the new job is in another city, or simply in a factory down the road, the loss of trained personnel is a financial burden to the enterprise concerned just the same. Invariably the reasons for dissatisfaction are '... a direct consequence of the lack of housing and sociocultural institutions, and poor working conditions' (Trubina, 1976, 29).

Throughout Siberia and the Far North, wage differentials are important in attracting labour. But housing plays a crucial role in stabilizing the labour force once it is in place. Inadequate housing produces predictable responses. In Bratsk, for example, nearly three-quarters of the workers leaving their jobs at the aluminium factory gave the impossibility of securing an apartment as the principal reason. Labour turnover at this plant was 14 per cent. This was low in relation to the 30 per cent figure which characterizes the Irkutsk region (Mel'nikov and Sudakov, 1974, 106–7). Higher wages for skilled employment no doubt played a part in keeping the level of turnover in the aluminium plant to a comparatively low level. But the loss of skilled employees who often have five or more years experience is a direct cost to the plant, and because of resultant lower levels of productivity, a cost as well to society as a whole. In the newer frontier settlements, such as those associated with the Baykal–Amur railroad construction project, housing is even more of a problem and so therefore is labour turnover. But it is in no sense peculiar to frontier regions (Logvinov, 1977, 10–11).

The inability of the planners to coordinate better the industrial and urban development processes is the principal reason for this state of affairs, as we indicated in the preceding chapter. The fact that some enterprises build housing for their own workers does not really help much either since it usually remains outside the allocative jurisdiction of the city Soviet authorities. The social costs which ensue from inadequate housing and high labour turnover are certainly recognized, and indeed have been for a long time:

> The absence of normal housing and living conditions does not attract and hold skilled personnel, which has a negative impact on the technical and economic indices relating to the work of new enterprises. Numerous cases are noted when newly activated industrial projects cannot reach their rated capacity for a long time for this reason (Antosenkov, 1973, 48).

A transient population by definition does not readily assimilate progressive social values such as a truly communal ethos. On the contrary, anti-social behaviour assumes a more important role. This is sometimes manifested through poor labour discipline (absenteeism) or sometimes in a high level of marital difficulties (divorce):

> Man's health, his mood, capacity for work, and life span depends in large measure on his housing conditions. Housing conditions play a large part in the formation and strengthening of the family, in the natural reproduction of the population (Antosenkov, 1973, 42).

Whether or not improved housing will bring about a transformation of values and lifestyles is very much a moot point. As we have tried to emphasize, the material conditions of daily life in Soviet cities are not what planning principles indicate they should be, but even in cities and regions which seem relatively well endowed, the same problems and trends we have been discussing are in evidence. Nonetheless, in the attempt to bring about directed social change, a logical first step would be to ensure that town planning norms are met. Oddly enough, it is precisely the success authorities have had in manipulating the movements of certain categories of the Soviet population which have created some severe social problems for specific types of cities.

Population migration and the distribution of criminality

Soviet socialism has not yet produced the perfect man—self-reliant, self-disciplined and selfless in his attitude and actions. As in all countries, crime exists in the USSR and is nurtured by urbanization. Rapid city growth is dependent upon large-scale rural-urban migration, a process which seemingly contributes to a sense of alienation, frustration and various forms of anti-social behaviour. Transient urban populations help sustain such behaviour patterns. Thus, in many Soviet cities criminal acts of one kind or another pose serious problems for the maintenance of law and order. In this regard there is nothing unique about the Soviet city. What tends to help differentiate the phenomenon of urban crime from West European and North American society, however, are the various restrictions on the movement of the Soviet population, and in particular on those with criminal records.

Convicted criminals from major cities who have been incarcerated for five years or more lose the right to return to those cities upon expiration of their sentence (Serebryakova, 1975, 116; Shelley, 1978, 3). Those convicted of especially serious crimes have an extremely limited choice of cities in which to take up residence. Thus, the major cities are able to reject once and for all particular categories of convicted criminals. But obviously they end up somewhere. Typically, the labour-deficient, fast growing industrial centre absorbs but seldom assimilates them. The less desirable the urban environment, the less choosy the authorities can be in providing the necessary *propiska*. While the converse holds for the large city the restrictions on in-migration of ordinary people may be playing some part in the increased incidence of other forms of anti-social behaviour.

Major Soviet cities have comparatively low levels of crime, but criminal acts of one kind or another obviously do occur. Moscow's record by the standards of other major world cities is quite exemplary. But none of its citizens are exempt, for example, from the possibility of being robbed, most especially not the wealthier ones (Juviler, 1974, 210). However, it is the problem of hooliganism and juvenile delinquency which, on the rise in all cities, is of particular concern. It is in this context that youthful commuters from outside the city limits figure disproportionately. The fact of the matter is that many people who are denied the right to live in a major city, end up working or going to school there just the same. The successful restriction on in-migration simply results in people taking up residence in nearby towns. Hooliganism and juvenile delinquency being at a higher rate amongst the commuting young is attributable in some degree to the fact that many of them are obliged to spend three to four hours travelling to work or school and back each day, doing so in largely unsupervised circumstances (Shelley, 1978, 17). Successful restriction of in-migration inevitably will lead to more commuting. As it is, most large cities are experiencing labour shortages, a problem exacerbated by the demographic 'ageing' of the population. The imposition of controls over in-migration simply exaggerates this feature. With a growing volume of commuter traffic, an increase in the incidence of juvenile delinquency and hooliganism may be expected. Thus, aside from the obvious social costs directly related to the long hours of commuting to work and school, Soviet society it seems must bear the additional cost of the various forms of anti-social behaviour associated with it. But these social costs pale in comparison with the problems created by ex-criminals who take up residence in the smaller, usually more remote, cities.

We need not dwell long on the problem of crime in the smaller city, which because of its location and environment, seemingly must accept any and all who wish to obtain a job and a *propiska*. Data on crime are patchy, but available information is at one in conveying the impression that the level of criminal activity in such places is singularly high and not unrelated to the presence of small, but disruptive numbers of ex-criminals (Serebryakova, 1975, 116; Shelley, 1978, 15). In some cities, though probably a distinct minority, the usual lack of concern about one's safety while on the streets at night is absent. In a recent report from Grozny, for example, it was remarked that '... it's unsafe to go out on the street at night in some parts of the city' (Ryabukhin, 1979, 16). Such fears are not widespread, but do seem more common in the new industrial centres of the eastern regions. There, wage incentives have been a factor in encouraging migration of all types, including ex-criminals. Indeed, the fact that wage differentials are necessary in the first place speaks to the problems in attracting labour under normal circumstances. The transient nature of the generally youthful and un-married population in frontier settlements is no doubt also a factor in accounting for higher rates of crime (Kutsev, 1974; Nefed'yev, 1974). There are only limited data on regional variations in rates of crime, but that available does confirm the general pattern suggested here (Sakharov, 1977, 75–84; Krylov, 1977, 6–8). It is not our purpose to explore the reasons for criminality in Soviet cities. Rather we are simply drawing attention to one possible consequence of the successful imposition of controls over the movement and residence of ex-criminals. To the extent that crime in cities where they are permitted is increased by their presence, then clearly the residents of those cities do shoulder a social cost of an especially onerous kind.

The environmental costs of Soviet town planning

Cities everywhere exhibit some evidence of environmental degradation and Soviet cities are no exception in this regard. From the earlier discussion of industrial location and zoning it was evident that strict segregation of non-conforming land uses has not yet been achieved. Even in Moscow industrial enterprises still are to be found in sizeable number in the areas zoned for residential use and in 'green' belts. While the environmental consequences of breaches in zoning regulations vary, it would appear that in most cities the consequences are more a nuisance than a threat to public health inasmuch as they are most commonly manifested in noise and air pollution. Yet it would be incorrect to imply a lack of real concern over water, air and noise pollution in Soviet cities, or to underestimate the dimensions of the problem (Bykov, 1978, 3).

Water pollution

It was the inadequate municipal water and sewage systems in Russian cities which played such an invidious role in the spread of infectious disease during the rapid urban-industrialization of the late imperial era (Bater, 1979, 50–53). Thus, one of the first tasks facing Soviet urban government was the revamping of city water and sewage networks. This was often achieved through the use of volunteer labour. While improved sanitation helped Soviet authorities to combat diseases like cholera and typhus, epidemics continued to be a fact of urban life. In the 1970s urban water-pollution problems and water-borne disease still persist, albeit with markedly less serious consequences than in the imperial era.

One of the main reasons for water pollution is that a sizeable com-ponent of urban housing is not yet part of municipal water and sewage systems. It may be recalled that about two-thirds of the European Russian housing stock were connected to municipal water and sewer networks, according to data provided by Mil'ner and Gilinskaya in 1975 (60). In the eastern regions of the RSFSR the proportion was only one half. Moreover, the data apparently refer just to the state housing sector, which comprises about 70 per cent of the total stock. As the privately owned house is often unserviced, save for electric power, the overall level of housing integrated into urban water and sewer systems is lower still. Even in cities where the level of servicing is above average, problems sometimes arise because domestic waste is inadequately treated (ZumBrunnen, 1976, 38–41). For downstream users of water courses into which untreated municipal effluent is dumped, the difficulties of ensuring supplies of potable water are obvious enough. The fact that disease is rarely of epidemic proportion testifies to the vigilence of public health authorities and to the adequacy of most water-purification facilities. Still, the population is from time to time reminded of the seriousness of the threat of polluted waters to public health. The closure of a public beach near Odessa in September of 1974 owing to cholera being traced there, is a case in point (Herlihy, 1978, 440).

To the extent that industrial effluent is not properly treated, then, the problems created by inadequate domestic waste treatment are simply compounded. And, indeed, in many regions water systems are seriously polluted by industry (ZumBrunnen, 1976; Bater, 1972, 11). While legislation to prevent water pollution has long been on the books, it is only in the last decade or so that enforcement has been undertaken with anything like real zeal. The usual nominal fine of the past still occurs to be sure, but in serious cases of pollution criminal proceedings are being initiated more often, a development in marked contrast to past experience (Powell, 1971, 628; Butler, 1975, 135). As in most industrialized countries, principle and practice in Soviet water-resource management are seldom entirely in harmony. While much money and effort have been expended in recent years to put right both municipal and industrial waste-treatment facilities, rapid urban-industrialization still poses problems in terms of water supply.

Shortages of potable water exist in many regions. In European Russia shortages are frequently acute in the Donetsk Basin and Krivoy Rog industrial regions. In the Central Industrial District focused on Moscow, many cities and towns face curtailment of supplies during parts of the year. In the cities of the Urals, and in some Siberian towns, regular interruptions in the water supply are a fact of life. Serious shortages have been forecast for the urban populations of Central Asia (Matlin, 1973, 17–18). There is, of course, a basic imbalance between the distribution of supply and demand for water. European Russia including the Urals, accounts for about three-quarters of the demand but has only about one-fifth of the country's fresh water resources. However, even in regions of positive balance maintaining adequate supplies is complicated by the fact that norms for water consumption in industry and agriculture frequently are exceeded.

Complaints about water shortage often refer to inadequate pressure. In many cities having a flat in the upper floors of an apartment block is a distinct disadvantage owing to reduced water pressure (Jacobs, 1975, 75). While running a basin full of water can be a time-consuming exercise in such circumstances, during periods of low water supply, even this trickle may stop. Only a small segment of the urban population is so affected, but the current trend of rapid urban-industrialization in regions where there is a delicate balance between supply and demand suggests that urban water deficits will become more acute.

Air pollution

Most observers reckon that air pollution in Soviet cities is not a major environmental issue (Mote, 1976, 3–4; Belousov, 1975, 9–11). This is not to say that problems do not exist, but that in comparison with the air-pollution problems in so many American and European cities, Soviet cities appear to be decidedly better off. From the standpoint of environmental management Soviet town planning does afford some real advantages. For example, the development of centralized heat and power generating and distribution facilities has reduced greatly the number of pollution prone, small oil-fired boilers. Individual boilers, of course, still do exist in considerable number in a great many cities, but there has been a steady process of removal. In Moscow in recent years thousands of such units have been replaced by communal facilities which for part of the year at least are fueled by the comparatively cleaner natural gas (Belousov, 1975, 9). The result of this programme of extending communal heat and power networks has been to reduce significantly the level of air pollution, an achievement by no means restricted just to the national capital (Stetsenko, 1978, 19). Another advantage follows from the initial decision to have spatial mobility dependent upon public transport. Thus, as we noted in the preceding chapter, the level of private ownership of automobiles is minute by comparison with West European and American societies. The contribution of the automobile to urban air-pollution problems is sufficiently well known not to require elaboration. But the additional advantage of the Soviet approach to public transport is that electric traction remains important. Trolley bus and tram lines each year are extended rather than curtailed (Narodnoye, 1978, 327).

The traditional means of controlling air pollution from industry has been to assign factories to specific zones within the city, to construct smoke stacks of sufficient height to ensure some degree of dispersal of particle and chemical pollutants, and during the last decade or so, to install purification facilities at the factory. Since land-use zoning has not been entirely successful in separating non-conforming activities, industry in some cities still adversely affects residential areas. Nor could it be claimed that all industrial-enterprise managers have responded with alacrity to the task of reducing air pollution. Though real achievements in reducing air pollution were registered in Leningrad during the 1960s, it was noted in 1972 that 'The smokestacks of individual enterprises are still spewing smoke' (Sterlikov, 1972, 18). In an increasingly clean air basin such occurrences are not readily tolerated, but criticism does not always produce the desired results:

> The Woodworking Plant imeni Khalturin is situated in the very centre of the city not far from the Nevskiy Prospect. For a time, it did not bother the inhabitants of Smol'ninskiy Rayon but in recent years its nearness has come to be sensed perceptibly: around it there are piles of sawdust and in the air one constantly smells the odour of formaldehyde, i.e. the residues of wood processing. The fact is that the plant production has almost doubled, the amount of waste has increased while the actual questions of conserving the environment are 'minor' against the background of raising production and they have been forgotten (Sterlikov, 1972, 18–19).

In smaller centres, where the authority of civic officials is usually less influential than in major cities like Moscow, Leningrad or Kiev, such transgressions of existing legislation are more common. The problem in Kirovakan, a small resort town in Armenia, is perhaps unusual in its severity, but is scarcely so in its evolution.

> ... the Armenian Republic's chief sanitary inspector, turned to the Republic prosecutor's office with the request that criminal action be taken against the managers of the Myasnikyan Kirovakan Chemical Plant. They are to blame for heavily polluting the air and water of the resort city.
> ... At one time the enterprise was far outside the city limits, but eventually it found itself surrounded by housing areas.... Particles discharged into the atmosphere from the carbide production facilities and from the lime shop settles in Kirovakan itself, over which a 'fox tail' from the production of nitric acid hovers in a poisonous trail (Arakelyan, 1978, 26).

Urban expansion puts obviously antediluvian industrial operations in the limelight. In this particular situation the facilities are so outmoded that modernization is seemingly precluded. Yet production continues —'We are given a plan, and it's out job to fulfil it' is the rationale, and a not uncommon one at that. Still, the fact that criminal proceedings were being initiated speaks to the potential clout of the legislation when recourse to litigation is demanded.

Old, central-city located, industrial enterprises and outmoded plant swallowed up by urban expansion are common elements in the process of environmental degradation everywhere. But what is all too often occurring in Soviet new towns is thwarting rational town planning, and producing air pollution in the process. In the haste to get both plant and housing up, the development of communal facilities falls behind and individual boilers are put into operation to provide heat (Sinelnikov,

1971, 22). The situation in Tynda, a new town on the Baykal-Amur railroad project is typical; '... the city's heat is presently being provided by 38 small, separate boilers, which operate inefficiently, pollute, and fail to meet the city's heating needs' (Pekarsky, 1977, 16). Perhaps this type of environmental degradation is a necessary price to be paid for the rapid urban-industrialization of frontier regions.

Major industrial areas like the Donetsk Basin in the southeast Ukraine, the southern Urals and the Kuznetsk Basin in western Siberia do suffer from serious air pollution (Mote, 1976, 12–20). As major centres of the heavy metallurgical industry this comes as no real surprise. To the extent that the technique of dilution through super stacks and sanitary buffers is replaced by the installation of purification facilities real improvements in air quality will be achieved—but this is an expensive and slow process. Slow, too, is the process of rectifying past mistakes in the intra-urban location of industry, a major contributory factor to the air-pollution problems in many cities. Gokhberg has noted, for example, that approximately one-quarter of the housing in Tula, an industrial centre south of Moscow, is adversely affected by the presence nearby of the city's two major metallurgical works. West of Moscow in Kalinin, he notes that a chemical complex was sited without due regard to the direction of the prevailing wind (Gokhberg, 1974, 133). Despite all the benefits accruing from more sensitive ecological planning of new urban construction, and from technological advances in development of air purification facilities to mitigate the effects of past mistakes, there is some indication that they could be compromised by the seemingly inexorable growth of automobile ownership and traffic.

We have already emphasized that one of the advantages of the Soviet town-planning principle that spatial mobility be based on public transport is a much lower level of air pollution than in Western cities. On a per capita basis automobile ownership in the USSR is low it is true. But in Moscow, Leningrad and the Republic capitals the ratio is much higher. Indeed, in Moscow the improvement of '... air quality is hampered by the rapidly growing number of cars on the city's streets. Motor vehicles already account for about 50 per cent of total air pollution in Moscow and 80 per cent of the carbon monoxide' (Konovalov, 1978, 6). Technological improvements to reduce the toxicity of exhaust fumes are being introduced, but as yet on a relatively small scale. The mechanisms for limiting automobile production for private ownership, of course, do exist. It is a moot point, however, as to whether curtailment of sales for the public good will occur (Jackson, 1974, 22–3).

Noise pollution

The fact that noise pollution has recently emerged as an issue in urban environmental quality reflects the growing public sensitivity to noise and the growing importance of ecological considerations in Soviet town planning. Indeed, until quite recently '... noise had a very low priority on the agenda of designers, builders and haulers' (Kashin, 1977, 11). So far as noise pollution is concerned, the formation of a national anti-noise committee in 1969 helped focus attention on this facet of environment planning (Bush, 1974, 16). But how successful have noise abatement efforts been? The situation in Tashkent is probably fairly typical of the larger cities.

A city commission was formed in 1969 in order to monitor noise pollution, and, to the extent possible, to promote a variety of noise-abatement measures. Since it is reckoned that 80 per cent of outside noise in a large city is generated by transport, a variety of measures to restrict, or redirect, vehicular traffic has been introduced. The construction of a ring road has cut down on truck traffic in the city centre, and indeed, on 20 streets truck traffic has been prohibited altogether. On these same streets no motorcycle or moped traffic is permitted after eleven o'clock in the evening. While modification of traffic patterns is undoubtedly a benefit, it is also a rather straightforward matter. Less easy is the introduction of specific noise-reduction measures into building design. Apartment buildings still are being put up with bedrooms fronting on main thoroughfares. Design solutions to this problem are at hand but are not yet widely implemented (Konovalov, 1978, 6). Thus, so far as the Tashkent commission is concerned, an opportunity to ameliorate the noise problem in apartment buildings built during the last decade has been lost. However, some progress in establishing more realistic set-back allowances from thoroughfares has been made. And with the creation of a noise map for the city, problem areas can be more easily singled out, and, where possible, measures introduced to improve the situation. Legislation now exists to prohibit industrial operations from making excessive noise during the night. Just how successful enforcement of these anti-noise regulations has been in Tashkent is not clear (Tyurikov, 1977, 11). What is beyond doubt, however, is the growing preoccupation with noise pollution, a justifiable concern given the steady growth in vehicular traffic each year.

Breaches of town-planning principles have certainly helped to create a noise problem through the incorrect location of industrial enterprises and major rail and road transport arteries. But the very different order of vehicular traffic on Soviet city streets still means that the average decibel count is probably less than on comparable European or American city streets. There is also the clear advantage that in the Soviet city noise pollution already is widely perceived as a problem and hence pressure is mounting for remedial and preventive action (Agayev, 1977, 11).

Environmental management

Since one of the traditional claims made for the Soviet socialist system of priorities and decision-making process was that the common good takes precedence, an obvious question is why should water, air and noise pollution occur at all? Indeed, for a long time the problem of environmental degradation was simply assumed to be the inevitable by-product of the quest for profit under conditions of capitalism, and that such a problem almost by definition could not exist under socialism. While we have touched upon some of the reasons for environmental degradation in specific Soviet cities in the preceding discussion, there are some inherent contradictions in the Soviet system itself which often result in environmental pollution, and to which we ought to give brief consideration.

External diseconomies of urban-industrial development are not specific to any one political-economic system. The fact that land and water are at best only nominally accounted for in the Soviet price system and accounting practice perhaps makes accurate determination of the benefits and costs of a particular development more difficult, but the mere existence of a set of market-determined prices for such resources is certainly no assurance of easy and accurate benefit-cost calculations (McIntyre and Thornton, 1978, 173–92). There is still the fundamental question, from whose perspective should benefits and costs be calculated? Simply contending that the best choice is that of the common good does not resolve the problem of determining whether cleaner air is preferable to a higher standard of living. In the final analysis, decision-makers with the greater economic and political power as a rule win out in such conflict situations.

The systemic weaknesses of the Soviet approach to environmental management are the absence of an environmental interest group within the upper echelons of the Party apparatus where fundamental policy decisions are taken, and the absence of a single authority at the level of the All-Union ministry which could serve as a countervailing influence to the economically and politically important industrial ministry. What tends to happen is that responsibility for environmental management is turned over to the ministries themselves. They create internal but subordinate units to implement and monitor environmental protection legislation and practice. The fragmentation of authority assures that less vital standards are often ignored if they impinge on the principal ministerial objective of meeting output targets. Thus, as we have already seen, antediluvian factories continue to produce and pollute, non-conforming locations of factories in cities are overlooked when the closing or relocating of such facilities could jeopardize production goals. From the standpoint of industrial managers, the choice is perfectly rational *within* the context of their priorities. Moreover, the proliferation of environmental agencies within different ministries and on an *ad hoc* basis amongst public interest groups can and does result in conflict situations amongst the very agencies and interest groups with an ostensibly identical objective (Kelley, 1976, 572).

The seemingly inevitable administrative fragmentation of the centralized economy into quasi-autonomous ministries, what Nove labels 'centralized pluralism', inevitably produces a set of mutually contradictory goals (Nove, 1977, 74–9). That this decision-making system has produced environmental pollution, contrary to long-standing Soviet claims, has been taken as some observers as evidence of the validity of the convergence argument. Put simply, the thesis is that political and institutional systems do not influence environmental management (Goldman, 1970, 37–42). However, we have shown already that some Soviet town-planning principles do create a qualitatively better urban environment, the instance of public transport and centralized heating policies being but two examples. Problems exist to be sure, but as we have implied, the structure of the decision-making system itself does offer a partial solution to some current environmental management dilemmas. The creation of an environmental protection agency with the status and clout of an All-Union ministry would go some way toward ensuring greater recognition throughout the system of the importance of proper environmental management. Different priorities would continue to exist. However, in the weighing up of alternative strategies the balance might well be shifted toward further improving the quality of the environment in the Soviet city.

Maintenance of public space

It is difficult to assess the Soviet perception of the quality of public space. Given the absence of much criticism it would seem that insofar as the central city is concerned all is quite satisfactory. And certainly initial impressions of the standards of maintenance of central thoroughfares, squares, parks and so forth would bear out this judgment. Indeed, return visits and widespread travel tend to reinforce rather than alter this impression. The general absence of litter is both a function of the diligence of sanitation departments and the now well entrenched collective behaviour patterns of the population. To drop litter is like smoking on a bus—it is uncultured and to do either is just as likely to bring forth a public rebuke from a total stranger as not. Where social responsibility seems to break down most evidently is not in the central city, which is maintained regularly by municipal employees and volunteers, but in the less closely supervised residential areas. Throughout the country the escalation in housing-maintenance expenditures is of growing concern and has resulted in the publicizing of socially irresponsible behaviour which has a familiar ring to it for the European or North American.

In a recent discussion of the problems of maintaining urban housing in Belorussia, the following observation was made

> ... Altogether 110 million roubles was spent on major repairs and modernization of apartment buildings in the cities and urban-type communities of Belorussia during the Ninth Five-Year Plan. In fact, the yearly expenditures on housing repair are approximately 25 per cent as large as total investment

in new apartment construction. Naturally, we cannot help being upset by the way tenants treat their own living quarters.

It is dismaying to see what some new apartment buildings look like after only a year or two. Stairways are dirty, elevators are a wreck, doors are peeling. Balconies show evidence of creativity run wild: Some are enclosed with sheets of some material, others are piled with junk, still others resemble a cross between a greenhouse and a dovecote.

We still have not learned how to give people a proper sense of proprietorship (Bezlyudov, 1977, 10).

Certainly the cost of unnecessary repairs is an issue of no small importance. After all, rent for state housing is so small a share of family budgets that collectively the revenues raised are barely sufficient to cover routine maintenance and repairs. But it would be incorrect simply to impute a financial motive alone to the recent spate of publicity about what is obviously perceived as an important social problem. Incorrect attitudes are attributed to a number of factors.

One reason for the careless treatment of property in state apartment buildings is that people who have not adjusted to modern urban living treat heating systems, plumbing and modern appliances as though they were dealing with the relatively simple implements of rural housekeeping. Another problem is that some people think it is sufficient to keep their own apartments clean and tidy inside, but fail to show any concern for the common areas of their apartment buildings. This is why one finds the hallways cluttered with trash, piles of boards, shabby trunks, or whatever people choose to deposit outside their doorways. Some apartment buildings have barely been occupied when the stairwells need repairing. Handrails are broken off and the freshly painted walls are covered with cigarette burns and graffiti (Shcherbakov, 1977, 13).

Lack of familiarity with modern conveniences no doubt plays some part in the ill treatment of personal and collective property. It also has been noted time and again that the waste of natural resources and the abuse of socialist property and benefits are related to the fact that the real costs of resources, property, and benefits are not appreciated. Moreover, acts of vandalism seem to be on the rise. In the opinion of some observers the

very belief that benefits underwritten by the state are 'free' may account for the disregard that some people show for their social obligations. Such disregard is evident, for example, in vandalism to apartment buildings—entryway doors torn off their hinges, graffiti gouged on elevator walls, stair railings knocked out. In 1975, 3,670 people were fined for damaging housing in Minsk alone (Shelokov, 1978, 12, 20).

Vandalism it would seem is a problem indifferent to political, economic and social ideologies.

The quality of the urban environment in the Soviet Union cannot be evaluated in anything other than quite subjective terms. The little hard evidence available indicates that although environmental pollution of one kind or another exists, it is probably no worse, and quite possibly is rather less serious, than is to be found in the cities of Western Europe and North America. Certainly in the case of air pollution the problem does appear to be less serious owing to the comparatively low level of automobile traffic. But as we have emphasized, achievements of Soviet town planning in this regard are being put at risk as the 'automobilization' process gathers momentum. Although water quality steadily improves, patterns of urban-industrialization portend difficulties in maintaining adequate supplies for domestic and industrial consumers alike.

Social planning and the city

The concept of social planning for cities is of much interest for several reasons. Confrontation with difficulties in the planning process has elicited two traditional responses. The first has already been mentioned in the discussion of decision making and entails centralization of authority at a higher administrative level. The second, and probably less frequent response, has been to initiate a grassroots movement, to enhance production as in the 'stakhanovite' movement of the 1930s, or to improve the management of urban affairs as in the case of social planning (Deruzhinskiy, 1974, 92).

The concept of social planning is closely associated with the post-economic reform effort to offset flagging labour productivity at the enterprise level and the growing role of the sociologist in industrial management. First tried in the Svetlana Electronic Instrument enterprise in Leningrad, it soon proved effective in reducing labour turnover and thereby improving productivity (Meleshchenko, 1975, 69). The main objective is to improve social relationships, which in the first instance boils down to enhanced workers' participation in enterprise operations and the provision of work-related facilities (Bitunov, 1976, 3–6; Korenevskaya, 1977). The latter range from enterprise-owned apartments to day-care facilities, canteen services and so on, none of which are especially innovative (Aitov, 1973, 12). The idea spread rapidly throughout Soviet industry but it was quickly conceded that many of the important factors bearing on workers' dissatisfaction and high labour turnover—it was frequently of the order of 30 to 40 per cent per annum —were borough or *mikrorayon* social problems (Bayramov, 1972, 10). More often than not dissatisfaction with the urban environment was directly related to the inability of planners to carry out their mandate (Dmitriyev, 1976, 12; *Problemy sotsial'nogo planirovaniya*, 1974, 192–203). What was especially innovative about the social planning approach was the broadening of the perspective to the city, even in a few cases to the city region. The Communist Party seems to be playing a major, although not necessarily overt, organizational role in creating a structure which runs in tandem with the existing town-planning bureaucracy (Dumachev, 1972, 30; Aitov, 1972b, 137). While not specifically dealt with in the 1971 municipal reform, the whole movement is very much in keeping with its spirit and purpose. It is probable that no more than a few score cities now have what is described as social planning but the innovation is being adopted rapidly (Bezrukov and Dmiterko, 1977, 151–2; Aitov, 1973, 12; Kachalovsky, 1971, 27–8).

Social planning usually encompasses three broad issues: wages and means of improving labour productivity and therefore national production; improving the material well-being of the population at large; and raising the level of public participation at the place of work and in the community as a whole. It has been argued on more than one occasion that social planning at the city level is more than simply the sum of enterprise social planning (Aitov, 1972a, 143). Whether or not this is borne out in practice is still far from clear (Lewis and Sternheimer, 1979, 124–35). The process has been frequently described and while there are slight variations the following are consistent features: determination of the demographic structure of the population at future dates; integration of economic development plans with manpower availability; ensuring that the basic norms of consumer well-being are met; further development of cultural and ideological work amongst the populace; expediting the upgrading of educational qualification and at the same time the technological capability of the workforce (Kholyuk, 1974, 139–40; Aitov, 1972b, 137). Many of the concerns clearly overlap with those normally within the compass of the town planner, and intentionally so. All serious discussions of social planning are conducted within the context of a less than ideal urban environment and its direct or indirect influence on labour productivity (Borshchevskiy *et al.*, 1975). The situation in Vladimir (0.3 million) an industrial town east of Moscow is typical, both in terms of urban-economic problems and of the development of a programme of social planning (Boldyreva, 1973, 33–40).

Rapid urban-industrialization in Vladimir in the post-war period has produced the usual lag in the development of urban infrastructure. Housing construction could not keep pace, and by the early 1970s more than 14,000 families were acknowledged to need improved accommodation. But in the new *mikrorayons* improved housing was the only benefit for the provision of items of collective consumption was abysmally low. Inadequate numbers of shops, public catering and personal service establishments, schools, and sport and recreation facilities made day-to-day life very difficult. The quality of the environment was also adversely affected by the rapid development. In the scurry to boost industrial production, zoning and effluent-treatment regulations were often ignored thus air and water pollution problems were serious. Indeed, the pollution of one of the local rivers was so severe that aquatic life was threatened and swimming prohibited. Part of the pollution problem was attributable to inadequate basic municipal services. For example, only about three-quarters of the housing stock was connected to the sewer system, while only 30 per cent was part of the centralized heat-distribution system. In short, all of the negative consequences of un-balanced urban-industrial development were evident. And so was the customary response—a high rate of labour turnover and resultant low labour productivity.

The inability of the planners to integrate the requirements of the various enterprises and city departments was perceived as the principal reason for the unsatisfactory state of the social and economic environ-ments. Thus, in 1971 on the initiative of the local Communist Party a social-planning committee was formed. Its purpose was to resolve these problems by creating a development plan which integrated the require-ments of the various ministerial interests in the city with the interests of the city itself. The committee comprised eight sections, each of which had representatives from the Party, the city and the various branches of the municipal economy. The task of drawing up a social plan took a year and involved coordinating the plans of literally dozens of ministries and departments under whose jurisdiction were even more individual factories and enterprises. Though something of an extreme case because of the size of the city, the original complex social and economic plan for Leningrad entailed coordinating the development plans of more than 150 ministries and departments (Tolmachev, 1976, 51). The Vladimir social plan was approved at the plenum of the local Communist Party in January 1972 and then was forwarded to the city Soviet where it was confirmed in February. The plan for the integrated social and economic development of the city spanned the period from 1971 to 1975, that is, it was intended to coincide with the national Five-Year Plan.

The plan had three basic objectives: to improve economic perform-ance; to enhance the material well-being of the population; and to improve the educational qualifications and technical capability of the workforce. It was of special concern that four-fifths of the female workforce were engaged in unskilled labour. The need to improve skills in order to enhance productivity was urgent. The customary replenish-ment of the labour supply was dependent upon in-migration from the countryside and drawing 'socially unproductive' females out of house-holds into the labour force. Both sources were nearly exhausted and hence increases in production would have to come from greater labour productivity. Clearly, to the extent that material improvements in the standard of living reduced labour turnover, it would be easier to achieve this objective. Thus, a major part of the plan entailed ensuring that city enterprises did contribute the necessary funds for consumer and cultural facilities and basic municipal services. Significant progress was made in reducing turnover to an annual average of just over 12 per cent, a notable achievement in that it was significantly below the average for the RSFSR which was more than 20 per cent (Mel'nikov and Sudakov, 1974, 106–7). The social plan for Vladimir apparently has been successful in coordinating inter-branch and social development needs of the city. However, it should be pointed out that unlike the Leningrad and Moscow complex social and economic planning schemes, its jurisdiction does not extend beyond the city to the urban region. Still, what has been achieved in Vladimir and a handful of cities elsewhere serves as an important example of what can be accomplished through the creation of an effective coordinative body.

There can be no ignoring the role of the Communist Party in spearheading the social planning movement, nor its overt economic connotation. Nonetheless, the movement is certainly a positive one. Public participation in urban affairs may be enhanced, something which has not always been associated with either town planning or municipal government (Parkins, 1953, 208; Kogan, 1974, 19). For instance, there is growing evidence of decisions regarding the location of consumer service or cultural facilities being challenged as inappropriate, with alternatives suggested so as to make accessibility more equitable (Dumachev, 1972, 28). The upswell of social planning certainly has not, nor will it, quickly remedy the gap between town planning principle and practice. According to the available literature, however, in a few cities it has served well at least one intended purpose—reducing labour turnover and increasing productivity (Kachalovsky, 1971, 28). Thus, it may well be that the social planning movement, albeit economically motivated and expedited by the Communist Party, will ultimately serve the urban population better than the recounting of the legal rights of the city Soviet which was so much a part of the 1971 reform. If so, the quality of day-to-day life in the Soviet city can only improve.

Summary

There are many advantages of the normative approach to town planning which has evolved in the USSR. Established standards regarding things like journey-to-work times may be unattainable in every urban situation, but they provide useful benchmarks against which to set prevailing conditions. When fulfilled it is customary that the minimum standards are raised, providing once again an ideal toward which reality may be consciously directly. This is now happening in the case of the norms for living space. But it is not always that the changes required to improve the quality of life in the Soviet city are of a material kind. The discussion of the time-budget data revealed a continuing, and from the official standpoint socially undesirable, difference in the use of time amongst married men and women. Put simply, stereotyped sex-roles result in women carrying the major burden of household obligations, while invariably working full-time as well. The consequences of this imbalance are manifested in many ways, not least of which being the limited amount of discretionary free time available to women. In a society in which leisure time is growing, this situation provides a real basis for discontent. To some extent better organization in the provision of items of collective consumption and increased availability of labour-saving devices for the home would help. But the problem is clearly one of attitude and not so much of shops and machinery.

Social costs of one kind or another are related to both the failure of town-planning practice to meet established norms in consumer services and housing and the successful imposition of controls over population movement. In any social system there are costs related to the particular organization of people and things. Within the Soviet system there is at least the theoretical possibility of consciously attempting to minimize such costs and thereby providing an urban environment the quality of which is second to none. Anticipating problems and ensuring congruence of principle with practice are two of the essential prerequisites for the realization of the possible benefits of the system. At present the average Soviet urbanite does enjoy many of the fruits of past planning successes. Whether or not he is simply inured to some of the inadequacies is debatable. Problems are publicized increasingly, expectations are rising steadily, real improvements are being registered. The quality of the urban environment has increased measurably over the last decade. In some cities the advent of social planning has helped to bring about such changes.

7
The Soviet city:
Ideal and reality

We began this study by noting that the city long has served as both an agent and example of modernization. In the history of the city there is as yet no equivalent of the Soviet achievements in consciously manipulating the tempo and distribution of urban growth and in planning the city building process. In the foregoing chapters we have discussed various facets of the town-planning process and the urban environment it has produced. In so doing the relationship between town-planning principles and actual practice has been stressed. It remains now to offer a few summary remarks about the Soviet experience in town planning and about the relationship between the reality of the Soviet city and some of the goals and objectives of Soviet socialism.

From the outset a principal objective of Soviet locational decision making was to spread the benefits of socialism through removing regional inequalities and fostering the urban-industrialization of traditionally backward, largely non-Slavic regions. Progress over the past six decades in evening out regional disparities in fact has been very substantial. Nonetheless, regional imbalances in the distribution of the personal consumption fund persist and are part of the reason for unplanned internal migration, high rates of labour turnover and transient urban populations (Zwick, 1976). Cities in the eastern regions of the country have been especially affected by transient workforces. Yet out-migration from Siberia is frequently to Middle Asia where there continues to be a labour surplus. The surplus manpower there, however, is amongst the rural indigenous population. Over the years they have proven to be particularly resistant to the attractions of city life and to government attempts to promote rural-urban migration. While urban-industrialization in Middle Asia has been of large scale, it has been fuelled in the main by migration from the Slavic parts of the USSR. Thus, cities in the Asian Republics are largely Slavic in ethnic composition. To tap the surplus labour of the countryside may necessitate taking the factory to the village. This would ensure that the rhythm and regimentation of factory life reached far more of the indigenous population. Such a development might be seen as fulfilling one of the fundamental tenets of Marxist ideology, that is, the removal of the difference between town and countryside. But is this goal still valid in the context of late twentieth-century Soviet life? There is some reason to think not.

At least two benefits were to be gained by the imposition of controls over the growth of the large city, the planned development of the small cities and the industrialization of the countryside. In the first place, both Marx and Engels were acutely conscious of the abysmal state of the built environment in the nineteenth-century industrial city. The enormous congestion in cities gave rise to environmental degradation of every possible kind, which impinged directly on the material conditions of daily labour and life amongst the masses. Thus, controlled urban development would make possible the creation of a more habitable, and equitable, urban environment. What neither Marx nor Engels could predict was the way in which technological change since the nineteenth century would so profoundly alter the material basis of life in both city and village. Pollution problems about which Marx and Engels were particularly concerned were most severe in the large cities because of inadequate technology for handling effluents of one kind or another. Clearly, technology does not offer final solutions but the material basis of urban life has changed rather dramatically since the turn of the century. There is certainly no comparison between the state of the urban environment under the autocracy, or indeed in those European cities which served as laboratories for the theorizing of Marx and Engels, and the major cities of Europe and the Soviet Union at present. Indeed, it is entirely possible that the quality of the urban environment of the major city in the Soviet Union is substantially better than it is in the smaller city.

Secondly, eradicating the differences between town and country was aimed at abolishing the so-called 'idiocy of rural life'. However, the differences between city and countryside have changed markedly since the revolution of 1917. Collectivization of agriculture, the steady shift in balance from collective to state-farm operation (the latter being the more factory-like in operational procedures), and progress in communications technology, all have meant that the material and moral environment in the countryside is now much different. To be sure, there still exist agricultural regions which are technologically ill-equipped, marginal in production and deprived in every other sense. But rural folk are no longer necessarily unsophisticated, ill-educated, poor in material terms and retarded in terms of progressive social values. In short, whatever validity the notion of the 'idiocy of rural life' might once have had, it no longer seems appropriate to the Soviet milieu. Thus, the ideological significance of the need to eradicate the difference between city and countryside plays a small part in locational decision making. It is doubtful if it were ever otherwise. Indeed, whether desirable or not, decision making which affects the tempo and distribution of urban growth is now governed more by considerations of efficiency in the use of increasingly scarce resources than it is by the ideological precepts of the nineteenth century.

The inherent tension between efficiency and equality in locational decision making is manifested in many ways. In the Soviet Union patterns of urban growth sometimes have reflected which of the two is paramount. But there has not been an overall plan as to the desired distribution of urban places. In fact, it is only in the past few years that the concept of a unified settlement system has been developed, and there is still a long way to go before it is operationalized in terms of specific growth policies. Whether or not there are underlying universal forces shaping settlement systems, or indeed, the land-use patterns within cities, has not been demonstrated. The argument that technology and spatial efficiency are independent of ideology, for example, offers great scope for imaginative evaluation. Certainly some of the trends in Soviet urban development would suggest that there is a basis for such a contention.

Despite long-standing policies to control the growth of large cities, it is precisely the larger rather than the smaller urban places which have been growing most rapidly in both relative and absolute terms during the last decade or so. While the debate as to whether this is an acceptable course for Soviet society continues, ideas and debate are likely to be overtaken by events. Large cities within urban agglomerations are the present reality. Their proper management and planning demand that the planners' jurisdiction be extended beyond the city border to the city region. Such a spatial extension of authority has been very slow in coming. The evolving urban system thus lacks both the necessary regional basis and the policies and programmes to guide its development effectively.

The recent emphasis on efficiency in locational decision making has important implications for planning urban settlement systems and for planning the cities in them. The last decade has witnessed a growing preoccupation with making more efficient use of urban land. Despite the potential negative consequences for the inhabitants, apartment blocks are being built higher and higher each year. The pressure to build up is directly related to the apparent savings to be had in construction and in land used. The question not yet answered is, what are the social costs of this trend likely to be? A common Soviet position on this matter is that there will not be any negative consequences because apartments are intended to be used in the main just for sleeping. That is, as the provision of items of collective consumption increases more time will be spent outside the apartment by all members of the family. Such an argument is already being challenged by the inability of the state to meet the existing norms for items of collective consumption, by evidence showing the problems people face living in high-rise apartment complexes and by the steadily rising expectations about what facilities the state should provide to make greater leisure time more enjoyable, if not socially productive. The experience elsewhere of alienation and various forms of anti-social behaviour has prompted reconsideration of high-rise housing development, and in some cases outright rejection of them. The argument that the Soviet citizen is fundamentally different in his aspirations and needs at this point seems rather hollow.

Just as the quest for savings in construction and land have helped to push apartment buildings to ever higher heights, so too have the same forces worked to alter the central city. Moreover, there is some indication that the apparent benefits of the face-to-face contact associated with spatial clustering of various activities is now being recognized as of some importance. The customary central-city role of 'trading in intelligence' is not peculiar to any particular political-economic system. The disadvantages of the past policy of decentralizing many key administrative activities in the Soviet city now at least are being discussed. To the extent that the central city eventually embraces more of this type of activity, the less different in function will it be from the Western city. What will remain distinctive, and much less likely ever to be altered, is the consciously limited role of the central city in retailing.

The efficacy of the town-planning process has been impaired for a variety of reasons, not least of which being the inability of the town planner to countermand the political and economic power wielded by many ministries and their subordinate departments, enterprises and factories (Zile, 1963). Decision making in the Soviet Union is rigidly centralized in structure, but in practice the process necessarily tolerates independent action in order to get things done. Thus, contrary to first impressions of industrial managers as simply automatons responding to instructions from higher authorities, that is, showing no initiative, the fact is they must be possessed of considerable entrepreneurial skill if they are to be successful. However, the kind of decision-making environment in which they operate invariably means that regional interests, including those of cities, do not take precedence over sectoral interests. To the extent that the two are coincident there are no difficulties. But this has not been the case often, and is certainly not so at the present time. To a large degree then, successful town planning is dependent upon the ability of civic authorities to gain political support, to ensure participation in the real corridors of power in terms of decision making, to effect bargains and arrange compromises. The inherent contradiction between regional and sectoral interests makes this at best an extremely challenging task, at worst an impossible one. Still, the achievements and prospects are far from bleak. The Soviet city provides tangible evidence of past successes. With the advent of the social-planning movement political, economic and social forces have been harnessed, public participation in the planning process has been enhanced and for some cities improvements in the quality of the urban environment have been registered.

The urban environment itself testifies in a variety of ways to the successful application of socialist principles. Egalitarianism is reflected by the absence of residential segregation according to social stratum, by the predominance of public transport, by the nature of the distribution of items of collective consumption, both within cities and amongst regions, and by the decision to develop the central city in such a way as to afford the masses an opportunity to partake in cultural and political activities. Furthermore, the planned development of the Soviet city was intended to facilitate the realization of the long-run goals of a heightened social consciousness amongst the population, the dissolution of the various strata in Soviet society, the fusion of the many nationalities and the creation of the necessary conditions for the emergence of a communist ethos. Put simply, the city was to be an agent of directed social change (Strumilin, 1961). While both the physical and moral environments in cities are changing, it is not always in the desired direction.

There is no basis for questioning the successful application of egalitarian principles to the Soviet housing scene. Most people live in broadly similar conditions. Limits on living space, which the long-standing minimum sanitary norms has become, ensure that few are much better off in this regard. Indeed, in the late 1970s most urban inhabitants live with less living space than the sanitary minimum stipulates. While massive numbers of people have been rehoused, the housing situation is not yet adequate. Still, the enormous progress made in the last quarter of a century is quite remarkable by any standard of measurement. But in Soviet society the ownership and allocation of housing has created problems for the rational planning of cities. We have seen how slow ministries, departments and enterprises have been in turning housing over to municipal authorities in accordance with the intention of the 1971, and earlier, reforms of municipal government. Given the continuing competition amongst ministries for labour this situation is not likely to change over the short run. Fragmented authority over housing construction and allocation simply increases the probability that some segments of urban society will not fare as well as others. Jobs with enterprises or organizations owning modern, well located housing are prized for reasons which are obvious.

The pragmatic accommodation of socialist principles with the reality of housing supply in Soviet cities has resulted in the persistence of privately owned houses and the decision in the early 1960s once more to permit the creation of housing cooperatives. To some extent the latter go against the generally egalitarian mix of social strata within Soviet cities simply because cooperatives tend to comprise rather narrow segments of society. Thus, in cooperative apartment blocks not only is the quantity and quality of housing space usually of a higher than average standard, but the occupants, it would seem, tend to be more homogeneous in occupation and income. The same thing sometimes occurs when enterprises allocate more flats in an apartment complex to say management level personnel than to any other group, or when Party or government elites are housed in particular blocks of flats. Put simply, power and privilege in Soviet society

obviously exist, and are reflected, in among other ways in the housing
allocation process (Mathews, 1978). More often than not, however, it
is the quality and quantity of housing, rather than its spatial segregation
within the city, which sets elites apart. The same process is at work
in terms of the country house or *dacha*. Indeed, the substantial size and
sumptuous fitting out of the *dacha* is certainly one of the most tangible
expressions of elitism in Soviet society. In some cases spatial segregation
of a kind even occurs. Outside Frunze, the capital of Kirgiz Republic,
for example, is a cluster of less-than-modest *dachas* which belongs to the
urban elite (mostly Party and government officials). In no sense is this
exceptional. Within the Soviet city, however, such obvious expression
of privatism is rather rare.

If cooperative housing becomes spatially segregated then the general
picture of heterogeneity of social strata in the Soviet city could change.
As yet, however, there is no firm evidence that this is occurring. But
the growing importance of cooperative housing has another important
dimension. It has been argued, with good reason, that since cooperatives
are built with money from savings accounts and state loans, on which
interest is paid, they represent a kind of rent decontrol (Wiles, 1977,
550). The nominal rent for state housing scarcely covers maintenance
costs. The demand for ever better quality housing seems insatiable. Thus,
in an era of limited resources, shifting some of the burden of meeting
the housing demand makes sense. The long-run implications of a
growing share of cooperatives within the Soviet city, however, may
ultimately compromise the achievements in creating an essentially
egalitarian environment.

But does an admixture of social strata bring about the dissolution of those
same features which permit the differentiation to be made in the first place?
Just because a particular apartment block houses a full range of social strata
does not mean the people involved interrelate (Johnston, 1977, 24–5).
Sociological surveys have shown that most residents of apartment blocks
rarely know their neighbours. Indeed, one of the almost predictable
consequences of the massive rehousing programme is that of alienation
amongst many of the residents of new *mikrorayons*. Moreover, planning
mikrorayons on the assumption that the demands of most people will
be fulfilled within the local area contradicts the principal feature of the
large city, that is, the large city requires greater rather than lesser
mobility if its inherent advantages and opportunities are to be realized.
To the extent that they are realized by greater mobility amongst the
inhabitants, the less likely is it that such city regions will create a sense
of common purpose, that the built environment will help to effect the
long-run objective of the dissolution of social strata.

The greatest opportunity for realizing such long-run social goals is clearly in the new town (Underhill, 1976; Smolyar, 1972). Indeed, studies in
cities like Bratsk have revealed a higher than average level of marriage
between the different 'nationalities', thus facilitating the objective of the

fusion of all peoples. There is as well a lower level of baptism of the new born, an apparent indication of a measure of success in abolishing the socially backward links with the past (Badiyev, 1974). But Bratsk has all the problems of contemporary urban society. The divorce rate is the highest in the region, alcoholism is all too common, labour discipline is often poor and so on. Invariably it is the failure of townplanning which is singled out as one of the principal reasons for social problems. Environment plays a part to be sure. However, it seems likely that some of these currents of change within Soviet society which are thought to be related to a less than satisfactory urban environment, are in fact as much a product of the general urbanization process as they are of the circumstances of a particular city.

Perhaps the single most important obstacle to the realization of the goals for Soviet society is the use of various types of incentive to promote fuller participation in the system in general, in the production process in particular. The private automobile, the cooperative apartment, differential incomes, the special shops for elites, in short, all the forms of privatism and privilege which have been permitted have an impact on Soviet society, on the Soviet city. The more privilege there is, the more resistance to egalitarian measures there is likely to be (Gilison, 1975, 53; Kolakowski and Hampshire, 1977, 3–10). Perhaps such measures are a necessary, but ephemeral, stage in the process of building a socialist society (Lukes, 1977, 87). But it does seem clear that if the goals for Soviet society and its increasingly urbanized population are to be realized, more rather than less state intervention in the conditions of daily life and labour is required. Some continuities with the past stand out. Urban society in Russia was least beset by problems when totalitarian authority was at its strongest. When controls over urban development and population movement collapsed in the face of rapid urban-industrialization, an urban crisis of unparalleled dimensions took hold. Russian society was scarcely ideal. But what the experience of the past in this case does demonstrate is the absolute necessity to hold migration in check, to in effect, exploit the countryside for the benefit of the city. For a long while this was also done in the Soviet Union. As restrictions have eased, as mobility has increased, as various forms of privatism and materialism have grown in importance, so the state is put in a dilemma. Competent management of the whole system demands the supremacy of authority over individualism. It remains to be seen whether the evolution of the Soviet city will remain fixed on the lines originally laid down by the town-planning principles adopted nearly a half century ago, or move in some other direction which almost inevitably will ensure its hard-won individuality is put at risk.

Despite the tragic disruptions of World War, Civil War and internal upheaval, the Soviet city stands out as a remarkable example of what is possible to achieve in the application of socialist principles to town planning. Problems exist to be sure: indeed, they are frequently just the same as in the Western city. But because the system offers potential solutions to them, the Soviet experience in planned urban development stands out as both different from, and of instruction to, Western society. This study of the Soviet city has no doubt raised many more questions than it has been possible to answer. To the extent that it serves to provoke more interest, and more inquiry, one of its purposes will have been served.

Bibliography*

ADAMS, R. B. 1977: The Soviet metropolitan hierarchy: regionalization and comparison with the United States. *Soviet Geography: Review and Translation* **28** (5), 313–28.

AGAYEV, E. 1977: Shum v dome. *Literaturnaya Gazeta* 19 October, 11.

AITOV, N. 1972a: Planirovaniye sotsial'nogo razvitiya gorodov. *Planovoye Khozyaystvo* **3**, 143–6.

—— 1972b: Comprehensive social development of cities. *Joint Publication Research Service* (hereafter *JPRS*) 55580, Reel 382, R11815.

—— 1973: Social planning: problems and perspectives. *Zhurnalist* **3**, 44–6. Translated in The Current Digest of the Soviet Press (hereafter cited as CDSP), 1973, **25** (32), 12–13.

ANDRLE, V. 1976: *Managerial power in the Soviet Union*. Farnborough: Saxon House.

ANTOSENKOV, E. 1973: The availability of housing and personnel turnover. *Soviet Review* **14** (3), 42–59.

ARAKELYAN, YU. 1978: The order was signed, but . . . *Pravda* 29 November, 3. Translated in CDSP, 1978, **30** (48), 26–7.

ASTAF'YEVA-DLUGACH, M. 1976: Gorod smotrit v zavtra. *Stroitel'naya Gazeta* 22 October, 3.

AZAN, V. 1972: For one's own city. *Izvestiya* 24 August, 5. Translated in CDSP, 1972, **24** (34), 23.

BADIYEV, N. A. 1974: Novyy sotsialisticheskiy gorod—shkola inter-natsionalizma. In Mel'nikov, G. I. (ed.), *Sotsial'nye problemy novykh gorodov vostochnoy Sibiri*. Irkutsk: Irkutskiy Gosudarstvennyy Universitet imeni A. A. Zhdanova, 45–53.

BALEZIN, V. P. 1963: *Pravovoy rezhim zemel' gorodskoy zastroyki*. Moscow: Izdatel'stvo Yuridicheskogo Literatury.

—— 1970: *Pravo zemlepol'zovaniya grazhdan, prozhivayushchikh v gorodskoy mestnosti*. Moscow: Izdatel'stvo Moskovskogo Universiteta.

BARANOV, N. V. 1964: *Kompozitsiya tsentra goroda*. Moscow: Izdatel'stvo Literatury po Stroitel'stvu.

* This Bibliography includes only those works which have been cited in the text.

BARANOV, ,N. V. 1973: Perspektivy uluchsheniya planirovki, zastroyka inzhenernogo oborudovaniya i obshchego arkhitekturnogo oblika slozhivshikhsya gorodov. In *Perspektivy preobrazovaniya okruzhayushchey cheloveka gorodskoy sredy*. Moscow: Stroyizdat.

BARKHIN, M. G. 1974: *Gorod 1945–1970. Praktika, proyekty, teoriya*. Moscow: Stroyizdat.

BARRY, D. D. 1969: Housing in the USSR, cities and towns. *Problems of Communism* 18 (May–June), 1–11.

BATER, J. H. 1972: Hydroelectric power development in Central Siberia. *Water Power* 1, 5–12.

—— 1973: The development of public transportation in St Petersburg: 1860–1914. *Journal of Transport History* 11 (2), 85–102.

—— 1976: *St Petersburg: industrialization and change*. London: Edward Arnold.

—— 1977a: Soviet town planning: theory and practice in the 1970s. *Progress in Human Geography* 1 (2), 177–207.

—— 1977b: Planning problems in Siberian new towns. *The Bloomsbury Geographer* 9, 55–62.

—— 1978: Some dimensions of urbanization and the response of municipal government: Moscow and St Petersburg. *Russian History/Histoire Russe* 5, part 1, 46–63.

—— 1980: Transience, residential persistence and mobility in Moscow and St Petersburg, 1900–1914. *Slavic Review*, in press.

BAYRAMOV, M. 1972: Azerbaydzhan economist discusses social planning of cities. *JPRS* 56253, Reel 396, R12206.

BELCHENKO, V. 1974: When efforts are united. *Izvestiya* 26 September, 4. Translated in CDSP, 1974, 26 (39), 15–16.

BELOUSOV, V. N. 1973: Prognozy pereustroystva transportnykh sistem slozhivshikhsya gorodov. In *Perspektivy preobrazovaniya okruzhayushchey cheloveka gorodskoy sredy*. Moscow: Stroyizdat.

—— 1975: Gradostroitel'stvo na novom etape. *Arkhitektura SSSR* 10, 3–17.

—— 1976: Sovetskoye gradostroitel'stvo: vchera, segodnya, zavtra. In Listengurt, F. M. (ed.), *Gradostroitel'stvo: sbornik nauchnykh trudov*. Moscow: TSNIIP Gradostroitel'stva.

BEREZIN, V. A. 1973: Integrated development of urban industrial districts recommended. *JPRS*, 61916, Reel 988, R14888.

BESHKILTSEV, V. 1974: How to build in the north. *Izvestiya* 14 February, 2. Translated in CDSP, 1974, 26 (7), 14.

BEZLYUDOV, A. 1977: Our city, our homes. *Ogonyok* 23, 8. Translated in CDSP, 1977, 29 (30), 10.

BEZRUKOV, A. and DMITERKO, D. 1977: Sotsial'noye planirovaniye. *Planovoye Khozyaystvo* 1, 147–52.

BITUNOV, V. V. 1976: Kompleksnoye planirovaniye narodnogo khozyaystvo stolitsy. *Gorodskoye Khozyaystvo Moskvy* 11, 3–6.

BLIZNAKOV, M. 1976: Urban planning in the USSR: integrative theories.

In Hamm, M. (ed.), *The city in Russian history*. Lexington: The University Press of Kentucky, 243–56.

BLUMENFELD, H. 1942: Regional and city planning in the Soviet Union. *Task* **3**, 33–52.

—— 1944a: Russian city planning of the 18th and early 19th centuries. *Journal of the Society of Architectural Historians* **4** (1–4), 22–33.

—— 1944b: Soviet city planning; an example. *American Review on the Soviet Union* **6** (1), 53–65.

—— 1948: Reconstruction: USSR. *Task* **7–8**, 25–33.

BOCHAROV, YU. P. 1975: Problems in establishing industrial regions in general city plans. *JPRS* R66482, 44–6.

BOCHAROV, YU. and KUDRYAVTSEV, A. O. 1972: *Planirovonnaya struktura sovremennogo goroda*. Moscow: Stroyizdat.

BOCHAROV, YU. and LYUBOVNYY, V. 1976a: Kompleksnoye razvitiye krupnykh gorodov. *Planovoye Khozyaystvo* **12**, 78–86.

—— 1976b: A city in a single complex. *Pravda* 13 November, 3. Translated in CDSP, 1976, **28** (46), 8–9.

BOLDYREVA, T. R. 1973: Vladimir Party Chief and mayor comment on urban development. *JPRS* 61916, Reel 448, R14888.

BOCHKOV, M. 1974: Problemy rayonnogo planirovaniya. *Planovoye Khozyaystvo* **12**, 61–3.

BORSHCHEVSKIY, M. V.; USPENSKIY, S. V.; SHKARATAN, O. I. 1975: *Gorod. Metodologicheskiye problemy kompleksnogo sotsial'nogo i ekonomicheskogo planirovaniya*. Moscow: Izdatel'stvo Nauka.

BRONER, D. I. 1966: *Zhilishchnyy vopros i statistika*. Moscow: Statistika.

—— 1973: O demograficheskikh predposylkakh planirovaniya struktury zhilishchnogo stroitel'stva. In Shcherbakov, L. L. (ed.), *Narodonaseleniye*. Moscow: Statistika.

BROVKIN, V. and YERMOLAYEV, V. 1978: Greeting new settlers. *Pravda* 29 May, 3. Translated in CDSP, 1978, **30** (22), 10–11.

BROWDER, R. P. and KERENSKY, A. F. 1961: *The Russian Provisional Government. Documents* 1. Stanford: Stanford University Press.

BUKREYEV, YU. 1972: The factory's beauty. *Izvestiya* 2 September, 2. Translated in CDSP, 1972, **24** (35), 20.

BULGAKOV, G. N. 1973: Nastoyashcheye i budushcheye Leningrada. In *Perspekitivy preobrazovaniya okruzhayushchey cheloveka gorodskoy sredy*. Moscow: Stroyizdat.

BUNIN, A. V. *et al.* 1943: *Gradostroitel'stvo*. Moscow: Izdatel'stvo Akademii Arkhitektury SSSR.

BUSH, K. 1976: The Soviet response to environmental deterioration. In Volgyes, I. (ed.), *Environmental deterioration in the Soviet Union and Eastern Europe*. New York: Praeger, 8–36.

BUTLER, W. E. 1976: Soviet continental shelf· and anti-pollution legislation. *International and Comparative Law Quartlery* **24**, 131–136.

174   *The Soviet City*

BYKOV, R. 1978: Chistoye nebo, chistoye more, chistyy gorod. *Stroitel'naya Gazeta* 29 September, 3.

BYULINKIN, N. P. *et al.* 1962: *Istoriya Sovetskoy arkhitektury.* Moscow: Gosstroyizdat.

CARR, E. H. 1959: *Socialism in one country 1924–1926.* London: The Macmillan Company.

CATTEL, D. T. 1968: *Leningrad: a case study of Soviet urban government.* New York: Praeger.

—— 1976: Soviet cities and consumer welfare planning. In Hamm, M. (ed.), *The city in Russian history.* Lexington: The University Press of Kentucky, 257–75.

CHERNICHENKO, A. 1977: A light in the cottage window. *Komsomolskaya Pravda* 20 September, 2. Translated in CDSP, 1977, **29** (37), 15–16.

CHINN, J. 1977: *Manipulating Soviet population resources.* London: The Macmillan Company.

City under construction. *Pravda* 18 May, 1973, 2. Translated in CDSP, 1973, **25** (20), 24–5.

DAVIDOVICH, V. G. 1964: *Planirovka gorodov i rayonov inzhenerno-ekonomicheskiye osnovy.* Moscow: Izdatel'stvo Literatury po Stroitel'stvu.

—— 1968: Kolichestvennye zakonomernosti rasseleniya otnositel'no mest raboty. In Davidovich, V. G. and Kudryavtsev, O. K. (eds), *Rasseleniye v gorodakh.* Moscow: Izdatel'stvo Mysl', 5–74.

—— 1972: O podvizhnosti naseleniya v yedinoy sisteme gorodov, poselkov i sel SSSR. *Voprosy Geografii* **91**, 27–66.

DAVIDOW, M. 1976: *Cities without crisis.* New York: International Publishing Company.

DEMENTYEVA, I. 1974: The microborough and the rush hour. *Izvestiya* 2 October, 3. Translated in CDSP, 1974, **26** (40), 16–17.

DENISOV, I. 1978: Net zaboty vazhneye. *Stroitel'naya Gazeta* 15 September, 1.

DERUZHINSKIY, V. 1974: Plan sotsial'no-ekonomicheskogo razvitiya goroda. *Planovoye Khozyaystvo* **4**, 92–6.

DIMAIO, A. J. 1974: *Soviet urban housing: problems and policies.* New York: Praeger.

DMITRIYEV, A. V. 1976: Comprehensive planning in cities. *Sotsio-logicheskiye Issledovaniya* **4**, 52–63. Translated in CDSP, 1977, **29** (7), 12–13.

DROBNYS, A. 1978: The town is small. *Pravda* 21 May, 2. Translated in CDSP, 1978, **30** (20), 13.

DROBOTOV, V. 1979: An apartment for the newlyweds. *Sovetskaya Rossiya* 14 February, 3. Translated in CDSP, 1979, **31** (8), 13.

DRYAVNEV, O. 1974: Razvitiye grupp bol'shikh gorodov v SSSR. *Arkhitektura SSSR* **4**, 6–10.

DUBINSKY, V. 1972: An automobile has been purchased. *Pravda* 22 August, 3. Translated in CDSP, 1972, **24** (34), 23–4.

DUMACHEV, A. 1972: Economic and social development plans in Leningrad. *JPRS* 55551, Reel 382, R11813.

EFIMOV, A. 1977: Rostov-na-Donu smotrit v zavtra. *Stroitel'naya Gazeta* 1 April, 3.

EFIMOV, V. T. and MIKERIN, G. I. 1976: Avtomobilizatsiya v razvitom sotsialisticheskom obshchestve. *Sotsiologicheskiye Issledovaniya* 1, 128–38.

EGOROV, I. A. 1969: *The architectural planning of St Petersburg.* Athens, Ohio: Ohio University Press. Translated by Eric Dluhosch.

FEDUTINOV, YU. A. 1968: Dinamika svyazey mest truda i zhil'ya. In Davidovich, V. G. and Kudryavtsev, O. K. (eds), *Rasseleniye v gorodakh.* Moscow: Izdatel'stvo Mysl', 205–9.

FOMIN, G. N. 1974: Sovetskoye gradostroitel'stvo na sovremennon etape. *Kommunist* 11, 44–54.

FRENCH, R. A. 1965: Recent population trends in the USSR. *St Antony's Papers* 19, 68–95.

—— 1979: The individuality of the Soviet city. In French, R. A. and Hamilton, F. E. I. *The socialist city.* Chichester: John Wiley and Sons, 73–104.

FRENKEL', Z. 1910: Neskol'ko dannykh o sanitarnom sostoyaniy Moskvy i Peterburga za 1909g. *Gorodskoye Delo* 20, 1407–15.

FROLIC, B. 1964: The Soviet City. *Town Planning Review* 34, 285–306.

—— 1970a: Soviet urban politics. Unpublished Ph.D. thesis. Cornell University.

—— 1970b: The Soviet study of Soviet cities. *Journal of Politics* 32, 675–95.

—— 1971: Municipal administrations, departments, commissions and organizations. *Soviet Studies* 22 (3), 376–93.

—— 1972: Decision-making in Soviet cities. *American Political Science Review* 66 (1), 38–52.

FUCHS, R. and DEMKO, G. J. 1978: Commuting in the USSR. *Soviet Geography: Review and Translation* 19 (6), 363–72.

GABYSHEV, K. 1969: Ekonomicheskaya otsenka prirodnykh resursov i rentnye platezhi. *Vestnik Moskovskogo Universiteta. Seriya Ekonomika* 5, 17–23.

GALETSKAYA, R. 1974: The demographic situation in the CMEA, member-countries. *Voprosy Ekonomiki* 4, 103–13. Translated in CDSP, 1974, 26 (34), 1–3.

GENDZEKHADZE, E. N. 1976: *Zhilishchno—stroitel'nye kooperativy v gorode i sele.* Moscow: Izdatel'stvo Moskovskogo Universiteta.

GERASHCHENKO, M. and TSINGALENOK, V. 1974: How we build cities. *Pravda* 3 March, 2. Translated in CDSP, 1974, 26 (9), 28.

GERASIMOV, I. P. *et al.* 1975: Contemporary problems in the constructive geography of large cities. *Soviet Geography: Review and Translation* 16 (3), 133–45.

GEYDANE, I. M. *et al.* 1976: *Balans vremeni naseleniya Latviyskoy SSR.* Riga: Izdatel'stvo 'Zinatne'.

GILISON, J. M. 1975: *The Soviet image of utopia.* Baltimore: The Johns Hopkins University Press.

GLUSHKOVA, V. G. and KOPILOV, V. A. 1976: Interaction of large metropolitan cities and their suburbs. In Kovalev, A. A. and Khorev, B. S. (eds), *Geography of Population.* Moscow: International Geographical Union, 264–6.

GOKHBERG, M. YA. 1973: Moscow's industrial development problems reported. *JPRS* 61916, Reel 488, R14888.

—— 1974: Razvitiye krupnykh gorodov. *Planovoye Khozyaystvo* **6**, 129–35.

—— 1976: Dolgosrochnoye planovoye regulirovaniye TPK Moskvy i Moskovskoy oblasti. *Planovoye Khozyaystvo* **1**, 51–62.

GOLDMAN, M. 1970: The convergence of environmental disruption. *Science* **170**, 37–42.

GOL'TS, G. A. 1972: Vliyaniye transporta na prostranstvennoye razvitiye gorodov i aglomeratsii. In Pivovarov, Yu. (ed.), *Problemy sovremennoy urbanizatsii.* Moscow: Statistika, 159–90.

GORDON, L. A. and KLOPOV, E. V. 1972: *Chelovek posle raboty. Sotsial'nye problemy byta i vnerabochego vremeni.* Moscow: Nauka.

—— 1977: Ratsional'nyy byudzhet vremeni: podkhod k probleme i opyt nachal'nogo rascheta. *Sotsiologicheskiye Issledovaniya* **1**, 19–30.

GORNOSTAYEVA, G. A. 1979: Quantitative analysis of the spatial evolution of cities. *Soviet Geography: Review and Translation* **20** (1), 7–15.

GRADOV, G. A. 1973: Osnovnye napravleniya perspektivnogo razvitiya sistemy i tipov zdaniy kul'turno-bytogo obsluzhivaniya. In *Perspektivy razvitiya sovetskogo gradostroitel'stva.* Moscow: Stroyizdat, 321–371.

GRIGOR'YEVA, V. and LAGUSHKIN, V. 1976: Rol' planovykh komissiy v razvitii gorodskogo khozyaystva. *Planovoye Khozyaystvo* **10**, 85–6.

GUREVICH, B. L. 1967: Plotnost' naseleniya goroda i plotnost' veroyatnosti sluchaynoy velichiny. *Vestnik Moskovskogo Universiteta: Geografiya* **1**, 15–21.

GUSEV, V. 1975: How to build quality housing. *Pravda* 4 March, 3. Translated in CDSP, 1975, **27** (9), 28.

GUTNOV, A. *et al.* 1968: *The ideal communist city.* New York: George Braziller. Translated by Renee Neu Watkins.

HAMILTON, F. E. I. 1976: *The Moscow city region.* London: Oxford University Press.

HARRIS, C. D. 1970: *Cities of the Soviet Union. Studies in their functions, size, density, and growth.* Chicago: Rand McNally.

HERLIHY, P. 1978: Death in Odessa. A study of population movements in a nineteenth-century city. *Journal of Urban History* **4** (4), 417–442.

HOUSTON, C. J. 1979: Administrative control of migration to Moscow. *The Canadian Geographer* **23** (1), 32–44.

HUZINEC, G. A. 1977: A reexamination of Soviet industrial location theory. *The Professional Geographer* **29** (3), 259–65.

IL'IN, P. M. 1972: O geografii zhilishchnogo khozyaystva. *Voprosy Geografii* **91**, 164–75.

ILYIN, M. 1931: Russian urbanism. In El Lissitsky, *Russia: Architecture for world revolution.* 1970. Cambridge: Massachusetts Institute of Technology Press, 179–83. Translated by Eric Dluhosch.

Itogi vsesoyuznoy perepisi naseleniya 1970 goda. **1**, 1972. Moscow: Statistika.

IVANOVA, A. 1973: Voprosy ispol'zovaniya territorii proyektakh general'-nykh planov gorodov. *Arkhitektura SSSR* **8**, 26–8.

JACKSON, W. A. D. 1974: Urban expansion. *Problems of Communism* **23**, 14–24.

JACOBS, E. M. 1975: Urban housing in the Soviet Union. *Economic aspects of life in the USSR.* Brussels: NATO, 65–90.

JENSEN, R. G. 1976: Urban environments in the United States and the Soviet Union. In Berry, B. (ed.), *Urbanization and Counterurbanization.* Beverly Hills: Sage, 31–42.

JOHNSTON, M. 1977: Public policies, private choices, new town planning and lifestyles in three nations. *Urban Affairs Quarterly* **13** (1), 3–32.

JUVILER, P. 1974: Crime and its study. In Morton, H. W. and Tokes, R. L. (eds), *Soviet politics and society in the 1970s.* New York and London: Collier Macmillan, 200–238.

KABAKOVA, S. I. 1970: Razmeshcheniye obektov gorodskogo khozyaystva v podzemnom prostranstve. *Gorodskoye Khozyaystvo Moskvy* **3**, 30–3.

——— 1973: *Gradostroitel'naya otsenka territoriy gorodov.* Moscow: Stroyizdat.

KACHALOVSKY, YE. 1971: If one sees the long-range perspective. *Pravda* 6 December, 2. Translated in CDSP, 1972, **23** (49), 27–8.

KAK KHVORAYET I UMIRAYET STOLITSA. 1909: *Gorodskoye Delo* **11**, 543–7.

KASHIN, L. 1977: Noise in the home. *Literaturnaya Gazeta* 3 August, 12. Translated in CDSP, 1977, **29** (38), 11–12.

KELLEY, D. R. 1976: Environmental policy-making in the USSR. The roles of industrial and environmental interest groups. *Soviet Studies* **28** (4), 570–89.

KHAFIZOV, R. 1978: Integrated city development. *Planovoye Khozyaystvo* **8**, 139–42. Translated in CDSP, 1978, **30** (41), 7.

KHANIN, S. YE. 1971: Sovremennoye rasseleniye v Barnaule. *Vestnik Moskovskogo Universiteta: Geografiya* **2**, 102–6.

——— 1976: A wave-type model of population density in a city. *Soviet Geography: Review and Translation* **17** (9) 632–6.

KHODATAYEV, V. P. 1973: Prognozy razvitiya gorodskogo i vneshnego transport. In *Perspektivy razvitiya sovetskogo gradostroitel'stva.* Moscow: Stroyizdat, 212–43.

KHODZHAYEV, D. 1976: Kompleksnost'-glavnoye napravleniye v zastroyke gorodov. *Planovoye Khozyaystvo* **8**, 43–52.

KHOLYUK, G. S. 1974: *Opyt sotsiologicheskikh issledovaniye na dal'nem vostoke.* Khabarovsk-Vladivostok: Akademiya Nauk SSSR.

KHOREV, B. S. 1968: *Gorodskiye poseleniya SSSR.* Moscow: Mysl'.

—— 1972: *Malyy gorod.* Moscow: Izdatel'stvo Moskovskogo Universiteta.

—— 1975: *Problemy gorodov.* Moscow: Mysl'.

KHOREV, B. S. and MOISEYENKO, V. M. 1976: *Sdvigi v razmeshchenii naseleniya SSSR.* Moscow: Statistika.

KISHKAN, V. 1977: Problems of development of a mining capital. *Trud* 17 December, 2. Translated in CDSP, 1978, **29** (51), 6.

KOCHETKOV, A. V. 1975: Sotsial'no-ekonomicheskiye aspekty gradostroitel'stva. *Voprosy Ekonomiki* **10**, 23–34.

KOCHETKOV, A. V. and LISTENGURT, F. M. 1977: A strategy for the distribution of settlement in the USSR; aims, problems and solutions. *Soviet Geography: Review and Translation* **18** (9), 660–674.

KOGAN, L. 1974: The author is the collective. *Sovetskaya Rossiya* 1 November, 2. Translated in CDSP, 1975, **27** (8), 19.

—— 1976: Sotsial'no-kul'turnye svyazi v aglomeratsii krupneyshego goroda i yego razvitiye. *Arkhitektura SSSR* **1**, 20–3.

KOLAKOWSKI, L. and HAMPSHIRE, S. (eds), 1977: *The socialist idea: A reappraisal.* London: Quartet Books.

KOLPAKOV, B. T. and PATRUSHEV, V. D. 1971: *Byudzhet vremeni gorodskogo naseleniya.* Moscow: Statistika.

KONOVALOV, V. 1978: A city's health. *Literaturnaya Gazeta* 1 November, 10. Translated in CDSP, 1978, **30** (46), 5–6.

KONSTANTINOV, D. A. 1975: Novye goroda v' sisteme gorodskogo rasseleniya SSSR. *Izvestiya Vsesoyuznogo Geograficheskogo Obshchestva* **107**, 22–8.

KOPP, A. 1970: *Town and revolution: Soviet architecture and city planning 1917–1935.* New York: G. Braziller. Translated by Thomas E. Burton.

KORENEVSKAYA, E. I. 1977: *Mestnye sovety i sotsial'noye planirovaniye* Moscow: 'Yuridicheskaya Literatura'.

KOSTIN, L. 1978: Managing the country's labour resources. *Planovoye Khozyaystvo* **12**, 16–27. Translated in CDSP, 1979, **31** (4), 1–4.

KRAVCHUK, YA. T. 1973: *Formirovaniye novykh gorodov.* Moscow: Izdatel'stvo Literatury po Stroitel'stvu.

KRUGLYAK, V. and DAL, R. 1972: What should the microborough be like? *Pravda* 23 July, 3. Translated in CDSP, 1972, **24** (29), 25–6.

KRYLOV, S. M. 1977: On the question of the nature of antisocial phenomena and a strategy for combating law violations.

Sotsiologicheskiye Issledovaniya **3**, 107–14. Translated in CDSP, 1978, **30** (3), 6–8.

KUBAL'CHICH, O. and LYUBOVNYY, V. 1976: Opyt i problemy regulirovaniya razvitiya krupnykh gorodskikh aglomeratsiy v Sovetskom Soyuze. In Pokshishevskiy, V. V. and Lappo, G. M. (eds), *Problemy urbanizatsii i rasseleniya*. Moscow: Izdatel'stva Mysl', 239–50.

KUDRYAVTSEV, A. O. 1971: *Ratsional'noye ispol'zovaniye territoriy pri planirovke i zastroyke gorodov SSSR*. Moscow: Stroyizdat.

KULIKOVA, G. B. 1976: Enhancing the local Soviet's role in the developed socialist society. *Istoriya SSSR* **5**, 20–40. Translated in CDSP, 1977, **29** (3), 12.

KURMAN, M. V. 1976: *Aktual'nye voprosy demografii*. Moscow: Statistika.

KUTSEV, G. F. 1974: Nekotorye sotsial'nye problemy trudovoy deyatel'nosti molodezhi v novom gorode. In Mel'nikov G. I. (ed.), *Sotsial'nye problemy novykh gorodov vostochnoy Sibiri*. Irkutsk: Irkutskiy gosudarstvennyy universitet imeni A. A. Zhdanova, 135–44.

LANDO, M. 1971: Improving economic work in planning mikroregions. *JPRS* 53433, Reel 349, R10861.

LAPPO, G. M. 1974: Problems in the evolution of urban agglomerations. *Soviet Geography: Review and Translation* **15** (9), 531–42.

LEVIKOV, A. and MOYEV, V. 1972: Bratsk lesson. *JPRS* 57470, Reel 417, R12782.

LEVITSKAYA, A. G. 1971: Dukhovnye potrebnosti molodezhi novykh gorodov i vozmozhnosti ikh udovletvoreniya. In Mel'nikov, G. I. (ed.), *Sotsial'nye problemy novykh gorodov vostochnoy Sibiri*. Irkutsk: Irkutskiy gosudarstvennyy universitet imeni A. A. Zhdanova, 143–60.

LEWIS, R. A. and ROWLAND, R. H. 1969: Urbanization in Russia and the USSR: 1897–1966. *Annals, Association of American Geographers* **59** (4), 776–96.

LEWIS, C. W. and STERNHEIMER, S. 1979: *Soviet urban management: with comparisons to the United States*. New York: Praeger.

LIBKIND, A. 1975: The architecture of the factory zone. *Pravda* 5 August, 3. Translated in CDSP, 1975, **27** (31), 8.

LISTENGURT, F. M. 1975: Criteria for delineating large urban agglomerations in the USSR. *Soviet Geography: Review and Translation* **16** (9), 559–68.

LITOVKA, O. P. 1976: *Problemy prostranstvennogo razvitiya urbanizatsii*. Leningrad: Izdatel'stvo Nauka.

LIVSHITS, D. M. 1971: Ekonomicheskaya reforma na gorodskom passazhirskom transporte. *Gorodskoye Khozyaystvo Moskvy* **7**, 32–4.

Loans for individual housing construction in cities. *Izvestiya* 29 April, 1977, 2. Translated in CDSP, 1977, **29** (17), 27–8.

LOGINOV, S. and LYUBOVNYY, V. 1975: Problemy malykh i srednikh gorodov Rossiyskoy Federatsii. *Planovoye Khozyaystvo* **2**, 47–56.

LOGVINOV, V. 1977: Without an apartment. *Pravda* 15 April, 2. Translated in CDSP, 1977, **29** (15), 10–11.

LORIMER, F. 1946: *The population of the Soviet Union: history and prospects.* Geneva: League of Nations.

LOYTER, M. N. 1975: Ekonomicheskaya otsenka gorodskikh zemel' i effektivnost' kapital'nykh vlozheniy. *Gorodskoye Khozyaystvo Moskvy* **5**, 26–7.

LOZBYAKOV, V. 1979: In the same room. *Sovetskaya Rossiya* 10 February, 3. Translated in CDSP, 1979, **31** (12), 14.

LUKES, S. 1977: Socialism and equality. In Kolakowski, L. and Hampshire, S. (eds), *The socialist idea: A reappraisal.* London: Quartet Books, 74–95.

LUPPOV, S. P. 1957: *Istoriya stroitel'stva Peterburga v pervoy chetverti XVIII veka.* Moscow: Izdatel'stvo Akademii Nauk SSSR.

LYASHCHENKO, P. I. 1949: *History of the national economy of Russia to the 1917 revolution.* New York: The Macmillan Company. Translated by L. H. Herman.

LYDOLPH, P. E. 1977: *A geography of the USSR.* New York: John Wiley and Sons.

—— 1978: Recent population trends in the USSR. *Soviet Geography: Review and Translation* **19** (8), 505–39.

LYUBOVNYY, V. 1976: A city is a single complex *Pravda* 13 November, 3. Translated in CDSP, 1976 **28** (46), 8–9.

LYUBOVNYY, V. and SAVELYEV, V. 1977: Russia's small and large cities. *Ekonomika i Organizatsiya Promyshlennogo* **4**, 110–23. Translated in CDSP, 1977, **29** (35), 7–8.

MANYUKHIN, V. 1977: Next to the giants. *Pravda* 4 December, 3. Translated in CDSP, 1978, **29** (49), 9.

MATHEWS, M. 1972: *Class and society in Soviet Russia.* London: Routledge and Kegan Paul.

—— 1978: *Privilege in the Soviet Union.* London: Allen and Unwin.

MATLIN, G. M. 1973: Methods suggested for economic assessment of water resources. *JPRS* 59463, Reel 448, R13750.

MATVEYCHUK, V. M. 1971: Nekotorye voprosy zhilishchnogo stroitel'stva v novykh gorodakh vostochnoy Sibiri (1956–1965 gg). In Mel'nikov, G. I. (ed.), *Sotsial'nye problemy novykh gorodov ostochnoy Sibiri.* Irkutsk: Irkutskiy Gosudarstvennyy Universitet imeni A. A. Zhdanova, 34–49.

MATVEYEV, S. 1972: Problems of urban transport. *Trud* 31 August, 2. Translated in CDSP, 1973, **25** (2), 17.

MAXWELL, B. W. 1935: *The Soviet state.* London: Selwyn and Blount.

MCINTYRE, R. J. and THORNTON, J. R. 1978: On the environmental efficiency of economic systems. *Soviet Studies* **30** (2), 173–192.

MELESHCHENKO, V. 1975: Kompleksnoye planirovaniye regiona. *Plano-voye Khozyaystvo* **11**, 67–75.

MELIKYANTS, G. 1971: How a plan becomes realized. *Izvestiya* 22 August, 3. Translated in CDSP, 1971, **23** (34), 10–11.

MEL'NIKOV, G. I. 1974: Novyy sotsialisticheskiy gorod kak obekt issledovaniya. In Mel'nikov, G. I. (ed.), *Sotsial'nye problemy novykh gorodov vostochnoy Sibiri*. Irkutsk: Irkutskiy Gosudarstvennyy Universitet imeni A. A. Zhdanova, 3–11.

MEL'NIKOV, G. I. and SUDAKOV, V. N. 1971: Nekotorye voprosy adaptatsii molodykh rabochikh. In Mel'nikov, G. I. (ed.), *Sotsial'nye problemy novykh gorodov vostochnoy Sibiri*. Irkutsk: Irkutskiy Gosudarstvennyy Universitet imeni A. A. Zhdanova, 102–109.

MEYER, H. 1942: The Soviet architect. *Task* **3**, 24–32.

MEZHEVICH, M. 1978: Comprehensive planning of large cities. *Planovoye Khozyaystvo* **3**, 110–15. Translated in CDSP, 1978, **30** (15), 14–15.

MIKHAYLOV, M. 1976: Bratsk industrial'nyy. *Ekonomicheskaya Gazeta* **51**, 24.

MILIUTIN, N. A. 1974: *Sotsgorod—the problem of building socialist cities*. Cambridge, Mass: Massachusetts Institute of Technology Press. Translated by Arthur Sprague.

MIL'NER, G. 1978: Questions of planning living standards on a territorial basis. *Planovoye Khozyaystvo* **4**, 55–62. Translated in CDSP, 1978, **30** (30), 20.

MIL'NER, G. and GILINSKAYA, E. 1975: Mezhrayonnoye regulirovaniye urovnya zhizni naseleniya. *Planovoye Khozyaystvo* **1**, 56–63.

MORTON, H. W. 1974: What have Soviet leaders done about the housing crisis. In Morton, H. W. and Tokes, R. L. (eds), *Soviet politics and society in the 1970s*. New York and London: Collier Macmillan, 163–99.

Moskvava v tsifrakh (1971–1975). 1976. Moscow: Statistika.

MOTE, V. 1976: The geography of air pollution in the Soviet Union. In Singleton, F. (ed.) *Environmental misuse in the Soviet Union*. New York: Praeger, 3–32.

MULLAGALYAMOV, M. 1977: The city's air. *Trud* 2 December, 3. Translated in CDSP, 1978, **29** (49), 8.

MURAV'YEV, E. P. and USPENSKIY, S. V. 1974: *Metodologicheskiye problemy planirovaniya gorodskogo rasseleniya pri sotsializme*. Leningrad: Izdatel'stvo Leningradskogo Universiteta.

MUSSALITIN, V. 1976: Why is it unpleasant in Neftekamsk. *Izvestiya* 1 March, 2. Translated in CDSP, 1976, **28** (13), 24.

MYASNIKOV, A. 1977: There should be one master. *Ekonomika i Organizatsiya Promyshlennogo Proizvodstva* **4**, 124–31. Translated in CDSP, 1977, **29** (35), 8–9.

Narodnoye khozyaystvo SSSR v 1974 g. 1975. Moscow: Statistika.
Narodnoye khozyaystvo SSSR v 1975 g. 1976. Moscow: Statistika.

Narodnoye khozyaystvo SSSR za 60 let. 1977. Moscow: Statistika.

Narodnoye khozyaystvo SSSR v 1977 g. 1978. Moscow: Statistika.

NEDACHIN, V. 1974: If one thinks of the passenger. *Pravda* 6 August, 3. Translated in CDSP, 1974, **26** (31), 11.

NEFED'YEV, YU. A. 1971: Organizatsiya svobodnogo vremeni—vazhnyy faktor v preduprezhdenii antiobshchestvennykh yavleniy sredi molodezhi. In Mel'nikov, G. I. (ed.), *Sotsial'nye problemy novykh gorodov vostochnoy Sibiri.* Irkutsk: Irkutskiy Gosudarstvennyy Universitet imeni A. A. Zhdanova, 161–76.

NETSENKO, A. V. 1975: *Sotsial'no-ekonomicheskiye problemy svobodnogo vremeni pri sotsializme.* Leningrad: Izdatel'stvo Leningradskogo Universiteta.

NOVE, A. 1977: *The Soviet economic system.* London: George Allen and Unwin.

OFER, G. 1973: *The service sector in Soviet economic growth: a comparative study.* Cambridge Mass.: Harvard University Press.

On measures for the further improvement of the work of the district city Soviets. *Pravda* 14 March, 1971, 1–2. Translated in CDSP, 1971, **23** (11), 1–6.

On rights and duties of the city and boroughs. *Izvestiya* 20 March, 1971, 4. Translated in CDSP, 1971, **23** (13), 27–30.

On the preliminary results of the 1979 All-Union population census. *Pravda* 22 April, 1979, 4. Translated in CDSP, 1979, **31** (16), 1–6.

OSBORN, R. J. and REINER, A. 1962: Soviet city planning: current issues and future perspectives. *Journal of the American Institute of Planners* **27** (4), 239–50.

OSIPENKOV, P. 1978: Problems of social development in new cities. *Planovoye Khozyaystvo* **1**, 112–16. Translated in CDSP, 1978, **30** (14), 14.

OTDEL'NOV, V. V. 1975: Perspektiva razvitiya predpriyatiy torgovli i obshchestvennogo pitaniya. *Gorodskoye Khozyaystvo Moskvy* **1**, 23–5.

OVCHAROV, M. 1972: How are things city? *Izvestiya* 30 June, 3. Translated in CDSP, 1972, **24** (26), 31.

OVESYAN, R. 1974: Yerevanskaya aglomeratsiya i yeye problemy. *Planovoye Khozyaystvo* **10**, 68–75.

OZIRANSKIY, S: and CHERKASSKAYA, A. 1968: Tsena vody i vozmozhnye puti yeye opredeleniya. *Otsenka prirodnykh resursov. Voprosy geografii* **78**. 67–75.

PARKER, W. H. 1968: *An historical geography of Russia.* London: University of London Press.

PARKINS, F. 1953: *City planning in Soviet Russia.* Chicago: University of Chicago Press.

PASKHAVER, B. I. 1972: *Rentnye problemy v SSSR.* Kiev: Izdatel'stvo 'Naukova Dumka'.

PAVLOV, B. 1977: The worker's dormitory. *Molodoy Kommunist* **5**, 81–5. Translated in CDSP, 1978, **30** (3), 4–6.

PAZHITOV, K. 1910: Kvartirnyy vopros v Moske i v Peterburge. *Gorodskoye Delo* **17**, 1162–6.

PCHELINTSEV, O. S. 1966–7: Problems of the development of large cities. *The Soviet Review* **7**, 15–23.

PEKARSKY, S. 1977: Let the young city grow. *Kommunist* **7**, 52–6. Translated in CDSP, 1977, **29** (21), 16.

PEN'KOV, V. I. 1971: Issledovaniye territorial'nogo raspredeleniya naseleniya g. Kazani merami geograficheskoy differentsiatsii. In Blazhko, N. I. (ed.), *Struktura naseleniya i gorodov Tatarii*. Kazan: Izdatel'stvo Kazanskogo Universiteta, 66–9.

PEREVEDENTSEV, V. 1971: Population migration and the utilization of labour resources. *Voprosy Ekonomiki* **9**, 34–43. Translated in CDSP, 1971, **23** (2), 1–6.

—— 1975: Demography and problems of Soviet life today. *JPRS* R66538, 14–33.

—— 1977a: The only child. *Literaturnaya Gazeta* 16 March, 12. Translated in CDSP, 1977, **29** (11), 1–2.

—— 1977b: Road to the 21st century. *Literaturnoye Obozreniye* **3**, 28–31. Translated in CDSP, 1977, **29** (14), 11.

PERI, G. A. 1971: Puti formirovaniya bazy stroitel'noy industrii Bratsk-Tayshetskogo promyshlennogo rayona. In Mel'nikov, G. I. (ed.), *Sotsial'nye problemy novykh gorodov vostochnoy Sibiri*. Irkutsk: Irkutskiy Gosudarstvennyy Universitet imeni A. A. Zhdanova, 19–33.

PETROV, M. N. 1955: Gorodskoye khozyaystvo. In *Istoriya Moskvy* **5**. Moscow: Izdatel'stvo Akademii Nauk SSSR, 690–713.

Planirovka gorodskikh promyshlennykh rayonov osnovnye polozheniya. 1965. Moscow: Stroyizdat.

POKSHISHEVSKIY, V. V. 1975: Differences in the geography of services and the characteristics of population structure. *Soviet Geography: Review and Translation* **16** (6), 353–66.

POLYAK, G. B. 1974: Ratsional'no ispol'zovat' gorodskiye zemli. *Gorodskoye Khozyaystvo Moskvy* **2**, 17–18.

POWELL, D. E. 1971: Social costs of modernization: ecological problems in the U.S.S.R. *World Politics* **23** (July), 618–34.

Problemy sotsial'nogo planirovaniya 1974. Moscow: Izdatel'stvo Mysl'.

PUDIKOV, D. 1977a: Novoye v zhilishchnoy kooperatsii. *Ekonomicheskaya Gazeta* **15**, 17.

—— 1977b: Kooperativnaya kvartira. *Stroitel'naya Gazeta* 17 August, 2.

P'YANKOV, I. 1978: Ot palatok k prospektam. *Stroitel'naya Gazeta* 30 June, 2.

RODGERS, A. 1974: The locational dynamics of Soviet industry. *Annals, Association of American Geographers* **64** (2), 226–40.

RODIN, YU. 1977: Strana novoseliy. *Stroitel'naya Gazeta* 22 May, 2.

ROMANENKO, A. I. 1974: Nekotorye voprosy ispol'zovaniya svobodnogo vremeni trudyashchimisya novykh gorodov vostochnoy Sibiri. In Mel'nikov, G. I. (ed.), *Sotsial'nye problemy novykh gorodov vostochnoy Sibiri*. Irkutsk: Irkutskiy Gosudarstvennyy Universitet imeni A. A. Zhdanova, 90–96.

ROSOVSKY, A. 1974: How is the city to grow? *Pravda* 30 July, 3. Translated in CDSP, 1974, **26** (30), 31–2.

ROZMAN, G. 1976: *Urban networks in Russia, 1750–1800, and premodern periodization*. Princeton: Princeton University Press.

RUTKEVICH, M. N. 1977: Results of the Soviet Sociological Association's five years of work. *Sotsiologicheskiye Issledovaniya* **3**, 9–21. Translated in CDSP, 1978, **30** (7), 13–14.

RYABUKHIN, A. 1979: This must not be tolerated. *Izvestiya* 27 March, 3. Translated in CDSP, 1979, **31** (13), 16.

RYAKHOVSKIY, V. 1977: Gorod i predpriyatiye. *Ekonomicheskaya Gazeta* **12**, 9.

RYBAKOVSKIY, L. L. 1973: *Regional'nyy analiz migratsiy*. Moscow: Statistika.

—— 1976a: *Territorial'nye osobennosti narodonaseleniya RSFSR*. Moscow: Statistika.

—— 1976b: Struktura i faktory mezhrayonnykh migratsionnykh protsessov. *Sotsiologicheskiye Issledovaniya* **1**, 45–52.

SAKHAROV, A. B. 1977: Opyt izucheniya vliyaniya sotsial'nykh usloviy na territorial'nye razlichiya prestupnosti. *Sotsiologicheskiye Issledovaniya* **1**, 75–84.

SCOTT, D. J. R. 1961: *Russian political institutions*. London: George Allen and Unwin.

SCOTT, J. 1942: *Behind the Urals*. London: Secker and Warburg.

SEGEDINOV, A. A. 1972: Obekty gorodskogo khozyaystva v podzemnom prostranstve. *Gorodskoye Khozyaystvo Moskvy* **7**, 21–5.

SELIVANOV, T. A. and GEL'PERIN, M. 1970: *Planirovaniye gorodskogo khozyaystva*. Moscow: Izdatel'stvo 'Ekonomika'.

SEMIN, V. 1975: So buildings will last a long time. *Izvestiya* 8 February, 2. Translated in CDSP, 1975, **27** (6), 24.

SEREBRYAKOVA, V. A. 1975: K voprosu izucheniya vliyaniya material'nogo urovnya na formirovaniye antiobshchestvennogo povedeniya. In *Voprosy izucheniya prestupnosti i bor'by s neyu*. Moscow: 115–26.

SEVOST'YANOV, V. N. 1972: Plotnost' naseleniya kak kharakteristika protsessa razvitiya goroda. *Vestnik Moskovskogo Universiteta: Geografiya* **2**, 40–46.

SHABAD, T. 1977: Soviet migration patterns based on 1970 census data. In Kosinski, L. (ed.), *Demographic developments in Eastern Europe*. New York and London: Praeger, 173–96.

SHAROV, A., KOCHETKOV, A. and LISTENGURT, F. 1973: Kompleksnaya territorial'naya organizatsiya proizvodstva i rasseleniya. *Planovoye Khozyaystvo* 2, 112–18.

SHAW, D. J. B. 1978: Planning Leningrad. *Geographical Review* 1, 183–200.

—— 1979: Recreation and the Soviet city. In French, R. A. and Hamilton, F. E. I. (eds), *The socialist city*. Chichester: John Wiley and Sons.

SHCHERBAKOV, V. 1977: The homeland begins at home. *Literaturnaya Gazeta* 23 November, 11. Translated in CDSP, 1977, 29 (46), 13.

SHELLEY, S. 1978: The geography of criminality in the Soviet Union. Unpublished manuscript.

SHELOKOV, A. 1978: Prosperity and our needs. *Zhurnalist* 12, 40–42. Translated in CDSP, 1979, 31 (6), 12, 20.

SHEYNIN, L. B. 1976: Vnimaniye 'Beskhoznym' Zemlyam. *Gorodskoye Khozyaystvo Moskvy* 1, 24–7.

—— 1977: Zemlya ne imeyet tseny. *Stroitel'naya Gazeta* 8 July, 2.

SHINKAREV, L. 1973: Siberian passes. *Izvestiya* 2 June, 2. Translated in CDSP, 1973, 25 (22), 6–7.

SHKVARIKOV, V. A. 1939: *Planirovka gorodov Rossii xviii i nachala xix veka.* Moscow: Izdatel'stvo Vsesoyuznoy Akademii Arkhitektury.

—— 1954: *Ocherk istorii planirovki i zastroyki Russkikh gorodov.* Moscow: Izdatel'stvo po Stroitel'stvu Arkhitektura.

—— 1964: *Rekomendatsii po planirovke i zastroyke zhilykh rayonov i mikrorayonov.* Moscow: Izdatel'stvo Literatury po Stroitel'stvu.

SHKVARIKOV, V. A. et al. 1971: *Zhiloy rayon i mikrorayon: posobiye po planirovke i zastroyke.* Moscow: Izdatel'stvo Literatury po Stroitel'-stvu.

SILANT'YEVA, M. N. 1975: Effektivnost' ispol'zovaniya territorii Moskvy. *Gorodskoye Khozyaystvo Moskvy* 10, 33–4.

SIMON, E. D. et al. 1937: *Moscow in the making.* London: Longmans, Green and Co.

SINELNIKOV, G. et al. 1971: The order has been given but there is no housing. *Pravda* 29 July, 3. Translated in CDSP, 1971, 23 (30), 22.

SLAVKINA, T. KH. 1976: Ot otdel'nykh predpriyatiy do promyshlennykh zon. *Gorodskoye Khozyaystvo Moskvy* 6, 18–21.

SMOLYAR, I. M. 1972: *Novye goroda.* Moscow: Stroyizdat.

SOKOLOV, A. 1971: The city is developing, but is transport? *Pravda* 30 May, 2. Translated in CDSP, 1971, 23 (22), 20.

SOKOLOV, L. 1971: O nekotorykh problemakh tsentrov krupnykh gorodov. *Arkhitektura SSSR* 1, 32–5.

SOLOVYEV, N. 1971: Urban industrial development problems discussed. *JPRS* 54262, Reel 365, R11296.

SOSNOVY, T. 1954: *The housing problem in the Soviet Union.* New York: Research Program on the USSR. Translated by T. S. Lindstrom.

—— 1959: The Soviet housing situation today. *Soviet Studies* **11** (1), 1–21.

STARR, F. S. 1971: Writings from the 1960s on the modern movement in Russia. *Journal of the Society of Architectural Historians* **30**, 170–78.

—— 1976: The revival and schism of urban planning in twentieth-century Russia. In Hamm, M. (ed.), *The city in Russian history*. Lexington: The University Press of Kentucky.

STERLIKOV, A. 1972: Smoking pipes threaten air basin's purity. *JPRS* 57756, Reel 421, R12894.

STETSENKO, YU. 1978: Ekologiya i gorod *Ekonomicheskaya Gazeta* **46**, 19.

STRIN'KOVSKIY, V. 1978: Proniknuv v sut' traditsiy. *Stroitel'naya Gazeta* 22 September, 2.

STRONGINA, M. L. 1970: *Sotsial'no-ekonomicheskiye problemy razvitiya bol'shikh gorodov v SSSR*. Moscow: Izdatel'stvo 'Nauka'.

—— 1974: Sotsial'no-ekonomicheskiye problemy urbanizatsii. *Voprosy Ekonomiki* **1**, 134–42.

Stroyka druzhby. *Stroitel'naya Gazeta* 10 September, 1976, 3.

STRUMILIN, S. 1961: Family and community in the society of the future. *The Soviet Review* **2**, 3–24.

SVETLICHNYY, B. 1960: Soviet town planning today. *Problems of Economics* **3**, 29–36.

—— 1974: Planirovaniye gradoobrazuyushchikh protsessov i problemy rasseleniya. *Planovoye Khozyaystvo* **9**, 140–44.

SYSIN, A. N. 1955: Sanitarno-lechebnoye delo. In *Istoriya Moskvy* **5**. Moscow: Izdatel'stvo Akademii Nauk SSSR, 718–29.

SZALAI, A. (ed.) 1972: *The use of time*. The Hague–Paris: Mouton.

TAUBMAN, W. 1973: *Governing Soviet cities*. New York: Praeger.

TOLMACHEV, V. 1976: Pol'za kompleksnykh planov. *Sovety Deputatov Trudyashchikhsya* **6**, 50–54.

TRUBINA, I. 1976: Problems in reducing labour turnover viewed. *JPRS* R 67200, 29–30.

TRUFANOV, I. 1977: *Problems of Soviet life*. Newtonville, Mass.: Oriental Research Partners. Translated by J. Riordan.

TSITSIN, P. 1976a: Gorodskoy rayon kak obekt upravleniya. *Ekonomicheskaya Gazeta* **5**, 15.

—— 1976b: Iz opyta raboty mestnogo soveta po razvitiyu khozyaystva rayona. *Planovoye Khozyaystvo* **7**, 79–85.

——1976c: Upravleniye stroitel'stvom v gorodskom rayone. *Ekonomicheskaya Gazeta* **36**, 9.

—— 1977: Gorodskoy rayon: problemy upravleniya. *Ekonomicheskaya Gazeta* **7**, 12.

TYURIKOV, V. 1977: Oknami vo dvor. *Literaturnaya Gazeta* 14 December, 11.

UNDERHILL, J. A. 1976: *Soviet new towns: housing and national urban growth policy*. Washington: US Government Printing Office.

VASHANOV, V. 1972: Planirovaniye ispol'zovaniya zemel' pod stroitel'-stvo. *Voprosy Ekonomiki* **8**, 94–102.

VISHNEVSKIY, A. G. 1972: Ekonomicheskiye problemy razvitiya form gorodskogo rasseleniya. In Pivovarov, Yu., (ed.), *Problemy Sov-remennoy Urbanizatsii*. Moscow: Statistika, 51–73.

WEBB, SIDNEY and BEATRICE 1937: *Soviet communism: a new civilisation*. London: Victor Gollancz.

WEBER, A. F. 1899: *The growth of cities in the nineteenth century. A study in statistics*. Ithaca, New York: Cornell University Press.

WILES, P. J. Ď. 1962: *The political economy of Communism*. Oxford: Basil Blackwell.

—— 1977: *Economic institutions compared*. Oxford: Basil Blackwell.

YANOVSKIY, A. G. 1973: Ekonomike gradostroitel'stva-kompleksnye obosnovaniya. *Gorodskoye Khozyaystvo Moskvy* **1**, 29–32.

YARALOV, YU. 1975: Silhouettes of new cities. *Izvestiya* 29 March, 3. Translated in CDSP, 1975, **27** (13), 24–5.

ZAGAYNOVA, E. E. 1974: Rasseleniye trudyashchikhsya kak sotsial'noye usloviye formirovaniya planirovochnoy struktury novogo goroda. In Mel'nikov, G. I. (ed.), *Sotsial'nye problemy novykh gorodov vostochnoy Sibiri*. Irkutsk: Irkutskiy Gosudarstvennyy Universitet imeni A. A. Zhdanova, 32–44.

ZAMULA, V. 1971: Combining forces. *Izvestiya* 2 October, 3. Translated in CDSP, 1971, **23** (40), 17–19.

ZAOZERSKAYA, E. I. 1953: Naseleniye. In *Istoriya Moskvy* **2**. Moscow: Izdatel'stvo Akademii Nauk SSSR, 55–75.

ZELNIK, R. E. 1971: *Labor and society in tsarist Russia*. Stanford: Stanford University Press.

ZHELEZKO, S. N., MOROZOVA, G. F. and SERDITYKH, B. G. 1976: Opyt sotsiologicheskogo issledovaniya migratsii naseleniya dal'nego vostoka. *Sotsiologicheskiye Issledovaniya* **2**, 75–81.

Zhilishchnaya perepis v g. S. Peterburga. 1906. *Izvestiya Moskovskoy Gorodskoy Dumy* **23**, 160–61.

ZILE, Z. 1963: Programs and problems of city planning in the Soviet Union. *Washington University Law Quarterly* (February), 19–59.

ZUMBRUNNEN, C. 1976: Water pollution in the Black and Azov Seas. In Singleton, F. (ed.), *Environmental misuse in the Soviet Union*. New York: Praeger, 33–59.

ZUZANEK, J. 1979: *Work and leisure in the USSR: A time-budget analysis*. New York: Praeger.

ZUZANEK, J. 1980 *Work and leisure in the Soviet Union: A time-budget analysis*. New York: Praeger.

ZWICK, P. 1976: Intrasystem inequality and the symmetry of socio-economic development in the USSR. *Comparative Politics* **8**, 501–23.

Author index

Subject index

DATE DUE